Pathways to Belonging

I0091760

Pathways to Belonging

Contemporary Research in School Belonging

Edited by

Kelly-Ann Allen and Christopher Boyle

BRILL

SENSE

LEIDEN | BOSTON

All chapters in this book have undergone peer review.

The Library of Congress Cataloging-in-Publication Data is available online at
http://catalog.loc.gov

ISBN 978-90-04-38657-0 (paperback)
ISBN 978-90-04-38659-4 (hardback)
ISBN 978-90-04-38696-9 (e-book)

Copyright 2018 by Koninklijke Brill NV, Leiden, The Netherlands.
Koninklijke Brill NV incorporates the imprints Brill, Brill Hes & De Graaf,
Brill Nijhoff, Brill Rodopi, Brill Sense and Hotei Publishing.
All rights reserved. No part of this publication may be reproduced, translated,
stored in a retrieval system, or transmitted in any form or by any means, electronic,
mechanical, photocopying, recording or otherwise, without prior written
permission from the publisher.
Authorization to photocopy items for internal or personal use is granted by
Koninklijke Brill NV provided that the appropriate fees are paid directly to The
Copyright Clearance Center, 222 Rosewood Drive, Suite 910, Danvers, MA 01923,
USA. Fees are subject to change.

This book is printed on acid-free paper and produced in a sustainable manner.

It is easier to build strong children than it is to repair broken adults.
– Frederich Douglass

CONTENTS

Part 3: Contemporary Issues for School Belonging

Part 4: Interventions for School Belonging

JOHN HATTIE

FOREWORD

As a father, I have long been convinced by the research of Henry Levin (1970), an education economist. He argued that the best predictor of adult health, wealth, and happiness is not achievement but the number of years of schooling. Hence, how to make schools inviting places for young people to want to belong; to come back and learn; and experience the moment-by-moment joy of giving, receiving, and learning. As parents, we encourage our sons and daughters to stay in schooling as long as possible and admire the schools who find ways to attend to their interests, passions, and learning. In my home state of Victoria in Australia, 97% of adults in prison did not finish school – the costs to them and society are huge. Schooling clearly was not inviting to them. Instead, they found a less formal form of schooling that led to bars, loss of freedom, and often financial and personal hells.

The topic of this book is crucial for every student and for our society as a whole. As humans, we strive to belong, some more than others, and there are skills to be taught and to be learned about joining, maintaining and shifting our sense of belonging. Yes, sometimes we strive for solitude, but to paraphrase Honore de Balzac, solitude is fine, but you need someone to tell you that solitude is fine. For many, particularly adolescents, it hurts to be lonely; and too many are lonely. There is an increased risk for mortality related to loneliness, approximately double the odds ratio for increased mortality for obesity and quadruple the odds ratio for air pollution (Holt-Lunstad, Smith, & Layton, 2010). Loneliness and a lack of a sense of belonging should be added to the list of major public health concerns.

In our work on adolescent development, we developed a model of reputation enhancement (Carroll, Houghton, Durkin, & Hattie, 2008). Adolescents like to enhance their reputations amongst their peers. Those who do not have a reputation to enhance, or peers to share this enhancement, often have major difficulties – indeed for these students not belonging can be persistent and painful. We (Houghton et al., 2014) outlined four major factors relating to these concerns: friendship related loneliness, isolation, negative attitude to solitude, and positive attitude to solitude; and found that it is not the *number* of friends that adolescents have that is important because one can have many friends and still be lonely, yet have few friends and not be lonely. For many, having at least one quality friend helps a sense of belonging and is a positive predictor of positive mental wellbeing. When a person shifts to a new school, to a new class, making a friend in the first month is among the best predictors of later success (Galton, Morrison, & Pell, 2000).

As noted in this book, school belonging relates to an attachment to school underpinned by feelings of being accepted and valued by others (including peers) within the school community. This places much attention on the adults in school to develop a high sense of trust, fairness, and safety so that it is ok to learn, fail, explore, and sense-make in the class and school. These attributes can be challenging to develop for all students, and some may not engage in these challenges for fear of damaging their perceptions of their sense of self, and others may seek safe challenges and not extend themselves for the same reasons. This highlights that it is not only developing positive relations between teacher and student, but also between students that is critical to developing a sense of belonging in this place of learning. Similarly belonging is crucial at the university level; and lack of belonging is one of the best predictors of school drop out (O'Keefe, 2013). The study by Moffa et al. in this volume, underlines these ideas.

There are many strengths to the research contributions of this book – longitudinal studies of university students sense of belonging (Moffa et al.), with refugee students (Due et al.), the role of parent joint decision making (Gowing & Jackson), the role of extracurricular activities as a source of belonging to school (Cocker et al.), the importance of family (McKenzie & Smead). We need more longitudinal studies, more meta-analyses, and more evidence about successful programs to enhance school belonging.

There have been at least two meta-analyses. Moallem (2013) completed a meta-analysis of 27 studies exploring the relation between belonging and academic achievement. She found a correlation of .22 (d=.45), and this correlation was larger when school belonging was conceptualised as belonging as peer group acceptance/ rejection compared to conceptualizing school belonging as emotional engagement (e.g., quality of teacher-student relationships, school safety, relationship with peers, and harmony among the different racial groups) yielded smaller effects. Allen et al. (2016) located 51 studies in their meta-analysis (from 67,378 students) and found a correlation of .31 between school belonging and academic motivation.

It is only through a sense of belonging that students can try and fail, succeed and seek more, see errors as opportunities to learn, think aloud with peers to explore conceptions and misconceptions, engage in productive failure, laugh and cry about not knowing and about the discovery of knowing. This book is timely as social media expands to make even more people vulnerable to not belonging or being told they do not belong. It is as schools become even more important to making sense of the global world that students are now expected to belong.

REFERENCES

Allen, K., Kern, M. K., Vella-Brodrick, D., Hattie, J. A. C., & Waters, L. (2016). What schools need to know about fostering school belonging: A meta-analysis. *Educational Psychology Review, 30*(1), 1–34.

Carroll, A., Houghton, S., Durkin, K., & Hattie, J. (2008). *Adolescent reputations and risk: Developmental trajectories to delinquency*. New York, NY: Springer.

Galton, M., Morrison, I., & Pell, T. (2000). Transfer and transition in English schools: Reviewing the evidence. *International Journal of Educational Research, 33*(4), 341–363.

Holt-Lunstad, J., Smith, T. B., & Layton, J. B. (2010). Social relationships and mortality risk: A meta-analytic review. *PLoS Medicine, 7*(7), e1000316.

Houghton, S., Hattie, J., Carroll, A., Wood, L., & Baffour, B. (2016). It hurts to be lonely! Loneliness and positive mental wellbeing in Australian rural and urban adolescents. *Journal of Psychologists and Counsellors in Schools, 26*(1), 52–67.

Levin, H. M. (1970). A new model of school effectiveness. In A. M. Mood (Ed.), *Do teachers make a difference?* Washington, DC: U.S. Office of Education.

Moallem, I. (2013). *A meta-analysis of school belonging and academic success and persistence* (Unpublished doctoral dissertation). Loyola University, Chicago, IL.

O'Keeffe, P. (2013). A sense of belonging: Improving student retention. *College Student Journal, 47*(4), 605–613.

John Hattie
Melbourne Graduate School of Education
University of Melbourne
Australia

PREFACE

Student success and wellbeing in school have become the perennial goals in good quality education. However, the latter seems to always be in the shadow of the former. Most countries have developed a metric approach to measuring educational quality in schools. This is seen as progress by many governments, however the Editors of this book and many commentators, regard this view of progress as, if we are kind, requiring some additional development. Or if we were to stretch to the more impolite version- this view of progress is bordering on the unhinged. For many students the school experience can be positively or negatively life changing. Success in education is much wider than the measurable. There has to be a recognition that school belonging is as important an aspect of schools as any set of academic results. The editors and authors of this book highlight the importance of wellbeing in school and the absolute necessity to feel a sense of belonging in school. Maslow's Hierarchy of Needs tells us that belonging is a fundamental psychological necessity in order for us to function effectively. School can be a microcosm of life and for those compulsory years of education, belongingness in school is (almost) the food and water of psychological wellbeing.

This book presents recent international scholarly research and discourse on the topic of school belonging. This book not only offers a space for researchers and scholars interested in school belonging to present their work, but for an audience interested in this field to draw knowledge from reputable sources of work. Low rates of school belonging reported by students in school and university settings remain a pressing global concern. With knowledge of the benefits of belonging to school and groups- especially in respect to long and short term physical and psychological health outcomes and not limited to academic achievement, contributors of this book provide valuable insights into how the field can be progressed and enhanced for future generations.

This text is derived from a widely popular special issue for *The Educational and Developmental Psychologist* (for more information: http://journals.cambridge.org/action/displayJournal?jid=EDP). Both authors of this proposal were guest editors of the special issue and the latter is the former Editor in Chief of the journal. Specifically, the following chapters were adapted from the special issue for the purpose of this text:

- Chapter 1, The varied pathways to belonging by Allen and Boyle;
- Chapter 2, A historical account of school belonging: understanding the past and providing direction for the future by Slaten, Allen, Ferguson, Vella-Brodick and Waters;
- Chapter 3, Student and staff perspectives on school connectedness by Gowing and Jackson;

- Chapter 4, Perceptions of School Climate: The role of extracurricular Activities by Coker, Martinez, McMahon, Cohen and Thapa;
- Chapter 5, Does including school belonging measures enhance complete mental health screening in schools? by Moffa, Dowdy, and Furlong;
- Chapter 6, "This reminds me of my country": Exploring experiences of belonging at school for young children with refugee backgrounds, by Due, Riggs and Augoustinos; and
- Chapter 11, Rethinking school belonging: A socio-ecological framework by Allen, Vella-Brodrick and Waters.

ACKNOWLEDGEMENTS

We would like to acknowledge Cambridge University Press for their cooperation in compiling this book. The editors would like to thank all the contributors and the participants in studies without whom this volume would not have been possible. To all our colleagues, friends, and family we thank you for your patience, advice and support.

A special thanks to Heather Craig for her support and commitment to our work that ensured timely publication. We are sincerely grateful for her work in compiling the index.

Last, we would like to acknowledge everyone at Brill | Sense who also played a hand in our publication. A special thanks to Jolanda Karada, Evelien van der Veer, and Michel Lokhorst. Your hard work and dedication to our book is gratefully appreciated.

FIGURES AND TABLES

FIGURES

FIGURES AND TABLES

TABLES

NOTES ON CONTRIBUTORS

Kelly-Ann Allen, Ph.D., is an endorsed Educational and Developmental Psychologist. She is nationally and internationally recognised both as a researcher and practitioner in social connectedness, belonging, and social and emotional learning. Dr Allen holds sessional academic positions within the Melbourne Graduate School of Education, The University of Melbourne, the School of Psychology, Charles Sturt University, and provides professional supervision to psychologists at different stages of their career in both private practice and schools.

Martha Augoustinos, is Professor of Psychology at the University of Adelaide. She has published widely in the areas of discourse, race, gender, and social psychology.

Christopher Boyle, Ph.D., is currently based in the Graduate School of Education, University of Exeter in the UK. He is currently Associate Professor of Educational Psychology and the Director of Doctoral Studies. He has been an education and psychology practitioner for over 20 years. He is an internationally recognised and respected academic and author on the subjects of inclusive education, and psychology.

Jonathan Cohen, Ph.D., the Senior Scholar, co-founder and president emeritus at the National School Climate Center: Educating Minds and Hearts Because the Three Rs's Are Not Enough. Jonathan is also an Adjunct Professor of Psychology and Education at Teachers College, Columbia University; co-editor of the Journal of the International Observatory for School Climate and Violence Prevention in Schools; and a practicing clinical psychologist and psychoanalyst. He is the author over 50 peer reviewed papers and over 50 chapters and briefs as well as six books, including the award winning Educating Minds and Hearts: Social Emotional Learning and the Passage into Adolescence and Caring Classrooms/Intelligent Schools, and most recently, Integrating Prosocial Learning with Education Standards: School Climate Reform Initiatives. Jonathan consults to districts, State Departments of Education, foreign educational ministries, UNICEF's Child Friendly Schools Program and the World Bank around a range of school climate, social emotional learning and mental health promotion efforts.

Crystal Coker is a postdoctoral research associate examining income-based educational opportunity gaps. Her current research explores the relationship between high school experiences and postsecondary outcomes among high-achieving, low-income students. Her interests include education policy, out-of-school time use, and the effects of concentrated poverty on youth development. She received her doctorate in community psychology from DePaul University and her masters and bachelor's degrees in psychology from New York University and the University of California, Irvine.

Erin Dowdy, Ph.D., is a Professor in the Department of Counseling, Clinical, and School Psychology at University of California, Santa Barbara. She graduated from the University of Georgia in 2006 with a Ph.D. in educational psychology. She is a licensed psychologist and a nationally certified school psychologist. Her research career and scholarly publications have focused on behavioral assessment, particularly universal assessment for social and emotional health and risk. She is involved in grant-funded research projects including measurement work funded by the Institute of Education Sciences investigating universal screening in schools.

Clemence Due, Ph.D., is a senior lecturer in the School of Psychology at the University of Adelaide. Her research focus is on the health and wellbeing of people with refugee backgrounds, including children. She has published extensively on the intersections between education and wellbeing for refugee and migrant children and young people.

Jonathan K. Ferguson, MS, is a doctoral student in the Department of Educational, School, and Counseling Psychology at the University of Missouri-Columbia. Jonathan has a passion for doing critical research that uplifts and amplifies the voices of marginalized communities. In addition, he is interested in how marginalized identities experience belonging in educational spaces. Jonathan has displayed this passion through community outreach, mentorship, and talks at local high schools. Additionally he has shared this passion with others through national and regional presentations, as well as, peer-reviewed articles and daily interactions. He aims to continue devoting his scholarly efforts and resources toward social justice advocacy and equity in marginalized communities.

Sebastian Franke, Ph.D., is working as psychologist at the chair for Developmental Science and Special Education at the University of Siegen (Germany). He was trained in clinical practice as a psychologist at the Child and Adolescent Department of the University Clinic Cologne (Germany). His research focuses on attachment throughout the lifespan and transitions.

Michael J. Furlong, Ph.D., is a Distinguished Professor at University of California, Santa Barbara affiliated with the International Center for School Based Youth Development. He is also currently serving as the Associate Dean for Research in Gevirtz Graduate School of Education. He is a fellow of the American Psychological Association and the American Education Research Association and a member of the Society for the Study of School Psychology.

Annie Gowing, Ph.D., is a member of the Youth Research Centre and a lecturer in the Graduate School of Education at the University of Melbourne. Her key teaching portfolio is in the area of student wellbeing. She has a social work and education background and has worked extensively in schools in both counselling and leadership roles and in education policy development and delivery. Her PhD explored student and staff understandings of school connectedness. Her research interests are centred on student wellbeing with particular interest in connectedness, belonging, resilience and school climate.

John Hattie is Laureate Professor at the Melbourne Graduate School of Education at the University of Melbourne, and Chair of the Australian Institute of Teaching and School Leaders. His areas of interest are measurement models and their applications to educational problems, and models of teaching and learning. He has published and presented over 1000 papers, and supervised 200 theses students, and 31 books – including 8 on Visible Learning.

Alun C. Jackson, Ph.D., is Director, Australian Centre for Heart Health; Honorary Professor, Office of the Executive Dean (Health), Deakin University; Honorary Professorial Fellow, Melbourne Graduate School of Education, University of Melbourne; and Honorary Professor, Centre on Behavioural Health, University of Hong Kong. He was previously Director of the Problem Gambling Research and Treatment Centre and Head of the School of Social Work at the University of Melbourne. He has undertaken research on young people in relation to ethnic identity, gambling behaviours, coping with chronic illness, the impacts of family violence, and HIV/AIDS knowledge and sexual practices.

Divya Jindal-Snape, Ph.D., is Professor of Education, Inclusion and Life Transitions in the School of Education and Social Work at University of Dundee, UK. She is also Director of Transformative Change: Educational and Life Transitions (TCELT) Research Centre. For details see https://www.dundee.ac.uk/esw/staff/details/jindal-snapedivya.php

Andrew Martinez, Ph.D., is a Senior Research Associate at the Center for Court Innovation (CCI) in New York City. Andrew's current portfolio includes two studies funded by the National Institute of Justice; a randomized control trial examining the effects of restorative participatory peace circles in New York City high schools, and a mixed-methods study of young illegal gun carriers across five New York City neighborhoods. Andrew's interests include violence prevention, state anti-bullying laws, and school climate improvement practices. Andrew holds a Ph.D. in Community Psychology from DePaul University and a Master of Social Work Degree from Fordham University.

Daniel Mays, Jun.-Prof. Dr. phil., holds the professorship for special education with a focus on emotional and social development at the University of Siegen, Germany. His main research areas are the socio-emotional development of children and adolescents; Permeability of the school system/Transition research and multi-professional cooperation in school.

Susan D. McMahon, Ph.D., is Associate Dean for Research and Faculty Development for the College of Science and Health and Vincent dePaul Professor of Clinical-Community and Community Psychology at DePaul University. She is Past President, Fellow, and recipient of the Outstanding Educator Award for the Society for Community Research and Action (Division 27 of APA). She has over 70 peer-reviewed publications and book chapters and over 180 presentations. Her research focuses on understanding risk and protective factors at multiple ecological levels, school-based intervention and evaluation, teacher and student experiences with violence, and enhancing our educational systems.

Victoria L. McKenzie, Ph.D., is a senior lecturer at the University of Melbourne and is Coordinator of the Master of Educational Psychology. Dr McKenzie has experience as leader of a multi-disciplinary team of school support personnel working with schools on systemic intervention in the areas of student and community well-being. In her PhD, Dr McKenzie studied the resources, resilience and coping skills of disengaged students. Dr McKenzie has presented at national and international conferences on building coping skills and resilience in young people. Training psychologists for professional practice in schools has been a central component of Dr McKenzie's professional career, and she has also supervised many psychologists in gaining specialised status. She is currently Chair-Elect of the APS College of Educational and Developmental Psychologists, and is a Fellow of the Australian Psychological Society.

Franka Metzner, Dipl.-Psych., research assistant at the Professorship for Special Education, focussing the emotional and social development at the University of Siegen and at the Department of Medical Psychology at the University Medical Center Hamburg-Eppendorf in Germany. Interests: trauma-related disorders in children and adolescents, preventive interventions in educational settings.

Kathryn Moffa, M.Ed., is a doctoral candidate in the Department of Counseling, Clinical, and School Psychology at University of California Santa Barbara with an emphasis in school psychology. Her research interests include early identification of youths experiencing social emotional difficulties, school-based mental health and multi-tiered systems of support, and the utility of universal complete mental health screening.

Silke Pawils, Ph.D., in Psychology, since 2002 Head of the Research Group 'Prevention in childhood and adolescents' at University Medical Center, Hamburg-

Eppendorf, Institute of Medical Psychologie; main topics: Child Maltreatment and childhood trauma, Prevention of Family Violence, Prevention in medical and scholarship systems.

Damien W. Riggs, Ph.D., is an Associate Professor in social work at Flinders University and an Australian Research Council Future Fellow. He is the author of over 200 publications on gender, family, and mental health, including (with Clemence Due) A Critical Approach to Surrogacy: Reproductive Desires and Demands (Routledge, 2017).

Sue Roffey, Ph.D., is Honorary Associate Professor at Exeter and Western Sydney universities and affiliated to University College, London and the Institute of Wellbeing in Cambridge. She is on the Advisory Board of the Carnegie Centre of Excellence for Mental Health in Schools, and Editorial Board of Educational and Child Psychology. Sue is Founder and Director of Growing Great Schools Worldwide and a prolific author on wellbeing in education, including behaviour, belonging, relationships, resilience, and social-emotional learning.

Lisa Schneider is special needs teacher and criminologist and works as an assistant researcher at the Department for Special Needs Education at the University of Siegen. Before she joined the University she founded the Nonprofit Organization "EXIT – EnterLife" that commits to education for young people in juvenile detention centers.

Bini Sebastian is a PhD student in Counseling Psychology at the University of Missouri-Columbia. Her research focuses on cultural diversity, mindfulness, belongingness, and resilience. Bini has presented her research and offered workshops on mindfulness and belongingness at local and national conferences. She is interested in exploring the role of mindfulness in minority health and other issues related to cultural diversity.

Christopher D. Slaten, Ph.D., is an assistant professor in the Department of Educational, School, and Counseling Psychology at the University of Missouri-Columbia. Dr. Slaten researches the construct of belonging and how it impacts career and academic outcomes for youth and college students, particularly those students that have been marginalized by the educational system. Dr. Slaten's passion for this line of research has led to over 20 peer-reviewed publications, 25 national presentations, national press recognition (Wall Street Journal), and international keynote lectures in 6 years in the academy.

Jessica J. E. Smead completed her undergraduate degree in psychology at the Australian Catholic University, her graduate diploma at Deakin University and her Masters in Educational Psychology at the University of Melbourne. She is employed with the Department of Education and Training and works in two different school networks (Melbourne/Maribyrnong and Yarra Ranges). In this role Jessica supports schools with funding applications, cognitive assessments, counselling and consultation. The areas of challenging behaviour, learning difficulties and resilience are key areas of interest for Jessica.

Amrit Thapa, Ph.D., is a lecturer in the International Educational Development Program at Graduate School of Education, University of Pennsylvania. He received his M.Phil. and Ph.D. in economics and education from Columbia University. Dr. Thapa is also an Affiliated Researcher for the Center for Benefit-Cost Studies of Education at Teachers College, Columbia University and vice president for The Institute of Global Education (IGE), an NGO that has consultative status with the Economic & Social Council of the United Nations. Prior to Penn GSE, Amrit worked as a research director at the National School Climate Center (NSCC), an educational non-profit organization in New York. His current research focuses economics of education in developing countries, and school climate research.

Dianne Vella-Brodrick, Ph.D., is Deputy Director and Head of Research at the Centre for Positive Psychology at the Melbourne Graduate School of Education, University of Melbourne. Dianne has served as a journal editor, has published widely, is on numerous research advisory boards, regularly reviews scientific papers for leading journals and has received around $2.5 million funding for her internationally renowned research. Her research program focuses on the development and evaluation of school-based well-being initiatives, particularly positive education. She specialises in innovative mixed method designs which are youth friendly, utilise the latest technology and include physiological indices of well-being.

Lea Waters, Ph.D., is a registered psychologist, researcher, speaker and author who specializes in positive parenting, positive organizations and positive education. Lea is the President of the International Positive Psychology Association and has affiliate positions with University of Cambridge and the University of Michigan. Listed in the Marques 'Who's Who in the World' since 2009, she has published over 90 scientific articles. She was listed as one of Australia's Top 100 Women of Influence by the Financial Review and Westpac Bank. Her book 'The Strength Switch: how the new science of strength-based parenting can help your child and your teen to flourish' is published with Penguin Press.

Michelle Wichmann, M.Sc. Psych., research assistant at the Department of Medical Psychology (University Medical Center Hamburg-Eppendorf) as well as at the Junior-Professorship for special education with a focus on socio-emotional development (University of Siegen). Research focus: children and adolescents with post-traumatic stress disorders at school, socio-emotional development of children and adolescents.

Holger Zielemanns, Dipl.-Päd., Belongs as a teacher for special education to the team of the professorship for special education with a focus on emotional and social development of the University of Siegen. His work and research priorities are dealing with externalizing disorders in the classroom, autism spectrum disorders and Classroom Management.

KELLY-ANN ALLEN AND CHRISTOPHER BOYLE

1. THE VARIED PATHWAYS TO BELONGING

An Introduction to School Belonging

INTRODUCTION

School belonging is generally regarded as a student's sense of affiliation or connection to his or her school. Anyone who has personally navigated the sometimes tortuous terrain of secondary school is able to have some level of direct understanding of the importance that belonging, fitting in and identifying with a school holds for most people. Educators and practitioners often work with young people who feel that they do not belong to the school community which they attend. An absence of belonging can manifest itself in mental health concerns, school attrition and risk-taking behaviours. Opportunities for early intervention through fostering school belonging are born from a greater understanding and awareness of what school belonging is and how it is contextualised and fostered. This edited text aims to place a focus on school belonging and highlight it as a significant social issue of our time. Divided into four parts, Part 1 looks at the history and future of school belonging, Part 2 explores contemporary research on the subject, Part 3 investigates current issues, and Part 4 considers school belonging through an interventionist lens.

Part 1: The History and Future of School Belonging

A powerful impetus for this volume was to create a resource, which offers a high level of applied impact for both researchers and practitioners. This is evident in the high quality and variance in the collection of chapters that are presented. The first chapter of this special issue by Slaten, Allen, Ferguson, Vella-Brodick and Waters, *A historical account of school belonging: understanding the past and providing direction for the future*, provides an overview of school belonging through a review of literature that describes the current context, trends and relevancy for future research. Most notable in this chapter is a discussion of school belonging in the university context. Given that the overarching school belonging literature is mainly concerned with issues in primary and secondary schools, this chapter is unique in exploring new ground in tertiary settings. There is a dearth of academic research in this area, and this chapter provides a solid foundation from which to build upon a discussion of current research trends that follow-on in the next section.

© KONINKLIJKE BRILL NV, LEIDEN, 2018 | DOI:10.1163/9789004386969_001

Part 2: Current Research on School Belonging

Literature on school belonging often focuses on student experiences and perspectives. Gowing and Jackson rigorously extend the literature by drawing on school staff as well. In *Student and staff perspectives on school connectedness,* the authors contextualise school connectedness, "as a process rather than a state, fluctuating across time within the relational, experiential, and physical spaces of school life". The chapter highlights the importance of teachers and peer relationships for school belonging, but also presents seminal findings in relation to joint decision making between young people and parents on choice of school and distance of home from school, which may facilitate greater opportunities for extra-curricular activities.

Coker, Martinez, McMahon, Cohen and Thapa extend our understanding of extra-curricular activities in their chapter, *Perceptions of School Climate: The role of extracurricular Activities*. A central finding of their work is that extra-curricular activities are beneficial for school connectedness, which affords readers a greater understanding of the role of this predictor in school belonging. The authors examine how different extra-curricular activities (sports, clubs and the arts) interact with school connectedness, and find that greater involvement in extra-curricular activities does not necessarily equate to higher school connectedness. In fact, the types of extra-curricular activities and the way they combine play a fundamental role in a young person's sense of belonging.

The fifth chapter of this text, by Moffa, Dowdy, and Furlong provides further insight into the application of school belonging in school settings by examining the construct's value in mental health screening for psychological distress and life satisfaction. In their chapter, *Does including school belonging measures enhance complete mental health screening in schools?* the authors found that students who reported high levels of life satisfaction and normative distress ("thriving") reported a higher sense of belonging than students who experienced low life satisfaction and elevated distress ("troubled"). In the second part of their analysis, they found that school belonging served as a predictor for social and emotional wellbeing one year on, but offered very little explained variance towards psychological distress symptoms. The authors argue that, although school belonging did not contribute substantially to psychological distress, it still has an important place in the complete mental health screening of secondary school students.

The text is particularly interested in considering school belonging in a range of populations. This is exemplified by Due, Riggs and Augoustinos, who present a novel methodology of photographic elicitation techniques in their chapter, *"This reminds me of my country", Exploring experiences of belonging at school for young children with refugee backgrounds*. The authors found that students with refugee backgrounds were able to derive a sense of school belonging from their environment, which included their relationships with peers and teachers. The authors offer suggestions for schools catering for children with refugee backgrounds.

2

McKenzie and Smead bring us the final research chapter in this section. Their chapter, *The relationship between school connectedness, family functioning and resilience*, explores the impact of both the family environment and school connectedness on a student's ability to cope with adversity. Their study, drawing from four schools in Melbourne found significant associations between school connectedness and family functioning. The authors highlight the necessity of early intervention to enhance school belonging which, from their results, seemed to be especially necessary for students from low socioeconomic backgrounds.

Part 3: Contemporary Issues for School Belonging

Next the volume moves to address contemporary issues in the school belonging literature and begins with an examination of school belonging experiences of international students in the chapter titled, *The role of belongingness in international students' acculturation process* by Sebastian and Slaten. This chapter investigates how international students' sense of school belonging may influence their acculturation process and the barriers international students may face in feeling a sense of belonging. This chapter makes a remarkable contribution to the literature in fulfilling a gap where little discourse exists on international student experiences – especially in respect to school belonging.

Next, Roffey and Boyle present a seminal essay on, *Belief, belonging and the role of schools in reducing the risk of home-grown extremism*. The authors tackle a deeply complex topic that reflects a contemporary issue of our modern age. The authors explore the difference between inclusive and exclusive belonging and the importance of educational settings in enhancing a sense of inclusive belonging. Roffey and Boyle advocate action in schools so that young people learn to perceive and understand the 'humanity' and commonality of others, breaking down assumptions and stereotypes and ultimately offering an alternative lens from which we can address extremism in youth through fostering school belonging.

Finally in this section, Mays and colleagues present some important findings from their study on the often de-emphasised issue of transition points for students moving between schools. The extra pressure that students who have additional support needs come under during this period is emphasised. Students are more vulnerable during transitions than at other times in their schooling. Having psychologically strong students is the role of the school, and it is paramount that schools utilise evidence based interventions in order to strengthen school belonging for all students.

Part 4: Interventions for School Belonging

The penultimate chapter of this text aims to distil the research on school belonging and re-frame it into an applied practical format that can be used by school leaders and practitioners. In their chapter, *Rethinking school belonging: A socio-ecological framework*, Allen, Vella-Brodrick and Waters present a socio-ecological framework for schools. The authors argue that school leaders and educators should be encouraged to foster students' sense of belonging by building qualities within the students *and* by changing school systems and processes. The framework represents the importance of whole school approaches by discussing the role of governmental, organisational, relational and individual level variables in influencing school belonging.

The final chapter of this text brings together the main themes and findings from all the studies in this book. Boyle and Allen re-emphasise the collective considerations of many leading academics in school belonging and discuss them in relation to the wider literature. Taking cognisance of various findings, it is clear that, across many geographical boundaries, there is little emphasis and understanding as to the consequences of a lack of belonging in school for many students. Building psychologically robust students is a task undertaken by many people and agencies but, there can be no doubt, that this should be a kernel objective of the school, and rightly so.

School belonging is a vitally important psychological construct. Taken together, the findings of the studies featured in this volume on school belonging have relevance for intervention design and organisational structures within educational settings, especially in respect to policy and practice. School management, in particular, have an important role in building school belonging for individuals and ensuring that this concept is prioritised as a guiding principle in education. The applied practice outcomes derived from this text will help create stronger school communities and contribute to the practice and science of educational and development psychology.

ACKNOWLEDGEMENT

This chapter is an adapted version from Allen, K., & Boyle, C. (2016). Pathways to school belonging. *The Educational and Developmental Psychologist, 33*(1), ii–iv. doi:10.1017/edp.2016.13

Kelly-Ann Allen
The Melbourne Graduate School of Education
The University of Melbourne
Australia

Christopher Boyle
Graduate School of Education
University of Exeter
England

PART 1

THE HISTORY AND FUTURE OF SCHOOL BELONGING

CHRISTOPHER D. SLATEN, KELLY-ANN ALLEN,
JONATHAN K. FERGUSON, DIANNE VELLA-BRODRICK
AND LEA WATERS

2. A HISTORICAL ACCOUNT OF SCHOOL BELONGING

Understanding the Past and Providing Direction for the Future

INTRODUCTION

The literature reveals that an individual's sense of belonging is an important psychological construct with formative implications for both psychological and physical health across the life span (e.g., Poulton, Caspi, & Milne, 2002; Wadsworth, Thomsen, Saltzman, Connor-Smith, & Compas, 2001). Past research investigating belonging has found that those who report a high sense of belonging are more likely to report psychological benefits such as wellbeing, increased self-esteem, and positive mood (Begen & Turner-Cobb, 2015; Newman, Lohman, & Newman, 2007), improved memory (Haslam, Jetten, Bevis, Ravencroft, & Tonks, 2010), positive life transitions (Haslam et al., 2008; Iyer, Jetten, Tsivrikos, Haslam, & Postmes, 2009), and reduced stress (Newman et al., 2007). Benefits associated with physical functioning have also been reported and include reduced risk of stroke (Boden-Albala, Litwak, Elkind, Rundek, & Sacco, 2005), lowered disease risk (Cohen & Janicki-Deverts, 2009), and reduced mortality (Holt-Lunstad, Smith, & Layton, 2010; Jetten, Haslam, Haslam, & Branscombe, 2009) Moreover, the benefits associated with belonging, whether it be to a group, school, or community, have also been found to have lasting effects (Walton & Cohen, 2011; Walton, Cohen, Cwir, & Spencer, 2012). While the benefits of general belonging have been widely accepted, there has not been as much research on the less understood construct of school belonging. The purpose of this chapter is to provide an overview of school belonging research through setting the theoretical context, defining school belonging, discussing the key variables associated with school belonging, presenting the predictors of school belonging as identified in research, highlighting the relevancy of school belonging in university settings, and suggesting directions for future areas of research. The main objective of this literature review is to generate a greater understanding of school belonging that may assist future research and practice aimed at investigating school belonging to school and university levels. The implications of a greater understanding of this field may assist educational and developmental psychologists, researchers, and school leaders to address growing concerns related to drop out rates by students

© KONINKLIJKE BRILL NV, LEIDEN, 2018 | DOI:10.1163/9789004386969_002

in secondary schools (Kuperminc, Dranell, & Jimenez, 2008) and attrition rates at university level training (Slaten, Elison, Hughes, Yough, & Shemwell, 2015).

Theoretical Background

Belonging has a connection to seminal work within the field of psychology (Maslow, 1943; Rogers, 1951). Maslow (1943, 1954) first noted belonging in his *hierarchy of needs* through his theory of human motivation. His theory suggests five fundamental needs that drive the behavior of individuals in hierarchical fashion. Specifically, Maslow describes all people to have a fundamental need for love and belongingness. He theorized that the need for belongingness would emerge only after the physiological and safety needs have been satisfied. Maslow describes the motivation to belong as related to family, friends, community, and social groups and the connections gained through the establishment of these genuine relationships. Maslow's (1943) work describing the need for belonging has proven to be a powerful construct which has engendered a significant amount of work on human motivation (e.g., Brofenbrenner, 1977; Cohen, 1982; Glasser, 1986; Baumeister & Leary, 1995; Putnam, 2000; Fiske, 2004; Josselson, 1992). In addition to Maslow (1954), other early educational researchers brought the concept of belonging into educational settings specifically. These include: the work of Dewey (1938), the concept of supportive school environments; Vygotsky (1962) work on the role of social environment in schools; Erikson's (1968) work on social identification in educational settings.

Although there are other psychological and educational theories that allude to belonging (e.g., Bowlby, 1969; Bonfenbrenner, 1977; Josselson, 1992; Voekl, 1996; Solomon et al., 1996; Connel & Wellborn, 1991), one of the seminal conceptual foundations of belonging research was published by Baumeister and Leary in 1995. *The belongingness hypothesis* suggests the construct of belonging is a fundamental human motivator. They define the need to belong as "a need to form and maintain at least a minimum quantity of interpersonal relationships" (Baumeister & Leary, 1995, p. 499). The belongingness hypothesis suggests that the need for belonging is not only innate but based in evolution. They argue that belonging to or interacting with groups provides a greater opportunity for survival through protection, reproduction, shared resources, and eventually affection (Baumeister & Leary, 1995).

The belongingness hypothesis argues that belonging drives goal-directed activity, and the lack of belonging causes adverse reactions (Baumeister & Leary, 1995). The need to belong motivates people to engage socially, form bonds, and the absence of these bonds can often contribute to psychological distress or even physical health concerns. Baumeister and Leary (1995) suggest two main features of belongingness; the need for frequent personal contacts with others and the perception of a stable relationship. They also argue against the seemingly interchangeable nature of belonging and affiliation by making a sharp contrast between the two terms. Affiliation is not necessarily based on a reciprocal relationship whereas belongingness requires an in-depth social connection. An important idea of their hypothesis of belongingness is that the need to belong is fundamental to an individual's wellbeing (Baumeister & Leary, 1995).

Defining School Belonging

Although Baumeiester and Leary (1995) have defined the overall construct of belonging, belonging to school has been defined more specifically. Williams (2000) defines school belonging as a psychological construct related to attachment to school and underpinned by feelings of being accepted and valued by others (including peers) within the school community. Other definitions of school belonging have incorporated different constructs including a sense of community (Osterman, 2000), student engagement (Finn, 1993), positive interactions with others (Hamm & Faircloth, 2005), and social identity (Tajfel, 1972). Notwithstanding the broad variability in how school belonging (or belongingness) is conceptualized, the most commonly cited definition of school belonging in the literature is offered by Goodenow and Grady (1993) who define school belonging as "the extent to which students feel personally accepted, respected, included, and supported by others in the school social environment" (p. 80) (e.g., Anderman, 2002; Knifsend & Graham, 2012; Ma, 2003; Nichols, 2006). This definition has also been operationalized widely through the use of the Psychological Sense of School Membership (PSSM) scale (Anderman, 2002; Knifsend & Graham, 2012; Ma, 2003; Nichols, 2006) and applies both to secondary school and university settings.

It seems that a review of the literature reveals more consistency in how school belonging is defined than in the terminology used to describe it. School belonging as a psychological construct in empirical research is often described using a range of terms including, school connectedness (Jose, Ryan, & Pryor, 2012; Libbey, 2004), school bonding (Hawkins et al., 1996), school identification (Sirin & Rogers-Sirin, 2004; Wang & Eccles, 2012), school attachment (Hallinan, 2008) and a sense of community (Osterman, 2000). Often terminology is used interchangeably (Anderman, 2002; Rowe & Stewart, 2009), and a given term's meaning in a particular context might depend upon the individual author using it (Libbey, 2007). Some theorists have even suggested that belonging is a component of school connectedness (McNeely & Falci, 2004).

School belonging can be closely related to and sometimes included as an aspect of academic motivation research (Deci & Ryan, 1985; Glasser, 1986). For example, Glasser's (1986) control theory's classroom application is a theory of motivation. Control theory argues against the influence of external motivators altogether and suggests that all motivation is derived from basic human needs, one of which is belonging. Glasser (1986) suggests that if the basic need of belonging is not met, students will have difficulty achieving academic success.

Self-Determination Theory (SDT) was the catalyst for academic motivation research as it proposed three forms of motivation: intrinsic, extrinsic, and amotivation

(Deci & Ryan, 1985). It is theorized that intrinsic motivation consists of three innate psychological needs: competence, autonomy, and relatedness. For the purpose of this literature review, relatedness (Josselson, 1992) is the most salient psychological need identified by Deci and Ryan (2000), as it is often used interchangeably with belonging. Therefore an individual's sense of belonging at a theoretical and empirical level holds implications for the academic outcomes of students (e.g., Anderman, 2002; Baskin et al., 2010; Slaten et al., 2014), a central objective for schools. This has also been supported by specific outcome research that has shown that academic outcomes, amongst other variables related to school belonging, may play an important role in a student's connectedness to their school.

Variables Related to School Belonging

Research has identified a number of important variables related to school belonging (e.g., the Centers for Disease Control and Prevention [CDC], 2009; Wingspread Declaration on School Connections, 2004) such as extracurricular activities (Dotterer, McHale, & Crouter, 2007; Shochet, Smyth, & Homel, 2007), academic motivation (Anderman, 2003; Whitlock, 2006), mental health (Holt & Espelage, 2003; Shochet, Smith, Furlong, & Homel, 2011), gender (Ma, 2003; Sanchez, Col'on, & Esparza, 2005), and race and ethnicity (Bonny et al., 2000). Social and emotional characteristics and how these enhance feelings of school belonging for students and vice versa have also been investigated with positive findings (Samdal, Nutbeam, Wold, & Kannas 1998; Sirin & Rogers-Sirin, 2004; Uwah, McMahon, & Furlow, 2008). Social and emotional characteristics relate to an individual's ability to manage emotions and create positive relationships and include variables such as self-efficacy, self-esteem, and self-concept (Collaborative for Academic, Social, and Emotional Learning [CASEL], 2003). In addition, researchers have also found positive correlations between school belonging and variables concerned with support from others, such as peer support, teacher support, and parent support (Garcia-Reid, 2007; Hallinan, 2008; Wang & Eccles, 2012). Further research has focused on school type (Ma, 2003; Brutsaert & Van Houtte, 2002), school location (Anderman, 2002), and year level (Read, Archer, & Leathwood, 2003).

Of particular note in school belonging research, is the relationship between school belonging and academic achievement, mental health outcomes, and maladaptive behaviours.

Academic achievement. Sirin and Rogers-Sirin (2004) examined the impact of psychological and parental factors on academic achievement of African American students. Researchers selected 336 African American students and their mothers from a large database and administered questionnaires that included a measure of school engagement involving nine items, five of which examined school identification defined as a students' sense of belonging to their school. After analyzing the data researchers found that the strongest predictors of academic performance were educational expectations and school engagement. Results also indicated a significant relationship between school engagement and self-esteem (Sirin & Rogers-Sirin, 2004).

Mental illness.　The literature has also demonstrated that mental illness (e.g., anxiety and depression) may also contribute to low levels of school belonging (McMahon, Parnes, Keys, & Viola, 2008; Moody & Bearman, 2004; Shochet, Smyth & Homel, 2007). Newman, Newman, Griffen, O'Connor, and Spas (2007) found a significant inverse relationship between school belonging and depressive symptoms. They found that during transition from middle school to high school students' sense of school belonging tends to decrease and therefore depressive symptoms increase (Newman et al., 2007).

A study by Anderman (2002) examined the relationship between school belonging and psychological outcomes. The researcher accessed a large sample of students (n=20,745) from schools across the United States (n=132). Within the study measurements of school belongingness were selected (individual and aggregated), school problems, social rejection, optimism, self-concept, and depression. The results indicated a significant negative correlation between individual perceptions of school belonging and depression, social rejection, and school problems. However, Anderman's (2002) study also indicated a positive correlation between aggregated school belonging and Grade Point Average (GPA), social rejection, and school problems. These results suggest that the more students feel a collective sense of school belonging the more rejection those students on the outside feel, and the more problems they will encounter (Anderman, 2002).

Shochet, Smith, Furlong, and Homel's (2011) study of school belonging and psychological factors investigated the impact of school belonging on negative affect in adolescent students. Using the Psychological Sense of School Membership Scale (PSSM) (Goodenow & Grady, 1993) and the Children's Depression Inventory (CDI) (Kovacs, 1992), researchers surveyed 504 seventh and eighth grade students in Australia. Researchers found that school belonging was a significant predictor of negative affect in adolescents (Shochet et al., 2011).

Maladaptive behaviours.　Previous research has also shown a relationship between school belonging and behavior concerns (McNeely & Falci, 2004; Loukas et al., 2010). McNeely and Falci (2004) analyzed survey data from a large sample of adolescents (n=20,745) and found that the more connected students felt to their teachers in particular, the less likely they were to engage in what researchers referred to as six health-risk behaviors (cigarette smoking, drinking to the point of getting drunk, marijuana use, suicidal ideation, sexual behaviors, and weapon-related violence). More recently a study by Loukas and colleagues (2010) examined data from 476 6th and 7th grade students in order to determine the role of school connectedness on conduct problems. The results indicated that school connectedness was a moderator between negative family relationships and conduct concerns.

11

Therefore, school belonging has been shown to be highly effective in school dropout prevention (Pittman & Richmond, 2007; Kuperminc, Dranell, & Jimenez, 2008; Slaten, Elison, Hughes, Yough, & Shemwell, 2015).

PREDICTORS OF SCHOOL BELONGING

Although school belonging is a growing body of research, there has been some work to identify predictors of the construct (Goodenow & Grady, 2003; Blomfield & Barber, 2010; Shochet et al., 2007). Despite discrepancies in terminology, which might arguably dilute the potency of research drawn from the field, research has identified that while terminology varied considerably, consistent themes emerged from the broad variety of terms used in the literature; for example, school environment, student safety, teacher supportiveness and caring, parent support, and peer relationships through extra-curricular activities, were all noted as being important contributors to a sense of school belonging (Libbey, 2004).

This current literature shows that the school environment is a salient variable in predicting student belonging (Loukas, Roalson, & Herrera, 2010; Slaten et al., 2015). Studies investigating environmental contributions to school belonging have identified a number of influential themes such as classroom climate, the availability of recreational spaces, opportunities to play and socialize, and school size (Anderson, Hamilton, & Hattie, 2004; Chan, 2008; Waters, Cross, & Shaw, 2010). A study by Anderman (2002) found school location was a major predictor of school belonging. The research suggested that students' sense of belonging was lower in urban school settings as opposed to suburban schools (Anderman, 2002).

Most studies that have investigated school environment with a student's sense of belonging have focused on student safety (e.g., Cunningham, 2007; Garcia-Reid, Reid, & Peterson, 2005; Hallinan, 2008; Holt & Espelage, 2003; Shochet et al., 2007; Whitlock, 2006). Findings consistently demonstrate that perceived safety is positively associated with school belonging. Cunningham (2007) investigated *bullying norms* and whether or not students felt that teachers intervened effectively when bullying occurred and whether or not they felt teachers viewed it as a concern. Findings suggested that the perception of healthy norms concerning bullying was positively associated with school belonging. Similar findings were reported by Hallinan (2008), who concluded that feelings of safety positively influenced school attachment. The studies by Garcia-Reid et al. (2005) and Shochet et al. (2007) also demonstrated that feelings of safety at school influenced school belonging, but this influence was mediated by support from others. When feelings of safety had been jeopardised, as in the case of repeated victimisation, Holt and Espelage found that school belonging was reduced. Thus, these studies show a clear relationship between feelings of safety and school belonging. Therefore, a school's practices related to fostering a safe environment should be a consideration in supporting school belonging within a school setting.

The important role of the teacher in supporting school belonging has been widely supported across a range of studies (Anderman, 2003; Bowen, Richman, &

Bowen, 1998; Brewser & Bowen, 2004; Garcia-Reid et al., 2005; Garcia-Reid, 2007; Hallinan, 2008; Shochet et al., 2007). A study by Anderman (2003), found that teachers play a significant role in predicting the sense of school belonging students feel. The study surveyed 618 middle school aged students and found that when teachers are able to promote mutual respect among peers and provide a safe instructional environment for students there is a stronger sense of school belonging. This study also noted that school belonging decreased over time (Anderman, 2003).

Crouch, Keys, and McMahon (2014) also found the importance of teacher support for student school belonging in a cohort of students with disabilities. Using a mixture of self-report and objective measures (teacher observations), data were collected for 115 students, which explored the role of the teacher-student relationship in school belonging for young people with and without disabilities. As found by previous research, school belonging was lower for students who perceived their relationship with their teachers as negative, and higher in students who reported a positive relationship with their teacher. Interestingly, it was found that the teacher's ratings of a student's school belonging were consistent with the student's self-reported ratings of school belonging. This finding extends school belonging research, which is mostly conducted through self-report measures by students and emphasises the importance of the student-teacher relationship for school belonging.

Slaten and colleagues (2015) conducted a qualitative study examining the educational needs of marginalized youth in an alternative high school. Researchers analyzed the data collected from these interviews and generated several domains, which were related to the educational needs that participants felt their school was meeting. One of the salient themes cited by participants as an educational need was their sense of belonging in school, and as part of that the genuine relationships students felt with teachers and/or administrators. Students identified school belonging in the form of relationships with school faculty as a primary motivation to stay in school as opposed to dropping out (Slaten et al., 2015). Thus, there is a role for support from school administrators as well as teachers in concern to fostering student school belonging.

The literature also provides evidence that it is not only the social support of teachers that is found to correlate with school belonging, but it is the academic support provided by teachers as well. Stevens, Hamman, and Olivárez Jr (2007) explored the effect of teachers who used mastery goal orientation and academic pressure on a total of 434 early adolescents (average age 12.71 years). Mastery goal orientation involves teachers assisting students to acquire new skills and master new situations through the development of personal goals (*see* Dweck, 1986). The findings suggested that students reported feelings of school belonging more when their teachers were perceived to promote mastery goal orientation in the classroom. A second finding revealed that teachers who applied academic pressure were also more likely to influence school belonging (Stevens et al., 2007). These teachers were more likely to challenge students and encourage their ideas, and request they explain their academic work. Notwithstanding these results, the most important finding by Stevens et al. was that the more teachers promoted learning over performance, the more students felt like they belonged to school.

It is not only a supportive and caring relationship from teachers that appears to be an important variable for fostering school belonging, but parent support as well. Kuperminc et al. (2008) conducted a study to investigate the variables that may mediate the relationship between parental involvement and achievement of Latino students. Researchers surveyed 195 middle and high school aged students and assessed their perception of parent involvement, school belonging, and academic competence. Teachers were also asked to provide data in the form of rating their expectations for student academic attainment. For the sake of the study, researchers were able to access school records to use grades as a measure of academic achievement. The results of the study indicate that school belonging mediated the relationship between parent involvement and academic adjustment (Kuperminc et al., 2008). Slaten et al. (2014) examined the impact different types of belonging, including school, had on the way students make career decisions. The results demonstrated that school belonging significantly contributed to career decision-making, the more a student felt they belonged, the more confident they were in making a career-based decision (Slaten et al., 2014).

In addition to teacher support and parent support, peer support through extra-curricular activities has also shown to be a strong predictor of school belonging. Studies have found that students who engage in extracurricular activities report a higher sense of school belonging compared to their peers (Blomfield & Barber, 2010; Waters et al., 2010). Time spent on these activities is seen to be a positive predictor of school belonging for both boys and girls (Dotterer et al., 2007), and is largely influenced by the adolescent's relationship with his or her parents (Shochet et al., 2007). Knifsend and Graham (2012) found that students who are moderately involved in extracurricular activities (i.e., two activities) feel a higher sense of school belonging than either students who are not involved at all, or students who are involved in too many. Thus there appears to be an optimal level of extra-curricular activities for fostering a sense of school belonging. Booker (2004) surveyed African American students (n=61) in a mixed methods study. The researcher utilized the quantitative research to determine a relationship between school belongingness and academic achievement and the qualitative methods to gain a further understanding of what the students perceived to influence their sense of school belonging. The results indicated that the students perceived both teacher and peer relationships to be the most significant influences to school belonging. Additional research was conducted by Shin, Daly, and Vera (2007) who examined the relationship between school engagement and peer norms (both positive and negative), peer support and ethnic identity. Researchers surveyed 132 seventh and eighth grade students and found peer norms to be a strong predictor of school engagement (Shin et al., 2007). Thus, in respect to school belonging it appears that the relationships students have with teachers, parents, and peers are central in fostering positive connections with school

SCHOOL BELONGING IN HIGHER EDUCATION

As previously mentioned, the construct of school belonging can manifest differently across various groups and settings. A recent trend has started to focus school belonging research on young adults in collegiate settings. Among the college population, research has shown belonging to be related to psychological adjustment, motivation, and grade point average (Pittman & Richmond, 2007; Pittman & Richmond, 2008; Guiffrida, Lynch, Wall, & Abel, 2013). In addition, researchers have made attempts to make models of school belonging on college campuses more culturally relevant (Tierny, 1992; Guiffrida, 2006). The purpose of this section is to discuss the most recent trends within the body of school belonging literature and identify opportunities for future research.

Further research has suggested that while school belonging may be related to academic performance, it is not necessarily related to college students' persistence to graduation (Guiffrida et al., 2013). Guiffrida and colleagues (2013) made this distinction, noting that students with high GPA's are not always motivated to finish college for various reasons. The study examined the relationship between GPA, intention to persist and motivation as it relates to Deci and Ryan's (1985) Self-Determination Theory (SDT). A sample of college students (n=2,520) were asked to complete questionnaires including measures of competence motivation, autonomy motivation, need for relatedness, intent to persist, and GPA along with demographic information (SES, race/ethnicity, gender, and 2 or 4-year institution). After analyzing the data researchers determined there was a significant relationship between relatedness and GPA. With regard to students' intention to persist only the measure of relatedness to school faculty was shown to have a significant relationship. The results lacked support for the other measures of relatedness (relatedness to home-altruistic, relatedness to home-keep up, and relatedness to school/peers; Guiffrida, 2013).

In attempt to adequately research this growing body of work, scholars have made attempts at identifying predictors of school belonging that are specific to college population (Freeman, Anderman, & Jensen, 2007; Slaten, Yough, Shemwell, Scalise, Elison, & Hughes, 2014). Freeman and colleagues (2007) evaluated college students' sense of school belonging within the classroom and the university as a whole. They attempted to examine the relationships between school belonging, academic motivation, and instructor characteristics. Data were collected from a sample of college freshmen (N=238) and the results indicated that social acceptance and pedagogical concern of instructors were large predictors of school belonging on a college campus.

A more recent study by Slaten and colleagues (2014) employed a Consensual Qualitative Research (CQR) design in order to analyze the meaning of belonging to students on a college campus (Hill, 2012). Researchers were able to identify several domains related to university belongingness: valued group involvement, meaningful personal relationships, environmental factors, and interpersonal factors. With this study, Slaten and colleagues (2014) determined that school belongingness looks different at the university level than at the school age level. Previous studies of school belonging on college campuses have employed modified versions of the Psychological Sense of School Membership (PSSM; Goodenow, 1993) to measure school belonging (Pittman & Richmond, 2007; Pittman & Richmond, 2008). The results found by Slaten et al. (2014) do not disprove Tinto's (1988) theory nor does it disprove the results found by previous studies (Pittmann & Richmond, 2007, 2008; Guifford et al., 2013). However, the results do suggest the need for a more appropriate measure of school belonging at the collegiate level.

Although the study of belonging in higher education is rather sparse and is often mistaken for similar constructs such as support, there has recently been research that may help to define the construct more clearly and provide opportunities for future research (Slaten, Elison, Deemer, Hughes, & Shemwell, 2017). Slaten et al. (2017) utilized previous qualitative research conducted by the team as well as consulting the literature on belonging to construct a piloted scale to measure belonging in higher education, the University Belonging Questionnaire (UBQ). The scale was analysed utilizing a exploratory factor analysis, followed by a confirmatory factor analysis and validity checks by comparing the scale to other constructs (ie social support, social connectedness, and general belonging). The result was a three-factor solution that was deemed valid and reliable: (a) university affiliation, (b) university support, and (c) faculty and staff relations. The final scale was 24-items total and will allow future researchers to more accurately measure university belonging and further understand the construct as it relates to academic, career, and psychosocial outcomes.

Due to the fact that school belonging at the collegiate level is still a growing area of research there are opportunities of future research to be completed. As work by Slaten and colleagues (2014) suggests, school belonging looks different for students enrolled at a university than it does for students enrolled at a local high school and there are many different variables that could be researched within this topic. In addition, there is a growing desire for school belonging work that is culturally sensitive and/or specific (Guiffrida, 2006).

Discussion and Future Directions

Although school belonging as a construct has garnered a substantial amount of attention in the literature, there are still some gaps that need to be tended to by academic researchers. Some preliminary qualitative research has suggested that students on the margins of the educational system find it exceedingly difficult to experience a sense of belonging in school (Slaten et al., 2015, 2016). Previous school belonging research has been limited in understanding the needs of youth in poverty, underrepresented minorities, students with disabilities, students with behavioral problems, and other marginalized youth, as it relates to their experience of belonging in academic settings. Future quantitative studies should focus specifically on marginalized populations and how these students may or may not differ in their experience of school belonging from their majority peers.

In addition to the need for increasing research focused on marginalized populations' experience of school belonging, intervention researchers have neglected to design studies that involve testing interventions that may increase a students' sense of belonging in school (i.e., SEL interventions, student mentoring, restorative justice practices). The majority of the scholarly/productivity regarding the construct of school belonging has demonstrated how a strong sense of school belonging significantly improves student outcomes, and yet there has been little research on examining what interventions help enhance this sense of belonging for students in the school setting. Future research should include the measurement of school belonging alongside psychosocial interventions that are utilized in schools to ascertain whether or not current intervention strategies impact student level of belonging. In addition, new intervention strategies could be designed to target school belonging specifically and assessed through experimental and quasi-experimental studies.

Finally, although school belonging in the K-12 school system has received a significant amount of attention, researchers have neglected to examine how school belonging is different based on developmental level and school building (ie elementary versus secondary versus post secondary). Perhaps the most glaring deficit area is a sense of belonging for university students. Scholars have begun the process of attempting to define the construct as there are many differences between university and primary/secondary school settings (Slaten et al., 2014, 2017). There is a need for more research in this area, most notably to utilize the UBQ (Slaten et al., 2017) to more accurately ascertain how belonging is related to student retention, well-being, and academic outcomes. Future qualitative work is needed to inquire about how students define a sense of belonging at the university level in the hopes of using this information to create a future instrument to measure the construct and begin looking at outcomes and predictors of university belonging. The implications of a greater understanding of school and university belonging contribute to the field of educational psychology and how the psychological, social, and academic needs of students can best be met to ensure successful educational outcomes across their lifespan.

ACKNOWLEDGEMENT

This chapter is an adapted version from Slaten, C., Ferguson, J., Allen, K., Brodrick, D., & Waters, L. (2016). School belonging: A review of the history, current trends, and future directions. *The Educational and Developmental Psychologist, 33*(1), 1–15. doi:10.1017/edp.2016.6

REFERENCES

Anderman, E. M. (2002). School effects on psychological outcomes during adolescence. *Journal of Educational Psychology, 94*(4), 795–809. doi:10.1037//0022-0663.94.4.795

Anderman, L. H. (2003). Academic and social perceptions as predictors of change in middle school students' sense of school belonging. *Journal of Experimental Education, 72*(1), 5–22. Retrieved from http://www.jstor.org/stable/20152724

Anderson, A., Hamilton, R. J., & Hattie, J. (2004). Classroom climate and motivated behaviour in secondary schools. *Learning Environments Research, 7*(3), 211–225. doi:10.1007/s10984-004-3292-9

Baumeister, R. F., & Leary, M. R. (1995). The need to belong: Desire for interpersonal attachments as a fundamental human motivation. *Psychological Bulletin, 11*(3), 497–529. doi:10.1037/0033-2909.117.3.497

Begen, F. M., & Turner-Cobb, J. M. (2015). Benefits of belonging: Experimental manipulation of social inclusion to enhance psychological and physiological health parameters. *Psychology & Health, 30*(5), 568–82. doi:10.1080/08870446.2014.991734

Blomfield, C., & Barber, B. L. (2010). Australian adolescents' extracurricular activity participation and positive development: Is the relationship mediated by peer attributes? *Australian Journal of Educational & Developmental Psychology, 10*, 114–128. Retrieved from http://researchrepository.murdoch.edu.au/3109/1/Blomfield_and_Barber_2010.pdf

Blum, R. W., & Libbey, H. P. (2004). Wingspread declaration on school connections. *Journal of School Health, 74*(7), 231–232. doi:10.1111/j.1746-1561.2004.tb08278.x

Boden-Albala, B., Litwak, E., Elkind, M. S. V., Rundek, T., & Sacco, R. L. (2005). Social isolation and outcomes post stroke. *Neurology, 64*, 1888–1892. http://dx.doi.org/10.1212/01.WNL.0000163510.79351.AF

Bonny, A. E., Britto, M. T., Klostermann, B. K., Hornung, R. W., & Slap, G. B. (2000). School disconnectedness: Identifying adolescents at risk. *Pediatrics, 106*, 1017–1021. Retrieved from http://pediatrics.aappublications.org/content/pediatrics/106/5/1017.full.pdf

Booker, K. C. (2004). Exploring school belonging and academic achievement in African American adolescents. *Curriculum and Teaching Dialogue, 6*(2), 131. Retrieved from http://eds.b.ebscohost.com/eds/pdfviewer/pdfviewer?sid=8e323dbf-4f73-41da-bf54-d440b3d74101%40sessionmgr104&vid=0&hid=108&preview=false

Bowen, G., Richman, J. M., Brewster, A., & Bowen, N. K. (1998). Sense of school coherence, perceptions of danger at school, and teacher support among youth at risk of school failure. *Child & Adolescent Social Work Journal, 15*, 273–286. doi:10.1023/A:1007535930286

Brewster, A. B., & Bowen, G. L. (2004). Teacher support and the school engagement of Latino middle and high school students at risk of school failure. *Child and Adolescent Social Work Journal, 21*(1), 47–67. doi:10.1023/B:CASW.0000012348.83939.6b

Bronfenbrenner, U. (1977). Toward an experimental ecology of human development. *American Psychologist, 32*(7), 513. doi:10.1037/0003-066X.32.7.513

Brutsaert, H., & Van Houtte, M. (2002). Girls' and boys' sense of belonging in single-sex versus co-educational schools. *Research in Education, 68*, 48–57. doi:10.7227/RIE.68.5

Centers for Disease Control and Prevention. (2009). *School connectedness: Strategies for increasing protective factors among youth.* Atlanta, GA: U.S. Department of Health and Human Services.

Chan, K. (2008). Chinese children's perceptions of advertising and brands: An urban rural comparison. *Journal of Consumer Marketing, 25*(2), 74–84. doi:10.1108/07363760810858819

Cohen, A. P. (1982). *Belonging: Identity and social organization in British rural cultures.* Manchester, CA: Manchester University Press.

Cohen, S., & Janicki-Deverts, D. (2009). Can we improve our physical health by altering our social networks? *Perspectives on Psychological Science, 4*(4), 375–378. doi:10.1111/j.1745-6924.2009.01141.x

Collaborative for Academic, Social, and Emotional Learning (CASEL). (2003). *Safe and sound: An educational leaders' guide to evidence-based Social and Emotional Learning (SEL) programs.* Retrieved from http://www.casel.org

Connell, J. P., & Wellborn, J. G. (1991). Competence, autonomy and relatedness: A motivational analysis of self-system processes. In M. R. Gunnar & L. A. Sroufe (Eds.), *Minnesota symposium on child psychology* (Vol. 22, pp. 43–77). Hillsdale, MI: Lawrence Erlbaum Associates. Retrieved from http://psycnet.apa.org/psycinfo/1991-97029-002

Crouch, R., Keys, C. B., & McMahon, S. D. (2014). Student-teacher relationships matter for school inclusion: School belonging, disability, and school transitions. *Journal of Prevention & Intervention in the Community, 42*(1), 20–30. doi:10.1080/10852352.2014.855054

Cunningham, N. J. (2007). Level of bonding to school and perception of the school environment by bullies, victims, and bully victims. *Journal of Early Adolescence, 27*(4), 457–458. doi:10.1177/0272431607302940

Deci, E. L., & Ryan, R. M. (1985). The general causality orientations scale: Self-determination in personality. *Journal of Research in Personality, 19*(2), 109–134. doi:10.1016/0092-6566(85)90023-6

Dewey, J. (1938). *Experience and education.* New York, NY: Kappa Delta Pi.

Dotterer, A. M., McHale, S. M., & Crouter, A. C. (2007). Implications of out-of-school activities for school engagement in African American adolescents. *Journal of Youth and Adolescence, 36,* 391–401. doi:10.1007/s10964-006-9161-3

Dweck, C. S. (1986). Motivational processes affecting learning. *American Psychologist, 41*(10), 1040. doi:10.1037/0003-066X.41.10.1040

Erikson, E. H. (1968). *Identity: Youth and crisis.* New York, NY: Norton.

Finn, J. D. (1993). *School engagement and students at risk.* Washington, DC: National Center for Education Statistics. Retrieved from http://files.eric.ed.gov/fulltext/ED362322.pdf

Fiske, S. T. (2004). *Social beings: A core motives approach to social psychology.* Hoboken, NJ: Wiley.

Freeman, T. M., Anderman, L. H., & Jensen, J. M. (2007). Sense of belonging in college freshmen at the classroom and campus levels. *The Journal of Experimental Education, 75*(3), 203–220. doi:10.3200/JEXE.75.3.203-220

Furlong, M. J., O'Brennan, L. M., & You, S. (2011). Psychometric properties of the add health school connectedness scale for 18 sociocultural groups. *Psychology in the Schools, 48*(10), 986–997. doi:10.1002/pits.20609

Garcia-Reid, P. (2007). Examining social capital as a mechanism for improving school engagement among low income hispanic girls. *Youth & Society, 39,* 164–181. doi:10.1177/0044118X07303263

Garcia-Reid, P. G., Reid, R. J., & Peterson, N. A. (2005). School engagement among Latino youth in an urban middle school context: Valuing the role of social support. *Education and Urban Society, 37*(3), 257–275. doi:10.1177/0013124505275534

Glasser, W. (1986). *Control theory in the classroom.* New York, NY: Perennial Library/Harper & Row.

Goodenow, C., & Grady, K. E. (1993). The relationship of school belonging and friends' values to academic motivation among urban adolescent students. *Journal of Experimental Education, 62*(1), 60–71. doi:10.1080/00220973.1993.9943831

Guiffrida, D. A. (2006). Toward a cultural advancement of Tinto's theory. *The Review of Higher Education, 29*(4), 451–472. doi:10.1080/00220973.1993.9943831

Guiffrida, D. A., Lynch, M. F., Wall, A. F., & Abel, D. S. (2013). Do reasons for attending college affect academic outcomes? A test of a motivational model from a self-determination theory perspective. *Journal of College Student Development, 54*(2), 121–139. doi:10.1353/csd.2013.0019

Hallinan, M. T. (2008). Teacher influences on students' attachment to school. *Sociology of Education, 81*(3), 271–283. doi:10.1177/003804070808100303

Hamm, J. V., & Faircloth, B. S. (2005). The role of friendship in adolescents' sense of school belonging. *New Directions for Child and Adolescent Development, 2005*(107), 61–78. doi:10.1002/cd.121

Haslam, C., Haslam, S. A., Jetten, J., Bevins, A., Ravenscroft, S., & Tonks, J. (2010). The social treatment: The benefits of group interventions in residential care settings. *Psychology and Aging, 25*(1), 157–167. doi:10.1037/a0018256

Haslam, C., Holme, A., Haslam, S. A., Iyer, A., Jetten, J., & Williams, W. H. (2008). Maintaining group memberships: Social identity continuity predicts well-being after stroke. *Neuropsychological Rehabilitation, 18*(5–6), 671–691. doi:10.1080/09602010701643449

Hawkins, J. D., Guo, J., Hill, K. G., Battin-Pearson, S., & Abbott, R. D. (2001). Longterm effects of the Seattle Social Development intervention on school bonding trajectories. *Applied Developmental Science, 5*(4), 225–236. doi:10.1207/S1532480XADS0504_04

Holt, M. K., & Espelage, D. L. (2003). A cluster analytic investigation of victimization among high school students: Are profiles differentially associated with psychological symptoms and school belonging? *The Journal of Applied School Psychology, 19,* 81–98. doi:10.1300/J008v19n02_06

Holt-Lunstad, J., Smith, T. B., & Layton, B. (2010). Social relationships and mortality risk: A meta-analytic review. *PLoS Medicine, 7*(7), e1000316. doi:10.1371/journal.pmed.1000316

Iyer, A., Jetten, J., Tsivrikos, D., Haslam, S. A., & Postmes, T. (2009). The more (and the more compatible)

19

the merrier: Multiple group memberships and identity compatibility as predictors of adjustment after life transitions. *British Journal of Social Psychology, 48*, 707–733. doi:10.1348/014466608X397628

Jetten, J., Haslam, C., Haslam, S. A., & Branscombe, N. (2009). The social cure. *Scientific American Mind, 20*(5), 26–33. doi:10.1038/scientificamericanmind0909-26

Jose, P. E., Ryan, N., & Pryor, J. (2012). Does social connectedness promote a greater sense of well-being in adolescence over time? *Journal of Research on Adolescence, 22*(2), 235–251. doi:10.1111/j.1532-7795.2012.00783.x

Josselson, R. (1992). *The space between us.* San Francisco, CA: Jossy-Bass.

Knifsend, C., & Graham, S. (2012). Too much of a good thing? How breadth of extracurricular participation relates to school-related affect and academic outcomes during adolescence. *Journal of Youth and Adolescence, 41*, 379–389. doi:10.1007/s10964-011-9737-4

Kovacs, M. (1992). *Children's depression inventory.* North Tonawanda, NY: Multi Health System.

Kuperminc, G. P., Darnell, A. J., & Alvarez-Jimenez, A. (2008). Parent involvement in the academic adjustment of Latino middle and high school youth: Teacher expectations and school belonging as mediators. *Journal of Adolescence, 31*(4), 469–483. doi:10.1016/j.adolescence.2007.09.003

Libbey, H. P. (2004). Measuring student relationships to school: Attachment, bonding, connectedness, and engagement. *Journal of School Health, 74*(7), 275–283. doi:10.1111/j.1746-1561.2004.tb08284.x

Libbey, H. P. (2007). *School connectedness: Influence above and beyond family connectedness* (Doctoral dissertation). Retrieved from ProQuest Dissertations and Theses database. (UMI No. 3287822)

Lingard, B. (2010). Policy borrowing, policy learning: Testing times in Australian schooling. *Critical Studies in Education, 51*(2), 129–145.

Loukas, A., Roalson, L. A., & Herrera, D. E. (2010). School connectedness buffers the effects of negative family relations and poor effortful control on early adolescent conduct problems. *Journal of Research on Adolescence, 20*(1), 13–22. doi:10.1111/j.1532-7795.2009.00632.x

Ma, X. (2003). Sense of belonging to school: Can schools make a difference? *Journal of Educational Research, 96*(3), 340–349. doi:10.1080/00220670309596617

Maslow, A. H. (1943). A theory of human motivation. *Psychological Review, 50*(4), 370.

Maslow, A. H. (1954). *Motivation and Personality.* New York, NY: Harper.

Mcgraw, K., Moore, S., Fuller, A., & Bates, G. (2008). Family, peer and school connectedness in final year secondary school students. *Australian Psychologist, 43*(1), 27–37. doi:10.1080/00050060701668637

McMahon, S., Parnes, A., Keys, C., & Viola, J. (2008). School belonging among low-income urban youth with disabilities: Testing a theoretical model. *Psychology in the Schools, 45*(5), 387–401. doi:10.1002/pits.20304

McNeely, C., & Falci, C. (2004). School connectedness and the transition into and out of health-risk behavior among adolescents: A comparison of social belonging and teacher support. *Journal of School Health, 74*(7), 284–292. doi:10.1111/j.1746-1561.2004.tb08285.x

Moody, J., & Bearman, P. S. (2004). Suicide and friendships among American adolescents. *American Journal of Public Health, 94*(1), 89–95. Retrieved from https://galileo.seas.harvard.edu/images/material/2800/1140/Bearman_SuicideandFriendshipsAmongAmericanAdolescents.pdf

Newman, B. M., Lohman, B. J., & Newman, P. R. (2007). Peer group membership and a sense of belonging: Their relationship to adolescent behavior problems. *Adolescence, 42*, 241–263. Retrieved from http://ew3dm6nd8c.scholar.serialssolutions.com/?sid=google&auinit=BM&aulast=Newman&atitle=Peer+group+membership+and+a+sense+of+belonging:+Their+relationship+to+adolescent+behavior+problems&title=Adolescence&volume=42&issue=166&date=2007&spage=241&issn=0001-8449

Newman, B. M., Newman, P. R., Griffen, S., O'Connor, K., & Spas, J. (2007). The relationship of social support to depressive symptoms during the transition to high school. *Adolescence, 42*(167), 441. Retrieved from http://ew3dm6nd8c.scholar.serialssolutions.com/?sid=google&auinit=BM&aulast=Newman&atitle=The+relationship+of+social+support+to+depressive+symptoms+during+the+transition+to+high+school&title=Adolescence&volume=42&issue=167&date=2007&spage=441&issn=0001-8449

Nichols, S. L. (2006). Teachers' and students' beliefs about student belonging in one middle school. *Elementary School Journal, 106*(3), 255–271. doi:10.1086/501486

Osterman, K. F. (2000). Students' need for belonging in the school community. *Review of Educational Research, 70*(3), 323–367. doi:10.3102/00346543070003323

Pittman, L. D., & Richmond, A. (2007). Academic and psychological functioning in late adolescence: The importance of school belonging. *The Journal of Experimental Education, 75*(4), 270–290. doi:10.3200/JEXE.75.4.270-292

Pittman, L. D., & Richmond, A. (2008). University belonging, friendship quality, and psychological adjustment during the transition to college. *The Journal of Experimental Education, 76*(4), 343–362. doi:10.3200/JEXE.76.4.343-362

Poulton, R., Caspi, A., & Milne, B. J. (2002). Association between children's experience of socioeconomic disadvantage and adult health: A life-course study. *Lancet, 360*(9346), 1640–1645. doi:10.1016/S0140-6736(02)11602-3

Putnam, R. D. (2000). *Bowling alone: The collapse and revival of American community.* New York, NY: Simon & Schuster.

Read, B., Archer, L., & Leathwood, C. (2003). Challenging cultures? Student conceptions of 'belonging' and 'isolation' at a post-1992 university. *Studies in Higher Education, 28*(3), 261–277. doi:10.1080/03075070309290

Rogers, C. R. (1951). *Client-centered therapy: Its current practice, implications, and theory, with chapters.* Boston, MA: Houghton Mifflin.

Rowe, F., & Stewart, D. (2009). Promoting connectedness through whole-school approaches: A qualitative study. *Health Education, 109*(5), 396–413. Retrieved from http://www98.griffith.edu.au/dspace/bitstream/handle/10072/30069/57373_1.pdf?sequence=1

Ryan, R. M., Connell, J. P., & Deci, E. L. (1985). A motivational analysis of self-determination and self-regulation in education. *Research on Motivation in Education: The Classroom Milieu, 2,* 13–51.

Samdal, O., Nutbeam, D., Wold, B., & Kannas, L. (1998). Achieving health and educational goals through schools: A study of the importance of the climate and students' satisfaction with school. *Health Education Research, 3,* 383–397. doi:10.1093/her/13.3.383

Sanchez, B., Col´on, Y., & Esparza, P. (2005). The role of sense of school belonging and gender in the academic adjustment of Latino adolescents. *Journal of Youth and Adolescence, 34*(6), 619–628. doi:10.1007/s10964-005-8950-4

Shin, R., Daly, B., & Vera, E. (2007). The relationships of peer norms, ethnic identity, and peer support to school engagement in Urban Youth. *Professional School Counseling, 10*(4), 379–388. doi:10.5330/prsc.10.4.l0157553k063x29u

Shochet, I. M., Smith, C. L., Furlong, M. J., & Homel, R. (2011). A prospective study investigating the impact of school belonging factors on negative affect in adolescents. *Journal of Clinical Child & Adolescent Psychology, 40*(4), 586–595. doi:10.1080/15374416.2011.581616

Shochet, I. M., Smyth, T. L., & Homel, R. (2007). The impact of parental attachment on adolescent perception of the school environment and school connectedness. *Australian and New Zealand Journal of Family Therapy, 28*(2), 109–118. doi:10.1375/anft.28.2.109

Simons-Morton, B. G., & Crump, A. D. (2002). The association of parental involvement and social competence with school adjustment and engagement among sixth graders. *Journal of School Health, 73*(3), 121–126. doi:10.1375/anft.28.2.109

Sirin, S. R., & Rogers-Sirin, L. (2004). Exploring school engagement of middle-class African American adolescents. *Youth & Society, 35*(3), 323–340. doi:10.1177/0044118X03255006

Slaten, C. D., Elison, Z. M., Deemer, E. D., Hughes, H., & Shemwell, D. A. (2017). The development and validation of the university belonging questionnaire. *Journal of Experimental Education,* 1–19. doi:10.1080/00220973.2017.1339009

Slaten, C. D., Elison, Z. M., Hughes, H., Yough, M., & Shemwell, D. (2015). Hearing the voices of youth at risk for academic failure: What professional school counselors need to know. *The Journal of Humanistic Counseling, 54*(3), 203–220. doi:10.1002/johc.12012

Slaten, C. D., Yough, M. S., Shemwell, D. A., Scalise, D. A., Elison, Z. M., & Hughes, H. A. (2014). Eat, sleep, breathe, study: Understanding what it means to belong at a university from the student perspective. *Excellence in Higher Education, 5*(1), 1–5. doi:10.5195/ehe.2014.117

Solomon, D., Watson, M., Battistich, V., Schaps, E., & Delucchi, K. (1996). Creating classrooms that students experience as communities. *American Journal of Community Psychology, 24,* 719–748.

Stevens, T., Hamman, D., & Olivárez Jr, A. (2007). Hispanic students' perception of white teachers' mastery goal orientation influences sense of school belonging. *Journal of Latinos and Education, 6*(1), 55–70. doi:10.1080/15348430709336677

Stoddard, S. A., McMorris, B. J., & Sieving, R. E. (2011). Do social connections and hope matter in predicting early adolescent violence? *American Journal of Community Psychology, 48*(3–4), 247–256. doi:10.1007/s10464-010-9387-9

Summers, J. J., Svinicki, M. D., Gorin, J. S., & Sullivan, T. A. (2002). Student feelings of connection to the campus and openness to diversity and challenge at a large research university: Evidence of progress? *Innovative Higher Education, 27*(1), 53–64. doi:10.1023/A:1020420507339

Tajfel, H. (1972). *Experiments in a vacuum. The context of social psychology: A critical assessment.* Oxford: Academic Press. Retrieved from http://psycnet.apa.org/psycinfo/1973-28845-007

Tierney, W. G. (1992). An anthropological analysis of student participation in college. *The Journal of Higher Education, 63*(6), 603–618. Retrieved from http://www.jstor.org/stable/pdf/1982046.pdf

Tinto, V. (1988). Stages of student departure: Reflections on the longitudinal character of student leaving. *The Journal of Higher Education, 59*(4), 438–455. Retrieved from http://www.jstor.org/stable/pdf/1981920.pdf

Uwah, C., McMahon, G., & Furlow, C. (2008). School belonging, educational aspirations, and academic self-efficacy among African American male high school students: Implications for school counselors. *Professional School Counseling, 11*(5), 296–305. Retrieved from http://www.thefreelibrary.com/School+belonging,+educational+aspirations,+and+academic+self-efficacy...-a0180860878

Voekl, K. E. (1996). Measuring identification with school. *Educational and Psychological Measurement, 56,* 760–770.

Vygotsky, L. S. (1962). *Thought and language.* Cambridge, MA: MIT Press.

Wadsworth, M. E., Thomsen, A. H., Saltzman, H., Connor-Smith, J. K., & Compas, B. E. (2001). Coping with stress during childhood and adolescence: Problems, progress, and potential in theory and research. *Psychological Bulletin, 127*(1), 87–127. doi:10.1037/0033-2909.127.1.87

Walton, G. M., & Cohen, G. L. (2011). A brief social-belonging intervention improves academic and health outcomes of minority students. *Science Journal, 331*(6023), 1447–1451. doi:10.1126/science.1198364

Walton, G. M., Cohen, G. L., Cwir, D., & Spencer, S. J. (2012). Mere belonging: The power of social connections. *Journal of Personality and Social Psychology, 102*(3), 513–32. doi:10.1037/a0025731

Wang, M., & Eccles, J. S. (2012). Social support matters: Longitudinal effects of social support on three dimensions of school engagement from middle to high school. *Child Development, 83*(3), 877–895. doi:10.1111/j.1467-8624.2012.01745.x

Waters, S., Cross, D., & Shaw, T. (2010). Does the nature of schools matter? An exploration of selected school ecology factors on adolescent perceptions of school connectedness. *British Journal of Educational Psychology, 80*(3), 381–402. doi:10.1348/000709909X484479

Whitlock, J. (2006). The role of adults, public space, and power in adolescent community connectedness. *Journal of Community Psychology, 35*(4), 499–518. doi:10.1002/jcop.20161

Willms, J. D. (2000). Monitoring school performance for 'standards-based reform'. *Evaluation & Research in Education, 14*(3–4), 237–253. doi:10.1080/09500790008666976

Willms, J. D. (2003). *Student engagement at school: A sense of belonging and participation: Results from PISA 2000.* Retrieved from http://www.oecd.org/edu/school/programmeforinternationalstudentassessmentpisa/33689437.pdf

Zimmer-Gembeck, M. J., Hunter, T. A., & Pronk, R. (2007). A model of behaviors, peer relations and depression: Perceived social acceptance as a mediator and the divergence of perceptions. *Journal of Social and Clinical Psychology, 26,* 273–283. doi:10.1521/jscp.2007.26.3.273

Christopher D. Slaten
Department of Educational, School, and Counseling Psychology
University of Missouri-Columbia
USA

Kelly-Ann Allen
The Melbourne Graduate School of Education
The University of Melbourne
Australia

Jonathan K. Ferguson
Department of Educational, School, and Counseling Psychology
University of Missouri-Columbia
USA

Dianne Vella-Brodrick
The Melbourne Graduate School of Education
The University of Melbourne
Australia

Lea Waters
The Melbourne Graduate School of Education
The University of Melbourne
Australia

PART 2

CURRENT RESEARCH ON SCHOOL BELONGING

ANNIE GOWING AND ALUN C. JACKSON

3. STUDENT AND STAFF PERSPECTIVES ON SCHOOL CONNECTEDNESS

INTRODUCTION

School connectedness (SC) is one of a number of terms used to describe a student's relationship to school. SC is an ecological concept, consisting of affective, behavioural and cognitive dimensions, placing the individual in relationship with others. The transactional pathways of these relationships are multi-directional and shape and influence the individual's and others' experience of SC. With school being a compulsory feature of most young people's lives, the nature of their relationship with this institution can be highly influential in terms of the quality of their overall school experience. Young people with low connectedness to school are more likely to withdraw from school (Finn, 1989) and experience the precarious outcomes that often follow (Bloom, 2010; Lessard et al., 2008; Sum, Khatiwada, McLaughlin, & Palma, 2009).

The relationship between young people and school is the foundation on which the educational enterprise rests, therefore this relationship is seen as highly influential in terms of outcomes for students, including its impact on academic performance and health (Mouton, Hawkins, McPherson, & Copley, 1996; Prince & Hadwin, 2013; Samdal, Nutbeam, Wold, & Kannas, 1998). The list of terms used to describe this relationship is lengthy, including engagement, bonding, belonging, and attachment and the proliferation of terms has itself become a focus of comment and discussion (Allen & Bowles, 2012; Jimerson, Campos, & Greif, 2003; Libbey, 2004; O'Farrell & Morrison, 2003). Many researchers in this field preface their work with an acknowledgement of the variety of terms and lack of consistency in application and measurement (Faulkner, Adlaf, Irving, Allison, & Dwyer, 2009; Frydenberg, Care, Freeman, & Chan, 2009).

The Evolution of the Construct 'School Connectedness'

Described as a basic human need to belong and to experience relational mutuality (Baumeister & Leary, 1995), connectedness or social connectedness as it is frequently called, occurs in the exchanges between individuals and their social ecologies, which are broadly identified as family, school, and community or neighbourhood (Barber & Olsen, 1997; Shin & Yu, 2012).

SC has drawn increasing scholarly interest as a specific domain of social connectedness (Ripperger-Suhler & Loukas, 2012), first gaining a conceptual profile in 1993 when Resnick, Harris, and Blum named it as a key protective factor for boys and

© KONINKLIJKE BRILL NV, LEIDEN, 2018 | DOI:10.1163/9789004386969_003

girls against acting-out behaviours. Drawing on data from the National Longitudinal Study on Adolescent Health, Resnick et al.'s 1997 study identified SC as protective against a range of health-compromising behaviours and in the process firmly established its place in the field of adolescent health research. Newmann (1981) had referred to connectedness more than a decade earlier when discussing ways to reduce student alienation in schools. Although the term was used with no conceptual specificity at that time, Newmann's impassioned case for schools to be places of 'integration, engagement and connectedness' (p. 549) offered a blueprint for school reform that contained elements such as student voice, increased opportunities for extra-curricular involvement, and improved student-teacher relationships that continue to feature strongly in SC research. Newmann's 1981 vision appears remarkably prescient when read from a vantage point three and a half decades later. Since Resnick et al. conducted their 1993 and 1997 studies, SC has consolidated its presence in both education and health research as a key protective factor for young people, although its burgeoning profile has not produced greater conceptual clarity (Barber & Schluterman, 2008; Chung-Do, Goebert, Chang, & Hamagani, 2015; Millings, Buck, Montgomery, Spears, & Stallard, 2012).

The ambiguity surrounding SC can be partly explained by its location in the large set of constructs used to describe a student's relationship with school, including belonging and bonding. Whitlock, Wyman, and Moore (2014) in discussing connectedness and suicide prevention in adolescents identify nine conceptual frameworks that have shaped the definition of connectedness, including attachment theory, social support theory, resilience frameworks, and the bio-ecological model of human development. Additions to this list could comfortably include social control theory (Hirschi, 1969), motivation theory (Maslow, 1962) self-determination theory (Deci & Ryan, 2000; Ryan & Deci, 2000), and human relatedness theory (Hagerty, Lynch-Sauer, Patusky, & Bouwsema, 1993).

The definitions of SC that emerge from these theories range from Libbey's (2004, p. 274) pragmatic definition of SC as 'the study of a student's relationship to school' to more complex understandings, viewing SC as multi-dimensional (Tighezza, 2014) and generated by interactions among all members of a school's ecology (Rowe & Stewart, 2011; Waters, Cross, & Runions, 2009) Clearly an ecological understanding of connectedness, the overarching construct from which SC developed, is integral to its definition yet SC research has been slow to embrace its conceptual origins (Barber & Schluterman, 2008).

An ecological perspective has however, grown over the last decade. Blum (2005) noted that SC was influenced by the interplay between individuals, environment, and culture while Whitlock's (2006) definition marked a clear departure from earlier understandings, introducing the idea of SC as both given and received (Rowe & Stewart, 2009, 2010, 2011), used a whole-school approach, informed by the Health Promoting School Model, to identify ways in which SC could be enhanced and firmly located SC in the multiple ecologies of the school. Similarly, Waters et al. (2009) describe SC as a function of the dynamic interactions between individuals and their social and ecological environments.

While the definition of SC continues to evolve, a small number of early studies have continued to be highly influential in how it is understood. In 2004 the Wingspread Declaration on School Connections served as a clarion call for an increased focus on the relational dimension of young people's school experience, singling out students' relationships with adults, feelings of safety, and supportive environments coupled with high expectations for learning as the core elements of connectedness, and defined SC as students' belief that adults in the school care about them and their learning. In 2009 the Centers for Disease Control and Prevention co-opted this definition of SC and included peers as key relational influences.

Since Resnick et al. (1997) reported that SC was protective for young people against pregnancy, substance use, emotional distress, and involvement in violence, research into SC has accelerated and evidence of the reach of its protective qualities has accumulated. One reason for the positive reception of Resnick et al.'s findings may be that it reinforced previous research into the link between a student's relationship with school and health-risk behaviours. Wilson (2004, p. 298) rightly observed that research into social bonding, described as 'closely akin to connectedness' had already established that the quality of social bonds can lower delinquency rates. This research and associated studies into school bonding and delinquency (Hawkins, Guo, Hill, Battin-Pearson, & Abbott, 2001; Herrenkohl et al., 2003; Jenkins, 1995) provided a firm foundation on which research into the links between SC and various adolescent problem behaviours has developed.

More recently, SC has been studied in relation to Internet use (Yen, Ko, Yen, Chang, & Cheng, 2009), suicide prevention (Whitlock et al., 2014), depression (Joyce & Early, 2014; Shochet & Smith, 2014), and transport risk-taking behaviours (Chapman, Buckley, Sheehan, Shochet, & Romaniuk, 2011). The consistent findings from the research continue to be optimistic, situating SC as protective in young people's lives against a range of health risk behaviours.

Despite the bourgeoning research interest in SC, there continues to be little consensus on how it is defined (Loukas & Pasch, 2013) and the present study sought to address this gap by exploring the meanings of SC from both student and teacher perspectives. A small number of studies has begun to emerge in which teachers' views of connectedness are explored using qualitative approaches (Biag, 2016; Bower, van Kraayenoord, & Carroll, 2015; Chapman, Buckley, Sheehan, & Shochet, 2013), however student voices are largely absent. Notable exceptions in the Australian context are Rowe and Stewart's (2009) study exploring the influence of a whole-school approach to SC via a case study design in which both students and staff were represented and Thompson and Bell's (2006) use of focus groups to explore student, teacher, and parent perspectives on disconnection to school. More recently a New Zealand study by Neely, Walton, and Stephens (2015) used an ethnographic methodology involving students and teachers to explore the impact of shared school lunches on SC. Whitlock's (2006) study using surveys and student focus groups to explore contextual correlates of SC is also noteworthy, as is the study by Yuen et al. (2012) exploring Chinese adolescents' views on factors that shape SC. Such qualitative approaches however remain the exception and SC research continues to reside largely in the empirical domain with student surveys the default data source of most studies (Chapman et al., 2013).

The Current Study

To enhance the current understanding of SC, this study employed a qualitatively driven mixed methods approach to answer the following research questions and test the following hypotheses:

1. What are the meanings of being connected to school?
2. What factors are associated with students' connectedness to school?

   The hypotheses related to this research question are:

- A student's prior knowledge of Woodlands College, through having parents or siblings attend the College, would influence SC;
- A student's involvement in the decision to attend Woodlands College would influence SC;
- Starting secondary school with peers from primary school would influence SC;
- The more knowledge a student had about Woodlands prior to attending would influence SC; and
- The distance a student lived from school would influence SC.

METHOD

Design

This mixed methods study utilised both qualitative and quantitative data collection methods within a concurrent triangulation design (Cresswell, Plano Clark, Gutmann, & Hanson, 2003). This approach best suited the exploratory and confirmatory questions posed by this study and allowed both generation and verification of theory, which is considered a notable advantage of this approach (Teddlie & Tashakkori, 2006). The qualitative data were collected via student and staff focus groups, student diaries, and a student questionnaire with a series of open-ended questions and opportunities for additional comments, while the quantitative data were captured through single and multiple-choice items within the student questionnaire. The qualitative data enabled the exploration of meanings of SC as offered by students and staff, while the quantitative data, through identifying the factors associated with SC, allowed a profile of connectedness to be generated. Results from both data sources were triangulated.

Participants

The study was conducted in a co-educational secondary school, Woodlands College (a pseudonym), located in metropolitan Melbourne, Victoria, Australia. At the time the study was conducted, Woodlands had an enrolment of 1590 students and employed 167 teachers (68 males, 99 females). Participants ranged in age from 12 to 18 ($M = 15.09$, $SD = 1.67$). Indigenous students and students with a background other than English comprised less than 1% of the total enrolment. A total of 336 students (187 female, 149 male) participated in the study. In terms of living arrangements, most of the participating students lived with their immediate family consisting of

Table 3.1. Study participants by method of data collection

Data collection activity	Number of participants	Number of groups	Cohorts	Sex	
				M	F
Student questionnaire	206		Year 7	21	18
			Year 8	15	14
			Year 9	16	19
			Year 10	14	23
			Year 11	12	16
			Year 12	13	25
Student focus groups	118	2	Year 7	10	13
		2	Year 8	6	9
		2	Year 9	8	10
		2	Year 10	8	9
		2	Year 11	10	11
		2	Year 12	12	12
Student diaries	12		Year 7	2	2
			Year 8	1	1
			Year 10		3
			Year 11		1
			Year 12		2
Staff focus groups	71	3	Teachers	9	12
		1	Executive staff	4	1
		1	Year coordinators	4	3
		1	Student support	1	6
		1	Administrative		5
		1	Special education	2	4
		1	Resource centre		5
		1	Performing arts	3	4
		1	Physical education	5	4

parents and siblings (194, 94.2%), with the remainder living with extended family or friends (12, 5.8%). Seventy-one staff (43 females, 28 males) participated in focus groups. See Table 3.1 for participants by method of data collection.

For the quantitative data the required sample size based on the results of a power analysis conducted using G*Power v. 3.0.1. When conducting the a priori power analysis procedures, desired medium effect size, the error probability, the desired power of the test, and the type of statistical analysis procedures that were planned were all taken into account (Faul, Erdfelder, Buchner, & Lang, 2009). The results of the power analysis procedures are summarized in Table 3.2. A minimum sample size of 200 students was targeted for recruitment. A total of 206 students completed the questionnaire.

Measures

The student questionnaire constructed for this study drew on comprehensive SC research and consisted of 109 items in eight sections, containing 64 single response items, 23 multiple response items, and 21 open questions. The eight sections included questions regarding demographic details, teacher and peer relationships, engagement in learning and extracurricular participation.

The *School Connectedness Scale* (SCS; Resnick et al., 1997) has been widely used to measure SC, although considerable variations exist in how it has been applied (Furlong, O'Brennan, & You, 2011). While the original scale contained six items, other studies have used between three (Kaminski et al., 2010) and seven (Svavarsdottir, 2008). In this study four items from the School Connectedness Scale were included in the questionnaire. These questions pertained to whether the participant feels close to people at school, feels like a part of their school, feels safe at school, and whether the students at school are treated fairly. The 109-item questionnaire was piloted with five young people who had completed their final year of secondary education at Woodlands College in the year prior to data collection.

Item 26 in the questionnaire was a visual analogue scale (VAS), asking students to indicate their level of connectedness on a horizontal line with the anchor points being 'not connected at all' and 'very connected'. The VAS has been used extensively in health research to measure subjective experiences such as pain intensity, fatigue (Crichton, 2001), and patient quality of life (de Boer et al., 2004) and demonstrates reliability, validity, and sensitivity within health settings (Gift, 1989).

Table 3.2. Results of a priori power analysis for sample size

Statistical test	Effect size (Med)	Error probability	Desired power	Sample size
Correlation	0.30	0.05	0.80	82
ANOVA	0.25	0.05	0.80	200
Regression	0.15	0.05	0.80	109

The student focus groups were organised according to year level and included males and females, with the size of groups ranging from 6 to 13 with the lead researcher (AG) facilitating all groups. Staff focus groups drew participants from the different operational areas of staffing and teaching faculties with group size ranging from five to eight. Questions addressed how staff recognise connectedness in students, student-staff relationships and, how schools influence SC. The student and staff focus groups were developed and run according to protocols as described by Stewart and Shamdasani (1990). All focus groups were audio-recorded and transcribed by a professional transcription service.

Student diaries were used as another form of qualitative data collection. Diaries are regarded as an effective way to explore an individual's emotional and relational experiences and are popular in mixed methods approaches (Snowden, 2015). Students who volunteered for this activity were asked to record their daily experiences of school life both within and outside the classroom over a three-week period. Given the intimacy of the act of diary-keeping (Hayman, Wilkes, & Jackson, 2012) and the possibility of participant distress as a result, the researcher met weekly with young people to monitor their well-being and address any concerns that arose.

Procedure

Ethics approval was obtained from The University of Melbourne Human Research Ethics Committee and the principal at Woodlands College gave permission for the study to be conducted. Participant and parental consent were obtained and students were recruited from randomly selected classes at each year level. Students were then randomly assigned to complete a questionnaire or participate in a focus group, while students who kept a diary volunteered for this task. Engaging with both male and female students across year levels 7 to 12 and staff from different areas of school operations was considered important. As indicated in Table 3.1 the numbers of participants involved in each data collection method varied considerably but overall the goal of representation of different groups within the College was achieved. All data collection occurred in term 4 of the school year (early October to mid-December) in order to allow all students, but particularly the year 7 cohort who were in their first year at the College, to have experienced three terms of school life.

Data Analysis

Questionnaire data were examined using both descriptive and inferential statistical analyses. SC provided the dependent variable in the study and was derived from two sources. Each participant's connectedness response on the VAS was converted into a rating from Very Low (0–2) to Very High (9–10) and this rating was cross-tabulated against the independent variables in the questionnaire to identify significant associations.

SC was also derived by summing the scores attributed by the participants to the four questions in the questionnaire from the School Connectedness Scale

(Resnick et al., 1997). Each of the items was scored on a scale of 1 to 5, resulting in scores for the SC variable ranging from 5 to 25. A Pearson's correlation analysis was conducted to determine any significant relationships between the continuous variables of the study. The results of this analysis were also used as the basis to quantify the type and strength of relationship between the study variables, based on the r-coefficient. For the categorical variables, an analysis of variance (ANOVA) was conducted to determine whether the participants' characteristics were associated with differences in their school connectedness scores. A linear regression analysis was conducted to determine which study variables were significant predictors of school connectedness. In the linear regression analysis, the study variables identified to be significantly correlated with SC were used as the independent variables, while SC was used as the dependent variable. For all analysis procedures, statistical significance was set at $p = .05$. Excel 14.6.2 and SPSS v.22.0 were used to facilitate data analysis.

The qualitative data, drawn from open items in the questionnaire, focus groups, and diaries were thematically analysed allowing broad patterns to be identified. Thematic analysis is inductive, where the themes emerge from the data and are not predetermined by the researcher (Carroll, Booth, & Lloyd-Jones, 2012). In this study, the thematic analysis was conducted in accordance with the six steps identified by (Braun & Clarke, 2006). To facilitate the qualitative data analysis, NVivo v.8.0 was used. Both qualitative and quantitative data sets were analysed separately and results from each set were integrated during the analysis phase to identify areas of convergence or divergence (Terrell, 2012).

RESULTS

In addressing the research question about the meanings of SC, thematic analysis of the qualitative data from the student questionnaire, focus groups, and diaries provided a surprising result with a single meta-theme, *school is a place of opportunities*, distinctly emerging from each data source. Students used the word *opportunities* to describe what they liked about Woodlands, locating those opportunities within the three spheres of school life; relational, learning, and extracurricular with each of these spheres interconnected. The opportunities that school provided across these three spheres contributed to how young people understood the importance of school in their lives. There was consensus among students across all year levels that school was important, albeit to varying degrees and for different reasons. Many students regarded an education as offering a pathway to life beyond school with comments such as 'it's going to help in the future' and 'helps to get a good job' frequently expressed.

School was regarded however as providing more than a portal to options in the future. The importance of school for many students lay in the relational sphere where opportunities to interact with friends, peers, and staff members trumped other factors in how school was valued. The lead interpersonal relationships for students, both male and female, were friends and peers, with 192 of the 206 questionnaire respondents naming these relationships as the most valued aspect of school life. In focus groups and diaries students proclaimed the importance of friends, attesting to their central role in how they experienced school as revealed in a diary entry from a senior female student who wrote "I look forward to school because of my mates, because they make me feel so alive".

Learning opportunities were highly valued by most students and the learning opportunities at Woodlands were regarded as facilitating access to a quality educational experience which in turn was regarded as providing post-secondary pathways. Breadth of subject choice and well-resourced facilities and learning environments were frequently named as key factors shaping the educational experience, while teachers were also highly influential in terms of students' engagement with and enjoyment of their learning.

The opportunities offered within the extracurricular sphere of school life were also highly valued by many young people and contributed to how important school was seen to be in their lives. The diversity of offerings was referred to repeatedly although certain activities such as sport, music, and drama were frequently singled out for special mention. Overall, the range of options was viewed as broad and there was a strong sense that there was something for everyone. The interrelationship of these three spheres of school life was evident and the importance of school for many students existed across the three spheres with differences in emphasis, rather than valuing one to the exclusion of the others.

The meta-theme and sub-themes sat within a temporal and spatial domain so that opportunities occurred within particular places in the school (classrooms, school grounds, ovals) and within named time frames (a period, a lunchtime, a term, a year). Students in the focus groups and diaries consistently told a narrative that presented school as a journey with multiple episodes located across time and in a variety of spaces. These aspects are captured in a comment from a year 11 male student who observed that 'Everyday I'm creating history here with my mates'.

Five themes were identified from the staff focus group discussions in relation to how staff understood and recognised school connectedness in students: likes being at school, positive relationships with teachers and other school staff, belonging to a peer/friendship group, engagement in learning, and participation in extracurricular activities. Staff across all groups understood that the most fundamental expression of a students' connectedness to school was simply wanting to be there, enjoying being at school, and being happy to be present each day.

In addressing the research question about factors associated with students' connectedness to school, the correlations show that age ($r = .144$, $p = .039$), extracurricular activities ($r = .247$, $p < .001$), student voice ($r = .207$, $p = .003$), general health ($r = .187$, $p = .007$), and academic engagement ($r = .334$, $p < .001$) are significantly positively correlated with SC. The means, standard deviations, and correlations of the study variables are presented in Table 3.3. For SC, the dependent variable in the study, scores ranged from 5 to 24 ($M = 14.45$, $SD = 3.90$).

The categorical variables of the study were also analysed to determine whether these independent, grouping variables were associated with differences in the SC

Table 3.3. Means, standard deviations, and correlations for independent variables

School connectedness	M	SD	r	p
1. Age	15.09	1.67	.144	.039
2. Extracurricular Activities	1.05	1.08	.247	.000
3. Student Voice	2.72	1.03	.207	.003
4. General Health	4.56	1.15	.187	.007
5. Visits to School Nurse	2.38	.94	−.096	.169
6. Academic Engagement	7.92	1.07	.334	.000
7. Knowledge of School	3.28	1.02	.054	.444
8. Peers from Primary School	3.67	1.34	−.011	.876

scores of the participants. Based on the results of the ANOVA shown in Table 3.4, year level (F (5) = 4.026, p = .002), involvement in the decision to go to Woodlands College (F (5) = 2.598, p = .027), and cigarette use (F (1) = 9.617, p = .002) were significantly associated with differences in the SC scores of the participants. Students from the higher year levels had higher mean scores of SC compared to those from lower year levels. Similarly, students who made the decision to attend Woodlands with their parents had higher scores for SC. Students who reported cigarette smoking also had significantly lower SC scores than students who did not smoke cigarettes.

A linear regression analysis using SC scores as the dependent variable and the variables found to be significantly associated with SC as the independent variables was conducted. The results of the analysis indicate the proposed model is a significant predictor of SC (F (8) = 6.837, p < .001), accounting for 21.8% of the variance in the dependent variable (R2 = .218). Among the predictors included in the model, extracurricular activities (β = .515, p = .036), student voice (β = .607, p = .016), academic engagement (β = .626, p = .021), and cigarette use (β = 1.603, p = .015) were found to be significant predictors of SC.

Using the students' self-ratings of connectedness, significant associations were found with enjoyment in being a member of the school community (p = .001), the number of subjects a student liked (p = .001), the number of subjects the student was passing (p = .037), availability of an adult to talk to if the student was upset (p = .003), knowing at least one teacher well (p = .001), truancy for a whole school day (p = .004) and having received detentions (p = .041) or suspensions (p = .033).

Three of the five hypotheses were supported by this study. Students who made the decision with their parents to attend Woodlands had higher connectedness (p = .027). Students who knew "quite a lot" about Woodlands prior to entering Year 7 had higher levels of connectedness than students who knew "a few things" or "very little" (p = .030). Distance lived from school was also associated with connectedness, with students living within 10 kilometres of Woodlands having higher connectedness than students who resided over 10 kilometres from the college (p = .026). Having

Table 3.4. Results of ANOVA

	Mean	F	df	p
Sex				
Male	13.98	2.420	1	.121
Female	14.83			
Year level				
7th grade	13.95	4.026	5	.002
8th grade	14.69			
9th grade	13.89			
10th grade	12.70			
11th grade	15.57			
12th grade	16.18			
Parents from Woodlands				
Yes	15.43	1.732	1	.190
No	14.30			
Siblings from Woodlands				
Yes	14.61	.171	1	.680
No	14.37			
Involvement in school choice				
Students	12.20	2.598	5	.027
Parents	13.61			
Students with parents	15.02			
Other family members	11.00			
Family decision	15.63			
Cigarette use				
Yes	12.74	9.617	1	.002
No	14.85			

siblings or parents who had attended Woodlands and entering Woodlands with peers from primary school were not associated with connectedness.

DISCUSSION

This study aimed to explore the meanings of SC from a number of viewpoints. The study confirmed previously reported associations between SC and cigarette use, health status, extracurricular activities (Bonny, Britto, Klostermann, Hornung, & Slap, 2000; Brown & Evans, 2005), academic engagement and student voice

(Libbey, 2004). The study also identified new associations. Three of the hypothesised associations between SC were supported; joint decision making with parents about the choice of school, distance of residence from school and prior knowledge of Woodlands were associated with SC. Joint decision-making may lead to greater student investment in the decision and may also be an indication of parental involvement and interest in their child's educational experiences which has benefits for a young person's development (Davis-Alldritt, 2012). Closer residence to school may facilitate participation in extracurricular activities and increase familiarity with and access to school facilities and spaces, which in turn may promote incidental contact with other students (not necessarily in the same age group or year level). Prior knowledge of the school may allay anxieties and certainly many transition programs include induction activities aimed at familiarising the incoming students with the new school context and providing as much information as possible about the new environment (Flitcroft & Kelly, 2016; Mackenzie, McMaugh, & O'Sullivan, 2012). This study's finding supports the attention that many schools now place on the primary-secondary transition in the educational experience.

A key finding from this study concerns the way in which students understood their connection to school. For most students, this connection was experienced through the opportunities given to them by the school. Opportunities existed in relational, learning and extracurricular domains with considerable over-lap between each. Staff also understood SC in terms of a young person's relational and academic experiences as well as involvement in school life.

The lead relational experience for students in this study was the peer relationship. Although relationships with teachers were important, they did not have the intensity, the endurance, or the influence of peer relationships. This differs from much previous research, which has focused heavily on the teacher-student relationship and its influence on a student's experience of school. The gathering voice of young people regarding the importance of their peer relationships to their experience of school invites closer attention within SC research. Pianta, Hamre, and Allen (2012) acknowledged in their study on student engagement in the classroom that peer interactions are central to students' experience of the social environment of school, observing that the intensity of students' peer interactions outside the classroom are dynamic, brimming over with "youthful energy, excitement, and enthusiasm" (p. 369).

Most Woodlands students conveyed a similar message of exuberant delight in their peer interactions and were unequivocal in naming peer relationships as the most valued aspect of their school experience. In the present study, the teacher-student relationship emerged as more transitory and less influential than students' relationships with peers, which were repeatedly characterised as central to life at school. The narratives students told about school were biographical accounts in which they and their friends and peers were lead characters with teachers frequently appearing but occupying less prominent roles.

Limitations

Students and staff who participated in this study were drawn from a single school and therefore are not representative of all students or staff or the multiple school sectors within the education system in Victoria, Australia. The purposive sampling strategy may have excluded some participants whose experience of connectedness differed from those selected to participate. The voluntary nature of teacher participation in focus groups also means that not all teacher perspectives were represented. The self-reported data from the questionnaire, focus groups, and student diaries cannot be independently verified, however the congruence between the qualitative and quantitative data suggests that this was not a major limitation. It is worth noting, that due to its definitional ambiguity, some claims regarding SC are based on studies of different constructs. Engagement and belonging appear to be most frequently used as surrogates and this situation necessarily attenuates the strength of some claims regarding SC within this field of research in general.

Implications

SC emerges from this study as a process rather than a state, fluctuating across time within the relational, experiential, and physical spaces of school life. Reconceptualising SC as connec*ting* (and disconnec*ting*) to school requires responses that are both planned and spontaneous. Students are constantly building and dismantling their own and others' connection to school as they negotiate their educational pathways. These changes can be minor and transient or catastrophic, as when a young person drops out of school. The key challenge for schools is to become places of opportunity for every young person. This requires a commitment to delivering on the rhetoric or discourse of choice, increasingly favoured by schools in the competitive education marketplace (Yoon, 2016).

As Woodlands students so evocatively described, they understood their connectedness to school through a dynamic and complex inter-weaving of opportunities within the relational, educational, and extracurricular life of the school. Opportunities were rarely one-dimensional; an activity such as an excursion to the local park could offer opportunities in each domain. This understanding of SC asks much of schools. Opportunity settings across each domain must be flexible, inclusive, responsive and engaging. Students must be co-collaborators with school staff in this work, positioned as key players in any school improvement agenda (Fletcher, Fitzgerald-Yau, Wiggins, Viner, & Bonell, 2015; Simmons, Graham, & Thomas, 2015), and contributing to the imagining and design of an opportunity-rich school environment.

A priority in future SC research is the inclusion of student and teacher perspectives. Based on the current study, the peer-peer relationship invites further consideration. The influence of peer relationships on SC has to date been under-considered with definitions and measures of the concept too often either placing peer-peer relations in a subordinate position to the teacher-student connection or subsuming them in a catchall relational milieu that is unyielding to more nuanced analysis. This teacher-centric emphasis has obstructed a more robust exploration of the influence of peer relationships on SC. This study invited Woodlands students to tell their own stories about their connection to school and they foregrounded their peer relationships as central to their experience of school. Both the method and this finding have implications for future SC research.

In summary, SC has emerged from this study as a multi-dimensional, socio-ecological concept, placing the individual in relationship with others within the school and beyond. The transactional pathways of these relationships are multi-directional, shaping and influencing the individual's and others' experience of SC. Additionally, SC is fundamentally mediated through the individual's relational experience of school, and is therefore dynamic and fluid in nature, responsive to the relational opportunities or barriers that are thrown up within the school context. The malleability of a number of the factors associated with SC is good news for schools; they know where to focus their efforts – and this gives cause for optimism and energetic engagement with the task.

Further research is needed to arrive at deeper understandings of SC and to enable consolidation of its place as a unique concept among the multiple terms used to describe a young person's relationship to school. Qualitative research which seeks the views of students and staff to inform these understandings must be prioritised in the evolving research agenda. This study has demonstrated the value of listening to student and staff voices to arrive at richer, more nuanced, and complex understandings of connectedness to school.

ACKNOWLEDGEMENT

This chapter is an adapted version from Gowing, A., & Jackson, A. (2016). Connecting to school: Exploring student and staff understandings of connectedness to school and the factors associated with this process. *The Educational and Developmental Psychologist, 33*(1), 54–69. doi:10.1017/edp.2016.10

REFERENCES

Allen, K. A., & Bowles, T. (2012). Belonging as a guiding principle in the education of adolescents. *Australian Journal of Educational & Developmental Psychology, 12*, 108–119.
Anonymous. (2004). Wingspread declaration on school connections. *The Journal of School Health, 74*(7), 233–234. doi:10.1111/j.1746-1561.2004.tb08279.x
Barber, B. K., & Olsen, J. (1997). Socialization in context: Connection, regulation, and autonomy in the family, school, and neighborhood, and with peers. *Journal of Adolescent Research, 12*(2), 287–315. doi:10.1177/0743554897122008
Barber, B. K., & Schluterman, J. M. (2008). Connectedness in the lives of children and adolescents: A call for greater conceptual clarity. *Journal of Adolescent Health, 43*, 209–216.
Baumeister, R. F., & Leary, M. R. (1995). The need to belong: Desire for interpersonal attachments as a fundamental human motivation. *Psychological Bulletin, 117*(3), 497–529.
Biag, M. (2016). A descriptive analysis of school connectedness: The views of school personnel. *Urban Education, 51*(1), 32–59. doi:10.1177/0042085914539772

Bloom, D. (2010). Programs and policies to assist high school dropouts in the transition to adulthood. *The Future of Children, 20*(1), 89–108.

Blum, R. (2005). *School connectedness: Improving the lives of students.* Baltimore, MD: John Hopkins Bloomberg School of Public Health.

Bonny, A. E., Britto, M. T., Klostermann, B. K., Hornung, R. W., & Slap, G. B. (2000). School disconnectedness: Identifying adolescents at risk. *Pediatrics, 106*(5), 1017–1021.

Bower, J. M., van Kraayenoord, C., & Carroll, A. (2015). Building social connectedness in schools: Australian teachers' perspectives. *International Journal of Educational Research, 70,* 101–109. doi:10.1016/j.ijer.2015.02.004

Braun, V., & Clarke, V. (2006). Using thematic analysis in psychology. *Qualitative Research in Psychology, 3*(2), 77–101. doi:10.1191/1478088706qp063oa

Brown, R., & Evans, W. P. (2005). Developing school connectedness among diverse youth through extracurricular programming. *The Prevention Researcher, 12*(2), 14–17.

Carroll, C., Booth, A., & Lloyd-Jones, M. (2012). Should we exclude inadequately reported studies from qualitative systematic reviews? An evaluation of sensitivity analyses in two case study reviews. *Qualitative Health Research, 22*(10), 1425–1434. doi:10.1177/1049732312452937

Centers for Disease Control and Prevention. (2009). *Fostering school connectedness: Improving student health and academic achievement.* Atlanda, GA: Centers for Disease Control and Prevention.

Chapman, R. L., Buckley, L., Sheehan, M., & Shochet, I. M. (2013). Teachers' perceptions of school connectedness and risk-taking in adolescence. *International Journal of Qualitative Studies in Education, 27*(4), 413–431. doi:10.1080/09518398.2013.771225

Chapman, R. L., Buckley, L., Sheehan, M. C., Shochet, I. M., & Romaniuk, M. (2011). The impact of school connectedness on violent behavior, transport risk-taking behavior, and associated injuries in adolescence. *Journal of School Psychology, 49,* 399–410. doi:10.1016/j.jsp.2011.04.004

Chung-Do, J. J., Goebert, D. A., Chang, J. Y., & Hamagani, F. (2015). Developing a comprehensive school connectedness scale for program evaluation. *Journal of School Health, 85*(3), 179–188. doi:10.1111/josh.12237

Cresswell, J. W., Plano Clark, V. L., Gutmann, M. L., & Hanson, W. E. (2003). Adanced mixed methods research designs. In A. Tashakkori & C. Teddlie (Eds.), *Handbook of mixed methods in social and behavioral research* (pp. 209–240). Thousand Oaks, CA: Sage Publications.

Crichton, N. (2001). Information point: Visual Analogue Scale (VAS). *Journal of Clinical Nursing, 10,* 697–706.

Davis-Alldritt, L. (2012). School connectedness/parent engagement: Critical factors in adolescent health and achievement. *NASN School Nurse, 27,* 286–287. doi:10.1177/1942602X12462529

de Boer, A. G. E. M., van Lanschot, J. J. B., Stalmeier, P. F. M., van Sandick, J. W., Hulscher, J. B. F., de Haes, J. C. J. M., & Sprangers, M. A. G. (2004). Is a single-item visual analogue scale as valid, reliable and responsive as multi-item scales in measuring quality of life? *Quality of Life Research, 13,* 311–320.

Deci, E. L., & Ryan, R. M. (2000). The "what" and "why" of goal pursuits: Human needs and the self-determination of behavior. *Psychological Inquiry, 11*(4), 227–268.

Faul, F., Erdfelder, E., Buchner, A., & Lang, A.-G. (2009). Statistical power analysis using G*Power 3.1: Tests for correlation and regression analysis. *Behavior Research Methods, 41*(4), 1149–1160. doi:10.3758/BRM.41.4.1149

Faulkner, G. E. J., Adlaf, E. M., Irving, H. M., Allison, K. R., & Dwyer, J. (2009). School disconnectedness: identifying adolescents at risk in Ontario, Canada. *Journal of School Health, 79*(7), 312–318.

Finn, J. D. (1989). Withdrawing from school. *Review of Educational Research, 59*(2), 117–142.

Fletcher, A., Fitzgerald-Yau, N., Wiggins, M., Viner, R. M., & Bonell, C. (2015). Involving young people in changing their school environment to make it safer: Findings from a process evaluation in English secondary schools. *Health Education, 115*(3–4), 322–338. doi:10.1108/HE-04-2014-0063

Flitcroft, D., & Kelly, C. (2016). An appreciative exploration of how schools create a sense of belonging to facilitate the successful transition to a new school for pupils involved in a managed move. *Emotional and Behavioural Difficulties, 21*(3), 301–313. doi:10.1080/13632752.2016.1165976

Frydenberg, E., Care, E., Freeman, E., & Chan, E. (2009). Interrelationships between coping, school connectedness and wellbeing. *Australian Journal of Education, 53*(3), 261–276.

Furlong, M. J., O'Brennan, L. M., & You, S. (2011). Psychometric properties of the ADD health school connectedness scale for 18 sociocultural groups. *Psychology in the Schools, 48*(10), 986–997. doi:10.1002/pits.20609

Gift, A. G. (1989). Visual analogue scales: Measurement of subjective phenomena. *Nursing Research, 38*(5), 286–288.

Hagerty, B. M. K., Lynch-Sauer, J., Patusky, K. L., & Bouwsema, M. (1993). An emerging theory of human relatedness. *IMAGE: Journal of Nursing Scholarship, 25*(4), 291–296.

Hawkins, J. D., Guo, J., Hill, K. G., Battin-Pearson, S., & Abbott, R. D. (2001). Long-term effects of the Seattle social development intervention on school bonding trajectories. *Applied Developmental Science, 5*(4), 225–236.

Hayman, B., Wilkes, L., & Jackson, D. (2012). Journaling: Identification of challenges and reflection on strategies. *Nurse Researcher, 19*(3), 27–31.

Herrenkohl, T. I., Hill, K. G., Chung, I.-J., Guo, J., Abbott, R. D., & Hawkins, J. D. (2003). Protective factors against serious violent behavior in adolescence: A prospective study of aggressive children. *Social Work Research, 27*(3), 179–191.

Hirschi, T. (1969). *Causes of delinquency.* Berkeley, CA: University of California Press.

Jenkins, P. H. (1995). School delinquency and school commitment. *Sociology of Education, 68*(3), 221–239.

Jimerson, S. R., Campos, E., & Greif, J. L. (2003). Towards an understanding of definitions and measures of school engagement and related terms. *The California School Psychologist, 8*, 7–27.

Joyce, H. D., & Early, T. J. (2014). The impact of school connectedness and teacher support on depressive symptoms in adolescents: A multilevel analysis. *Children and Youth Services Review, 39*, 101–107. doi:10.1016/j.childyouth.2014.02.005

Kaminski, J. W., Puddy, R. W., Hall, D. M., Cashman, S. Y., Crosby, A. E., & Ortega, L. A. G. (2010). The relative influence of different domains of social connectedness on self-directed violence in adolescence. *Journal of Youth and Adolescence, 39*, 460–473. Retrieved from doi:10.1007/s10964-009-9472-2

Lessard, A., Butler-Kisber, L., Fortin, L., Marcotte, D., Potvin, P., & Royer, E. (2008). Shades of disengagement: High school dropouts speak out. *Social Psychology of Education, 11*, 25–42.

Libbey, H. P. (2004). Measuring student relationships to school: Attachment, bonding, connectedness and engagement. *The Journal of School Health, 74*(7), 274–283. doi:10.1111/j.1746-1561.2004.tb08284.x

Loukas, A., & Pasch, K. E. (2013). Does school connectedness buffer the impact of peer victimization on early adolescents' adjustment problems? *The Journal of Early Adolescence, 33*(2), 245–266. doi:10.1177/0272431611435117

Mackenzie, E., McMaugh, A., & O'Sullivan, K.-A. (2012). Perceptions of primary to secondary school transitions: Challenge or threat? *Issues in Educational Research, 22*(3), 298–314.

Maslow, A. H. (1962). *Towards a psychology of being.* New York, NY: D. Van Nostrand Company.

Millings, A., Buck, R., Montgomery, A., Spears, M., & Stallard, P. (2012). School connectedness, peer attachment, and self-esteem as predictors of adolescent depression. *Journal of Adolescence, 35*, 1061–1067. doi:10.1016/j.adolescence.2012.02.015

Mouton, S. G., Hawkins, J. D., McPherson, R. H., & Copley, J. (1996). School attachment: Perspectives of low attached high school students. *Educational Psychologist, 16*(3), 297–304.

Neely, E., Walton, M., & Stephens, C. (2015). Building school connectedness through shared lunches. *Health Education, 115*(6), 551–569. doi:10.1108/HE-08-2014-0085

Newmann, F. M. (1981). Reducing student alienation in high schools: Implications of theory. *Harvard Educational Review, 51*(4), 546–564.

O'Farrell, S. L., & Morrison, G. M. (2003). A factor analysis exploring school bonding and related constructs among upper elementary students. *The California School Psychologist, 8*, 53–72.

Pianta, R. C., Hamre, B. K., & Allen, J. P. (2012). Teacher-student relationships and engagement: Conceptualizing, measuring, and improving the capacity of classroom interactions. In S. L. Christenson, A. L. Reschly, & C. Wylie (Eds.), *Handbook of research on student engagement* (pp. 365–386). New York, NY: Springer.

Prince, E. J., & Hadwin, J. (2013). The role of a sense of school belonging in understanding the effectiveness of inclusion of children with special educational needs. *International Journal of Inclusive Education, 17*(3), 238–262. doi:10.1080/13603116.2012.676081

Resnick, M. D., Bearman, P. S., Blum, R., Bauman, K. E., Harris, K. M., Jones, J., Tabor, J., Beuhring, T., Sieving, R. E., Shew, M., Ireland, M., Bearinger, L. H., & Udry, J. R. (1997). Protecting adolescents from harm: Findings from the national longitudinal study on adolescent health. *JAMA, 278*(10), 823–832.

Resnick, M. D., Harris, L. J., & Blum, R. W. (1993). The impact of caring and connectedness on adolescent health and well-being. *Journal of Paediatric and Child Health, 29*(Suppl 1), S3–S9.

Ripperger-Suhler, K., & Loukas, A. (2012). School connectedness. In R. J. Levesque (Ed.), *Encyclopedia of adolescence* (pp. 2474–2481). New York, NY: Springer. doi:10.1007/978-1-4419-1695-2

Rowe, F., & Stewart, D. (2009). Promoting connectedness through whole-school approaches: A qualitative study. *Health Education, 109*(5), 396–413. doi:10.1108/09654280910984816

Rowe, F., & Stewart, D. (2010). *Promoting school connectedness: Using a whole-school approach.* Saarbrucken: Lap Lambert Academic Publishing.

Rowe, F., & Stewart, D. (2011). Promoting connectedness through whole-school approaches: Key elements and pathways of influence. *Health Education, 111*(1), 49–65. doi:10.1108/09654281111094973

Ryan, R. M., & Deci, E. L. (2000). Self-determination theory and the facilitation of intrinsic motivation, social development, and well-being. *American Psychologist, 55*(1), 68–78. doi:10.1037110003-066X.55.1.68

Samdal, O., Nutbeam, D., Wold, B., & Kannas, L. (1998). Achieving health and educational goals through schools: A study of the importance of the school climate and the students' satisfaction with school. *Health Education Research, 13*(3), 383–397. Retrieved from https://doi-org.ezp.lib.unimelb.edu.au/10.1093/her/13.3.383

Shin, H., & Yu, K. (2012). Connectedness of Korean adolescents: Profiles and influencing factors. *Asia Pacific Education Review, 13*, 593–605. doi:10.1007/s12564-012-9222-0

Shochet, I. M., & Smith, C. L. (2014). A prospective study investigating the links among classroom environment, school connectedness, and depressive symptoms in adolescents. *Psychology in the Schools, 51*(5), 480–492. doi:10.1002/pits.21759

Simmons, C., Graham, A., & Thomas, N. (2015). Imagining an ideal school for wellbeing: Locating student voice. *Journal of Educational Change, 16*, 129–144. doi:10.1007/s10833-014-9239-8

Snowden, M. (2015). Use of diaries in research. *Nursing Standard, 29*(44), 36–41.

Stewart, D. W., & Shamdasani, P. N. (1990). *Focus groups: Theory and practice* (Vol. 20). Newbury Park, CA: Sage Publications.

Sum, A., Khatiwada, I., McLaughlin, C., & Palma, S. (2009). *The consequences of dropping out of high school.* Boston, MA: Center of Labor Market Studies Northern University.

Svavarsdottir, E. K. (2008). Connectedness, belonging and feelings about school among healthy and chronically ill Icelandic schoolchildren. *Scandinavian Journal of Caring Sciences, 22*(3), 463–471. doi:10.1111/j.1471-6712.2007.00553.x

Teddlie, C., & Tashakkori, A. (2006). A general typology of research designs featuring mixed methods. *Research in the Schools, 13*(1), 12–28.

Terrell, S. R. (2012). Mixed-methods research methodologies. *The Qualitative Report, 17*(1), 254–280.

Thompson, G., & Bell, J. W. (2005). School connectedness: Student voices examine power and subjectivity. *The International Journal of School Disaffection, 3*(1), 13–22.

Tighezza, M. H. (2014). Modeling relationships among learning, attitude, self-perception, and science achievement for grade 8 Saudi students. *International Journal of Science and Mathematics Education, 12*(4), 721–740. doi:10.1007/s10763-013-9426-8

Waters, S., Cross, D. S., & Runions, K. (2009). Social and ecological structures supporting adolescent connectedness to school: A theoretical model. *Journal of School Health, 79*(11), 516–524.

Whitlock, J. (2006). Youth perceptions of life at school: Contextual correlates of school connectedness in adolescence. *Applied Developmental Science, 10*(1), 13–29.

Whitlock, J., Wyman, P. A., & Moore, S. R. (2014). Connectedness and suicide prevention in adolescents: Pathways and implications. *Suicide & Life-Threatening Behavior, 44*(3), 246–272. doi:10.1111/sltb.12071

Wilson, D. (2004). The interface of school climate and school connectedness and relationships with aggression and victimization. *The Journal of School Health, 74*(7), 293–299. doi:10.1111/j.1746-1561.2004.tb08286.x

Yen, C.-F., Ko, C.-H., Yen, J.-Y., Chang, Y.-P., & Cheng, C.-P. (2009). Multi-dimensional discriminative factors for internet addiction among adolescents regarding gender and age. *Psychiatry and Clinical Neurosciences, 63*(3), 357–364. doi:10.1111/j.1440-1819.2009.01969.x

Yoon, E.-S. (2016). Neoliberal imaginary, school choice, and "new elites" in public secondary schools. *Curriculum Inquiry, 46*(4), 369–387. doi:10.1080/03626784.2016.1209637

Yuen, M., Lau, P. S. Y., Lee, Q. A. Y., Gysbers, N. C., Chan, R. M. C., Fong, R. W., Chung, Y. B., & Shea, P. M. K. (2012). Factors influencing school connectedness: Chinese adolescents' perspectives. *Asia Pacific Education Review, 13*, 55–63. doi:10.1007/s12564-011-9176-7

Annie Gowing
Melbourne Graduate School of Education
The University of Melbourne
Australia

Alun C. Jackson
Melbourne Graduate School of Education
The University of Melbourne
Australia

CRYSTAL COKER, ANDREW MARTINEZ, SUSAN D. MCMAHON,
JONATHAN COHEN AND AMRIT THAPA

4. PERCEPTIONS OF SCHOOL CLIMATE

The Role of Extracurricular Activities

INTRODUCTION

School climate has been defined as the quality and character of school life (Cohen, McCabe, Michelli, & Pinkeral, 2009; National School Climate Council, 2007) and is based on patterns of student, parent, and school personnel experiences. School climate reflects norms, goals, values, interpersonal relationships, teaching and learning practices, and organizational structures (Thapa, Cohen, Guffey, & Higgins-D'Alessandro, 2013). While different models of school climate have been proposed, common dimensions include safety, relational (e.g., adult and student support), and environmental components (e.g., school connectedness) (Thapa et al., 2013). School climate has gained significant attention as a way to promote safer and more supportive schools.

As a multidimensional construct, school climate can be conceptualized as encompassing school belonging – a psychological construct characterized by feelings of attachment to school and relations with others in the school community. In other words, students' psychological connections to school or feelings of belonging to one's school could be considered one dimension of the broader construct of school climate. Further, school belonging and school climate have been shown to be directly correlated with one another (Huang, Xiao, & Huang, 2013). Thus, when students perceived their school climate positively, they also tend to feel a sense of belonging to their school and vice versa. Therefore, interventions that foster positive school climates have direct implications for school belonging.

As with school belonging, school climate has been associated with a range of student outcomes. For instance, school climate has been associated with motivation to learn (Eccles, Barber, Stone, & Hunt, 2003), decreased absenteeism (e.g., Gottfredson & Gottfredson, 1989), lower levels of aggression and violence (Gregory et al., 2010), and lower suspension rates (Lee, Cornell, Gregory, & Fan, 2011). In light of these outcomes, school climate reform has been identified as an important strategy for bully and dropout prevention in the United States (Centers for Disease Control and Prevention, 2009; Thapa et al., 2013).

Research has linked school climate with individual, classroom, and school-level factors (Koth, Bradshaw, & Leaf, 2008; National School Climate Council, 2015).

© KONINKLIJKE BRILL NV, LEIDEN, 2018 | DOI:10.1163/9789004386969_004

For example, factors such as race, gender, teacher-student ratio, and school size shape school climate. A focus on these different levels of the school environment and different settings within the school has helped to advance our understanding of school climate. Taking into account the various activities that students are involved in through their schools may yield additional nuance to our understanding of school climate.

Extracurricular Activities

School-based extracurricular activities provide additional experiences and have received increased attention as a way of supporting positive youth development (Ramey & Rose-Krasnor, 2012). Extracurricular activity participation has also been identified as a strategy to promote school connectedness (Centers for Disease Control and Prevention, 2009). School connectedness is a construct closely related to school belonging and sometimes used interchangeably with school belonging, and can also be conceptualized as a component of school climate (Anderman, 2011). Yet, scant research has examined how different types of extracurricular activities are associated with distinct dimensions of school climate.

According to the United States National Center for Education Statistics (2012), sports are the most common type of extracurricular activity among American secondary school students, with 44% of high school seniors reporting participation in some type of sport. In addition, 21% of students participate in music activities (band, orchestra or choir), as well as clubs, such as academic (21%), hobby (12%) (e.g., photography, chess), and vocational clubs (16%) (e.g., DECA, Future Farmers of America, Skills USA). Overall, extracurricular activities are associated with a range of positive outcomes such as higher grades, test scores, decreased school dropout, and greater educational attainment (Farb & Matjasko, 2012). Other studies have noted that the positive relationship between participation in extracurricular activities and academic outcomes may not apply across all activities (Farb & Matjasko, 2012). For example, Fredricks and Eccles (2008) found that participation in school clubs was related to higher grades whereas sports participation was related to less valuing of the school. Lleras (2008) found that participation in academic and sports activities was associated with higher educational attainment and job earnings while fine arts participation was associated with lower job earnings. Fredricks and Eccles (2008) suggest that these differences are a function of the unique ecological contexts consisting of distinct characteristics and relationships with peers and adults. For example, student athletes are more likely to associate with peers who drink alcohol (Eccles & Barber, 1999), and to have a higher social status (Barber, Eccles, & Stone, 2001). Sports have also been associated with opportunities to develop initiative while school clubs have been associated with experiences related to identity formation, and prosocial norms (Hansen, Larson, & Dworkin, 2003; Larson, Hansen, & Moneta, 2006). Thus, extracurricular activities afford students with different developmental opportunities, and research that examines extracurricular participation in relation to dimensions of school climate is needed.

Measurement of extracurricular activity involvement. Early research focusing on extracurricular activities suggested that participation in more activities is associated with more favorable outcomes; however questions were raised about the importance of the number of activities versus the combination of activities (Feldman & Matjasko, 2005). Participation in qualitatively different activities may increase exposure to different opportunities (Feldman & Matjasko, 2005), increasing the positive effects and compensating for negative associations of individual activities and developmental outcomes. Examining participation in extracurricular activities grouped together may mask the true relationship between specific extracurricular activities and specific student outcomes.

Research focusing on breadth of participation has grown in recent years and has supported the notion that more activities, up to a point, across different activity domains is better (Bohnert, Fredricks, & Randall, 2010; Farb & Matjasko, 2012). However, these studies do not yield information about student participation in different combinations of activities, such as participation in sports and clubs as compared to participation in arts and clubs (Linver, Roth, & Brooks-Gunn, 2009). Given that different types of activities offer unique developmental opportunities and experiences, specific combinations of activities may have varying implications for different student outcomes. Thus, examining specific activity combinations provides greater specificity to the literature on breadth of participation.

School Climate and Extracurricular Activities

Thapa and colleagues (2013) highlight four main dimensions of school climate: safety, relational, teaching and learning, and environmental. A review of the research on extracurricular activities suggests that various activities may support positive school climates. However, some extracurricular activities may support specific dimensions of school climate, more so than others. Below we focus specifically on the safety, interpersonal relations, and school environment dimensions of school climate.

Safety. Safety refers to social, emotional, and physical feelings of security within the school setting. Safe schools are characterized by low rates of verbal abuse, teasing, social exclusion, and physical violence (Cohen et al., 2009). Threats to safety can lead students to skip school (Centers for Disease Control and Prevention, 2009), which can undermine students' ability to learn. While scant research has examined the relation between extracurricular activities and perceptions of safety, Fleming and colleagues (2008) found that participation in extracurricular activities was related to less school misbehavior and delinquency. Moreover, Peguero (2008)

47

found that students who participated in classroom-related extracurricular activities (band, student government, yearbook, newspaper) were more likely to be bullied, as compared to student athletes. Thus, participation in certain types of activities may contribute to different treatment from peers, affecting their experiences and perceptions of school safety.

Interpersonal relations. The relational component of school climate involves interactions between people and how connected individuals feel (Thapa et al., 2013). Support from teachers and peers is associated with higher self-esteem and grades as well as psychological well-being (Jia et al., 2009). Extracurricular activities can contribute to positive student outcomes by allowing students to develop relationships with like-minded peers and supportive adults (Mahoney, Larson, Eccles, & Lord, 2005). However, scant research has examined the ways in which specific types of extracurricular activities may contribute to these interpersonal dimensions of school climate such as supportive or collaborative relationships with peers and adults.

School environment. The environmental dimension of school climate includes feeling cared for and as though one is part of the school community (McNeely, Nonnemaker, & Blum, 2002). School connectedness and school belonging have been used interchangeably within the research literature (Allen & Bowles, 2012; Guo, Choe, & D'Alessandro, 2011; Libbey, 2004), however, we use the term school connectedness in this study. Research on school connectedness has found that schools with higher rates of participation in extracurricular activities report higher levels of school connectedness (Blum, McNeely, & Rinehart, 2002). Using cluster analysis, Linver et al. (2009) examined five activity clusters – sports only, sports and other activities, little or no involvement, primarily school-based, and primarily faith-based activities. This study found that students who participated in the sports-only cluster reported higher levels of connectedness, but the study did not differentiate between specific types of school activities such as clubs or arts-based activities. Sports activities have been most extensively studied in the extracurricular literature, possibly because it is the most popular activity among high school (grades 9–12) students in the United States (National Center for Educational Statistics, 2012). However, given that students participate in other activities, such as clubs and arts, research is needed that examines how participation in multiple activities relates to student perceptions of school connectedness and belonging.

Current Study

The current study seeks to examine the relationship between participation in three of the most popular types of extracurricular activities among American youth (sports, clubs, and arts) and multiple dimensions of school climate (i.e., safety [social-emotional security], interpersonal relationships [adult support, student support], and school environment [school connectedness]), while controlling for student (e.g., race) and school-level characteristics (rate of extracurricular participation). Given the lack of research in this area, we test main effects in order to understand how each extracurricular activity is associated with perceptions of school climate. We also test interaction effects in order to examine how different combinations of extracurricular activities are associated with school climate. We hypothesize that the three activities will have differing associations with student perceptions of the school climate. Specifically, given the importance of sports and the status of athletes in American schools, we believe sports will be positively related to all dimensions of school climate. We further hypothesize that, when paired with sports, participation in other activities will result in more favorable perceptions of school climate.

METHOD

Participants

Participants consisted of 15,004 grade 9–12 students from 28 high schools across 11 states in the United States. The majority were 9th grade students (27%) followed by 10th (25.6%), 11th (25.1%) and 12th grade (22.3%) students. A slightly higher percentage of participants were female (51.5%). Regarding race/ethnicity, the majority of students self-identified as White (68.6%), followed African American (10.3%), Latino (8.4%), multi-racial (6.1%), Asian (4.7%), and American Indian/Alaska Native (1.5%). Most students participated in sports (54.1%), followed by clubs (37%), and arts (22.6%). Approximately one-fourth of the students in this sample were not involved in an extracurricular activity. The majority of schools were public (96.3%) and suburban (67.9%), followed by urban (25%) and rural (7.1%) settings. The average percentage of students across schools displaying financial need was 36.2% (data available for 24 schools).

Measures

Independent variables. We examined students who participated in sports, clubs, and art-related extracurricular activities. Each of these categorical variables consisted of binary measurement (1 = participated in the extracurricular activity; 0 = did not participate in the extracurricular activity). Students who did not participate in the extracurricular activity served as the reference group. Students who participated in arts consisted of students who reported involvement in music and performing arts (e.g., drama, acting).

Control variables. We controlled for three individual-level variables: gender (females as reference group), race/ethnicity (non-White as reference group), and grade-level (9th grade as reference group). We also included an aggregated school-level variable to account for extracurricular involvement at the respective schools, given school variation in extracurricular offerings and involvement. This variable is a percentage, which was computed by dividing the total number of students who reported involvement in at least one extracurricular activity by the total number of students sampled from that school.

Outcome variables.   The four outcome variables in this study were drawn from the Comprehensive School Climate Inventory (CSCI-V3.0). The CSCI evaluates student, parent, and school staff perceptions of school climate, and in this study we focus on student perceptions. Additionally, we focus on three of the four major CSCI domains, safety, interpersonal relationships, and institutional environment. Items on the CSCI are assessed using a 5-point Likert scale (1 = Strongly Disagree, 5 = Strongly Agree), with higher scores reflecting more favorable perceptions of school climate. The CSCI has good construct validity and internal consistency (Clifford, Menon, Gangi, Condon, & Hornung, 2012).

Safety: social-emotional security.   Social-emotional security refers to the extent to which students feel safe from verbal abuse, teasing, and exclusion within the school. This subscale consists of six items and is one of the three subscales within the safety domain of the CSCI. A sample item is "Adults in the school stop students if they see them insulting, teasing, and making fun of others". This scale demonstrated good internal consistency ($\alpha = .85$).

Interpersonal relationships: adult social support.   Adult social support is defined as the pattern of supportive and caring adult relationships for students, including high expectations for students' success, willingness to listen to students and to get to know them as individuals, and personal concern for students' problems. This subscale consists of eight items and is one of the three subscales within the interpersonal relationships domain of the CSCI. A sample item is "Adults who work in my school treat students with respect". This scale demonstrated good internal consistency ($\alpha = .86$).

Interpersonal relationships: student social support.   Student social support refers to the pattern of supportive peer relationships for students, including friendships for socializing, problems, academic help, and for new students. This subscale consists of five items and is one of the three subscales within the interpersonal relationships domain of the CSCI. A sample item is "Students have friends at school they can trust and talk to if they have problems". This scale demonstrated acceptable internal consistency ($\alpha = .73$).

Institutional environment: school connectedness.   School connectedness refers to positive identification with the school, and norms for broad participation in school life for students, staff, and families. This subscale consists of eight items and is one of the two subscales within the environment domain of the CSCI. A sample item is "I feel like I belong at my school". This scale demonstrated good internal consistency ($\alpha = .82$).

ANALYSIS

Due to the nested structure of these data, we used multilevel regression modeling to test our hypotheses, through four simultaneous models in which social-emotional security, adult social support, student social support, and school connectedness served as the respective outcome variables. The level-one (student-level) predictor variables include gender (female vs: male), race/ethnicity (White vs. Non-White), grade, and participation in sports, clubs, and arts, respectively. One school-level predictor variable, school-level extracurricular involvement, was included. Regarding extracurricular activities, the main effects compare students who participate in the activity (e.g., sports) versus students who do not participate in the activity, while accounting for participation in other extracurricular activities (arts and clubs). These main effects answer questions such as "Do students participating in sports report higher levels of school connectedness, as compared to students not participating in sports, while taking into account participation in arts and clubs?"

Students can participate in multiple extracurricular activities (sports and arts), and therefore we incorporated interaction effects between the different types of extracurricular activities (sports x arts; sports x clubs; arts x clubs; sports x arts x clubs) to test how involvement in combinations of activities are associated with dimensions of school climate. Due to the multiple interaction effects we set the critical value to .001. These interaction effects were all level-one variables.

RESULTS

There were significant demographic differences in perceptions of school climate (see Table 4.1). Male students reported more positive perceptions of social emotional security than female students, while White students reported more positive perceptions of adult support, peer support, and connectedness compared to non-White students. Perceptions of school climate appeared to decrease with age, as 9th grade students reported more positive perceptions of school climate than 10th, 11th, and 12th grade students. These demographic factors were controlled for in subsequent analyses.

Safety: Social-Emotional Security

The results revealed significant main effects for gender, grade, and participation in sports (see Table 4.1). Students who participated in sports ($M = 2.92$) reported more social-emotional security than students who did not participate in sports ($M = 2.83$).

C. COKER ET AL.

Table 4.1. Main effects and interactions

	Social-emotional security		Adult social support		Student support		Connectedness	
	B	SE	B	SE	B	SE	B	SE
Intercept	3.19*	.18	3.73*	.15	3.67*	.13	3.50*	.15
Gender								
Male	.05*	.01	−.002	.01	−.02	.01	.01	.01
Race/ethnicity								
White	−.03	.01	.08*	.01	.08*	.01	.07*	.01
Grade								
10	−.12*	.02	−.07*	.01	−.05*	.01	−.10*	.01
11	−.09*	.02	−.09*	.01	−.04	.01	−.15*	.01
12	−.04	.02	−.07*	.01	−.02	.01	−.12*	.01
Extracurricular activities								
Sports	.10*	.02	.08*	.01	.14*	.01	.21*	.01
Clubs	.04	.02	.19*	.02	.12*	.02	.23*	.02
Arts	.04	.03	.07	.02	.09*	.02	.13*	.02
Sports*Arts	−.06	.04	−.06	.03	−.04	.03	−.12*	.03
Arts*Clubs	−.11	.04	−.09	.02	−.03	.04	−.13*	.04
Sports*Clubs	−.03	.03	−.09*	.02	−.02	.02	−.10*	.02
Sports*Arts*Clubs	.04	.06	−.02	.05	−.09	.05	.04	.05
School-level extracurricular participation	−.004	.003	−.003	.002	−.002	0.002	−.003	.002

*Notes: N = 15,004; *p<.001*

Interpersonal Relationships

Adult social support. Results revealed significant main effects for grade, race/ethnicity, participation in sports, and participation in clubs (see Table 4.1). Students who participated in sports (M = 3.61) reported higher levels of adult social support than students who did not participate in sports (M = 3.57). Further, students who participated in clubs (M = 3.67) reported higher levels of school adult social support than students who did not participate in clubs (M = 3.55). The results also revealed an interaction effect between sports participation and participation in clubs (see Figure 4.1). While participation in clubs (M = 3.69) was associated with higher levels of adult support in comparison to students who were not involved in sports or

52

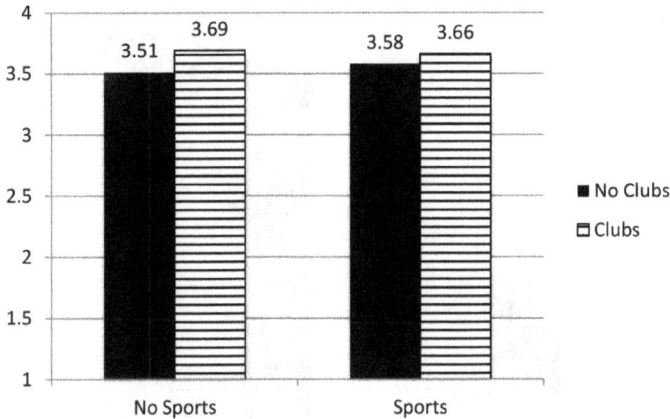

Figure 4.1. Adult support – interaction between sports and clubs

clubs ($M = 3.51$); when students participated in sports, clubs ($M = 3.66$) no longer contributed to more adult support.

Student social support. Results revealed significant main effects for race/ethnicity, and participation in sports, clubs, and arts, respectively (see Table 4.1). Students who participated in sports ($M = 3.72$) clubs, ($M = 3.73$) and arts ($M = 3.73$), respectively, reported more student social support than their counterparts who were not involved in these activities (no sports, $M = 3.59$; no clubs, $M = 3.64$, no arts, $M = 3.62$).

Institutional Environment: School Connectedness

Results revealed significant main effects for race/ethnicity, sports, clubs, and arts (see Table 4.1). Students who participated in sports ($M = 3.50$), clubs ($M = 3.52$), and arts ($M = 3.45$) reported higher levels of school connectedness than their counterparts (no sports, $M = 3.35$; no clubs, $M = 3.38$, no arts, $M = 3.43$).

Results also revealed three interaction effects (see Figures 4.2–4.4). A sports x arts interaction revealed that participation in arts was associated with higher levels of school connectedness ($M = 3.42$) in comparison to students who were not involved in arts or sports (3.33). However, when students participated in sports, arts ($M = 3.48$) no longer contributed to more school connectedness. The sports x clubs interaction revealed that participation in sports ($M = 3.46$) was associated with higher levels of school connectedness in comparison to students who were not involved in sports or clubs ($M = 3.28$); however, among students participating in clubs, sports ($M = 3.57$) no longer contributed to more connectedness. Finally, the clubs x arts interaction revealed that participation in arts ($M = 3.43$) was associated with higher levels of

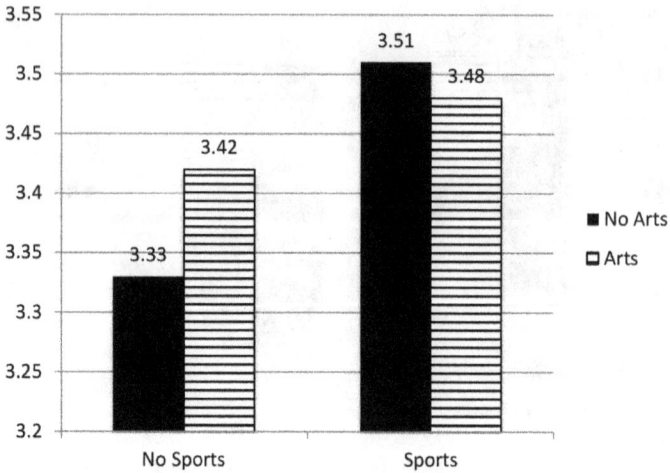

Figure 4.2. School connectedness – interaction of sports and arts

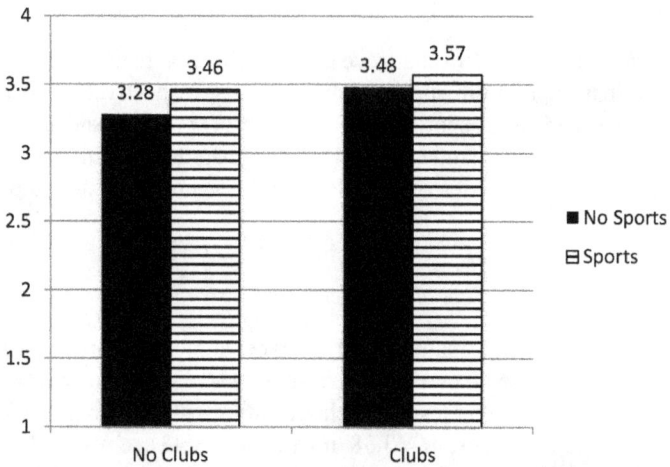

Figure 4.3. School connectedness – interaction of sports and clubs

school connectedness in comparison to students who were not involved in arts or clubs ($M = 3.36$). However, when students participated in clubs, arts ($M = 3.49$) no longer contributed to more school connectedness.

DISCUSSION

This study examined how involvement in different types of extracurricular activities (sports, clubs, arts) is associated with students' perceptions of school

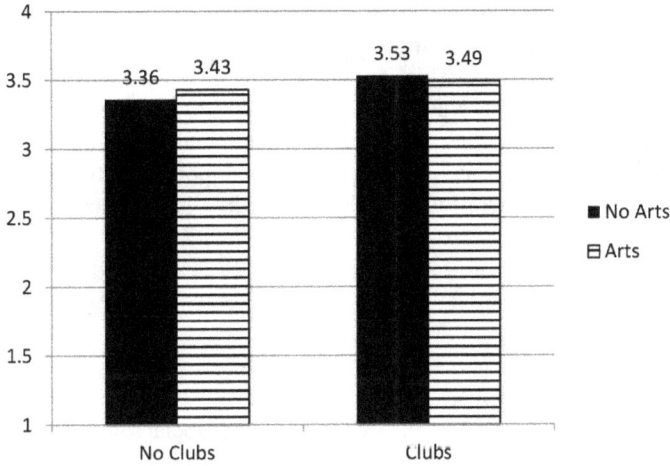

Figure 4.4. School connectedness – interaction of clubs and arts

climate, namely social-emotional security, student support, adult support, and school connectedness. We find that extracurricular participation is associated with multiple dimensions of school climate. Participation in various activities was associated with feelings of inclusion, connections with others in the school community, and attachment to school, factors that have important implications for school belonging.

This investigation extends the research on extracurricular activities by linking extracurricular involvement to school climate, a multidimensional construct that has not been fully explored within this body of work. Whereas previous studies have focused on specific activities and/or breadth of extracurricular participation, this study highlights how different extracurricular activities interact, and are associated with different dimensions of school climate.

Demographic Differences in School Climate

Although it is not the main objective of this study, some of the demographic differences in this study are noteworthy. Our findings show that non-White students, as compared to White students, reported less favorable views of school climate (i.e., adult support, student support, and connectedness). Previous research by Voight, Hanson, O'Malley, and Adekanye (2015) also found ethnic differences in school climate. These differences in perception are not surprising given the numerous documented disparities in educational outcomes and practices (e.g., academic achievement, school dropout, teacher racial bias, exclusionary disciplinary practices, tracking, etc.). These findings underscore the disparate experiences of school climate across racial/ethnic groups and suggest more research is needed to assess how student sub-groups experience and are connected to their schools. Our findings also show that 9th grade students report more favorable views of school climate than 10th, 11th, or 12th grade students, suggesting that perceptions of school climate decrease across high school. This is consistent with research showing a decline in student engagement across grades (Gallup, 2015). Our research adds to this by examining multiple dimensions of the school environment. The finding that students perceive their environment as less safe, feel less supported by teachers and peers, and are less connected overall to the school over time is disconcerting and worthy of further exploration.

Social-Emotional Security

We found that involvement in sports was the only activity associated with social-emotional security. Athletic participation is often associated with higher social status in the school context (Shakib, 2011). Given their higher social status, athletes may feel more socially and emotionally safe because they are less likely to be teased, ridiculed, or excluded relative to students who participate in other activities. Indeed, participation in sports has been associated with less social isolation (Barber, Eccles, & Stone, 2001) and less bullying victimization (Peguero, 2008). In contrast, participation in arts has been linked to decreased popularity and greater bullying victimization (O'Neill, 2005). Thus, sports offer a unique opportunity by allowing students to be socialized into a more popular peer group where students are safe from teasing and social exclusion. Nevertheless, these findings also suggest that students who participate in arts and clubs feel similar levels of social-emotional safety as students who are not involved in extracurricular activities. The connection between extracurricular involvement and perceptions of school safety warrants further investigation.

Adult Support

Being connected to a caring adult is commonly cited as promoting positive development (Mahoney, Larson, Eccles, & Lord, 2005). Sports and club participation, respectively, was linked to higher levels of adult social support. However, the interaction effects reveal a more complex picture. Participation in clubs contributes to more meaningful adult support among students who do not participate in sports. One explanation is that forging meaningful student-adult relations necessitates more time than is typically possible for students who are sports involved, given the time commitment (e.g., sport practices and competitions). Thus, any involvement in clubs, in addition to sports, may be limited to minimal involvement or certain off-season times of the school year; resulting in fewer and potentially sporadic interactions with adults.

Student Support

We found main effects for involvement in sports, arts, and clubs. A key feature of extracurricular activities is the opportunity to build supportive relationships with peers that are characterized by warmth, closeness, caring, and respect (Mahoney, Eccles, & Larson, 2004). Extracurricular activities link students to other school peers and the more time students spend in an activity, the more likely they are to develop connections and draw friends from the activity (Eccles, Barber, Stone, & Hunt, 2003). From a practical standpoint, the higher level of student support among students who participate in sports, arts, and clubs is encouraging and suggests that participation in general, regardless of activity type, can foster positive student relations. However, it is noteworthy that these three activities are linked to positive peer relations, but as previously discussed, only sports was associated with social-emotional security. Thus, more positive student relations associated with extracurricular activities do not necessarily lead students to feel socially and emotionally safe.

School Connectedness

Our findings indicate that participation in extracurricular activities may be particularly important for fostering school connectedness. Participation in the three respective extracurricular activities was associated with higher levels of school connectedness. These findings are in line with research showing that participation in extracurricular activities is associated with greater school attachment (McNeely, Nonnemaker, & Blum, 2002). However, unique combinations of extracurricular involvement seem to qualify these effects.

We found that participating in sports and clubs, respectively and combined, was associated with higher levels of school connectedness than not participating in these activities; however, participating in sports did not yield greater feelings of school connectedness among students participating in clubs. Thus, there does not appear to be an additive effect in which participation in both activities translates into higher levels of school connectedness, a finding contrary to research by the U.S. Centers for Disease Control and Prevention (2009) which suggests that students who report having friends from several peer groups also report feeling more connected to school. School clubs tend to consist of larger student groups, and the academic orientation of many clubs often connects students with the academic mission of schools (Feldman & Matjasko, 2005). As a result, participating in sports, in addition to clubs, may not bring forth a substantially meaningful added value in relation to school connectedness.

Finally, while students who participated in arts activities reported higher levels of school connectedness than students who did not, arts participation appeared to undermine the positive effects of being involved in sports. The decreased popularity and increased bullying associated with participation in art activities may partly explain these negative effects (O'Neill, 2005). For example, in a qualitative study of sports and arts participation, Patrick and colleagues (1999) found that participation in sports and arts provided students with opportunities to develop friendships. However, only students who participated in arts activities reported negative reactions from their peers such as being labeled as "strange" or teased. Thus, although arts activities allow students to build relationships with like-minded peers, negative reactions may undermine students' connectedness with the larger school context. These findings further underscore how unique combinations of these extracurricular activities qualify these effects, and how participation in more activities, does not necessarily lead to higher levels of school connectedness or belonging.

Implications for Theory, Research, Practice, and Policy

Theory. There is not a national consensus about how to define 'school climate' or 'effective school climate improvement processes'. This is a major challenge to school climate theory, research, policy, and practice as different definitions and measures are used in different studies (Iachini, Berkowitz, Moore, Pitner, Astor, & Benbenishty, 2017). The authors of this study endorse the definitions of "school climate" that were first proposed by the National School Climate Council (2007) and have been adopted by a growing number of U.S. districts and States (Cohen, 2015).

In addition to adopting the standard definition of school climate, we need to further specify our theories to incorporate multiple predictors, moderators, mediators, and outcomes. Theories need to take into account students' experiences in schools, the ecology of their schools and communities, the activities within and outside of schools that youth take part in, and relationships and supports from peers, parents, and teachers. We need robust theories that guide research, allow for assessment of multidimensional constructs and multiple reporters, and enable and promote predictions and hypothesis-testing.

Research. More research is needed to understand demographic differences in perceptions and experiences of school climate and the role of extracurricular activities in relation to these differences. Specifically causes, correlates, and associated outcomes should be further explored. It is possible that participation in extracurricular activities has different levels of impact on student experiences, depending on the subgroup of interest and their connections with school. Further, given our grade level differences in school climate, longitudinal studies are needed that examine how changes in participation are associated with changes in perceptions of school climate and academic experiences.

In terms of extracurricular activities, researchers have posited that greater breadth of participation is associated with more positive developmental outcomes. This study suggests that the effects of participation in multiple extracurricular activities depend on the types of activity combinations, and that the most notable gains exist when students participate in some type of activity rather than no activity. Further, some activities are more likely to align with and reinforce the values of the school community than others. Thus, research should not only consider the characteristics of activities that shape development, but also how activities fit into the overall school milieu. Characteristics of the school, such as a mission or a school culture that values sports or arts or academic rigor, may shape the significance and quality of these extracurricular experiences. Future work should also examine specific characteristics of these extracurricular activities such as quality, whether they are mandatory or optional, and time of operation (during the school day or during out-of-school-time hours).

Further, in light of the association between school climate and student outcomes, research can examine the extent to which school climate has a mediating or moderating affect in promoting academic success. Extracurricular activities may promote positive academic outcomes by fostering positive school climates, or through the development of neurophysiological pathways, as has been found with music participation (Kraus et al., 2014). Rigorous methodological techniques are needed that can isolate these different associations and pathways contributing to academic success.

Practice. This study has implications for educational, developmental, and community psychologists working with schools, as well as other researchers and practitioners seeking to foster positive school climates. Participation in extracurricular activities may be one way to promote a positive school climate, and schools should consider practices that promote student involvement in at least one activity. Our findings also suggest that school climate interventions should take into account the needs of specific student subgroups, as subgroups may have different needs and experiences of the school environment. Moreover, infusing practices within extracurricular activities that emphasize individual strengths and talents, teamwork, and skill development could further enhance the quality of these settings, interpersonal relations, and school belonging (Siperstein, Glick, & Parker, 2009). Extra-curricular activities may also serve as vehicles to infuse social-emotional related interventions. A burgeoning body of implementation science research has given attention to the conditions that allow for successful implementation of school-based interventions, and some extracurricular activities may be poised as viable contexts (Forman, Olin, Hoagwood, Crowe, & Saka, 2009).

When providing extracurricular activities, transportation also needs to be provided and funded. Graham, Keys, and McMahon (2014) found that transportation problems are related to fewer school resources, less school belonging, and more school stressors, anxiety, and depression. Transportation issues and access to students with disabilities are especially important in the context of providing and encouraging extracurricular activities (Graham et al., 2014; Graham, Keys, McMahon, & Brubacher, 2014).

Policy. From a policy standpoint, the importance of extracurricular activities is often overlooked in the U.S. educational system. Funding for extracurriculars has been threatened, and socioeconomic disparities in access and participation exist (Snellman, Silva, Frederick, & Putnam, 2014). However, extracurricular activities can complement the school curriculum, shape development, and shape student perceptions of the school environment. Policies that support extracurricular activities are important in creating environments where students feel they belong and thrive. At a local level, schools can offer a variety of activities and encourage students to participate in some type of extracurricular activity. At a broader governmental level, funding for extracurricular activities can support schools in ensuring extracurriculars are available for students.

Policy-level attention to school climate is also warranted. The U.S. *Every Student Succeeds Act* (ESSA) and the federal endorsement of school climate reform provide a platform for developing effective prevention strategies (Thapa et al., 2013). ESSA has dramatically increased interest in school climate improvement efforts. Such a focus on school climate is encouraging as it represents a more preventive movement toward the improvement of school environments and addressing student problem behaviors. However, preventive policy-level strategies that emphasize school climate are often the exception rather than the norm. For example, currently all 50 states have some form of anti-bullying policy. Yet, these policies are reactive, and often conceptualize the problem at the student-level rather than emphasize the contribution of the broader school context.

Finally, education policy can help to address how student sub-populations (e.g., race/ethnicity) experience school climate. Education policy has placed greater emphasis on school accountability and racial/ethnic achievement gaps within the past several decades (e.g., No Child Left Behind). However, such policies often emphasize student outcomes while placing less emphasis on the conditions of the school environment. The Every Student Succeeds Act has brought forth significant attention to school climate, and this marks a critical step in placing school climate on the political agenda. Further policy enhancements can be generated that seek to improve school climate across disparate student groups (e.g., gender, race/ethnicity).

Strengths and Limitations

This study possesses several limitations. Foremost, this study is cross-sectional, directionality cannot be determined, and fluctuations in involvement across time are not accounted for. Second, the schools were not randomly selected and therefore causation cannot be determined. Students may be more likely to participate in activities when they perceive their environment more favorably. Thus, participation in extracurricular activities may be a result of the school climate rather than extracurricular activities promoting feelings of connectedness, inclusion, and attachment with one's school. Further, it is likely that students self-select into extracurricular activities, and there may be a variety of personal characteristics that lead students to join specific types of activities. These characteristics may also contribute to perceptions of school climate. We do control for ethnicity, gender, or socioeconomic status, which are related to self-selection.

Despite these limitations, this study possesses several strengths. First, this study is strengthened by the large sample size of students across multiple schools. Second, this study examines individual activities as well as combinations of activities, which adds more specificity to the literature on extracurricular activities. Third, the use of multilevel modeling adds to the rigor of our analyses, by taking into account individual and school-level effects. Last, this study examines extracurricular activities in relation to multiple dimensions of school climate. Given the importance of school involvement and school climate, future research should continue to explore how extracurricular activities relate to school climate and how this relationship changes over time.

CONCLUSION

This study underscores the importance of furthering student engagement as an important goal. Extracurricular activities are one important and powerful strategy that supports students being engaged in school life. A recent commentary by the National School Climate Council (2015) in the United States indicates that efforts to improve school climate, including interpersonal relations and school belonging, should include three components. These include systemically engaging all members of the school community, focusing on instruction that promotes prosocial development (e.g., collaboration, co-leadership), and meaningful relationships. Extracurricular activities serve as vehicles that can engage a broad cross-section of school community members (teachers, coaches, parents), incorporate prosocial instruction, and enhance relationships among students and across stakeholders at different social-ecological levels. Ultimately, extracurricular activities can ignite students' inclination to become involved in school life and promote school belonging.

ACKNOWLEDGEMENT

This chapter is an adapted version from Martinez, A., Coker, C., McMahon, S., Cohen, J., & Thapa, A. (2016). Involvement in extracurricular activities: identifying differences in perceptions of school climate. *The Educational and Developmental Psychologist, 33*(1), 70–84. doi:10.1017/edp.2016.7

REFERENCES

Allen, K. A., & Bowles, T. (2012). Belonging as a guiding principle in the education of adolescents. *Australian Journal of Educational & Developmental Psychology, 12*, 108–119.

Anderman, L. (2011). *School belonging.* Retrieved from http://www.education.com/reference/article/school-belonging/

Barber, B. L., Eccles, J. S., & Stone, M. R. (2001). Whatever happened to the jock, the brain, and the princess? Young adult pathways linked to adolescent activity involvement and social identity. *Journal of Adolescent Research, 16*, 429–455. doi:10.1177/0743558401165002

Bohnert, A., Fredricks, J., & Randall, E. (2010). Capturing unique dimensions of youth organized activity involvement theoretical and methodological considerations. *Review of Educational Research, 80*, 576–610. doi:10.3102/0034654310364533

Blum, R. W., McNeely, C. A., & Rinehart, P. M. (2002). *Improving the odds: The untapped power of schools to improve the health of teens.* Minneapolis, MN: Center for Adolescent Health and Development, University of Minnesota.

Centers for Disease Control and Prevention. (2009). *School connectedness: Strategies for increasing protective factors among youth*. Atlanta, GA: U.S. Department of Health and Human Resources.

Clifford, M., Menon, R., Gangi, T., & Condon, C., & Hornung, K. (2012). *Measuring school climate for gauging principal performance: A review of the validity and reliability of publicly accessible measures*. Washington, DC: American Institute of Research.

Cohen, J. (2015). *School climate reform, and violence prevention policy and practice trends: Latin American, US, and the European Union*. Presentation at the VI World Congress on School Violence and Public Policies, Lima, Peru.

Cohen, J., McCabe, E. M., Michelli, N. M., & Pickeral, T. (2009). School climate: Research, policy, teacher education and practice. *Teachers College Record, 111*, 180–213. Retrieved from http://www.tcrecord.org/Content.asp?ContentId=15220

Eccles, J. S., & Barber, B. L. (1999). Student council, volunteering, basketball, or marching band what kind of extracurricular involvement matters? *Journal of Adolescent Research, 14*(1), 10–43.

Eccles, J. S., Barber, B. L., Stone, M., & Hunt, J. (2003). Extracurricular activities and adolescent development. *Journal of Social Issues, 59*, 865–889. doi:10.1046/j.0022-4537.2003.00095.x

Fan, W., Williams, C. M., & Corkin, D. M. (2011). A multilevel analysis of student perceptions of school climate: The effect of social and academic risk factors. *Psychology in the Schools, 48*, 632–647. doi:10.1002/pits.20579

Farb, A. F., & Matjasko, J. L. (2012). Recent advances in research on school-based extracurricular activities and adolescent development. *Developmental Review, 32*, 1–48. doi:10.1016/j.dr.2011.10.001

Feldman, A. F., & Matjasko, J. L. (2005). The role of school-based extracurricular activities in adolescent development: A comprehensive review and future directions. *Review of Educational Research, 75*, 159–210. doi:10.3102/00346543075002159

Fleming, C. B., Catalano, R. F., Mazza, J. J., Brown, E. C., Haggerty, K. P., & Harachi, T. W. (2008). After-school activities, misbehavior in school, and delinquency from the end of elementary school through the beginning of high school: A test of social development model hypotheses. *The Journal of Early Adolescence, 28*(2), 277–303. doi:10.1177/0272431607313589

Forman, S. G., Olin, S. S., Hoagwood, K. E., Crowe, M., & Saka, N. (2009). Evidence-based interventions in schools: Developers' views of implementation barriers and facilitators. *School Mental Health, 1*, 26–36. doi:10.1007/s12310-008-9002-5

Fredricks, J. A., & Eccles, J. S. (2008). Participation in extracurricular activities in the middle school years: Are there developmental benefits for African American and European American youth? *Journal of Youth and Adolescence, 37*, 1029–1043. doi:10.1007/s10964-008-9309-4

Gallup. (2015). *Engaged today – Ready for tomorrow*. Retrieved from http://www.gallupstudentpoll.com/188036/2015-gallup-student-poll-overall-report.aspx

Gottfredson, G. D., & Gottfredson, D. C. (1989). *School climate, academic performance, attendance, and dropout*. North Charleston, SC: Charleston County School District.

Graham, B., Keys, C. B., & McMahon, S. D. (2014). Transportation and socioemotional well-being of urban students with and without disabilities. *Journal of Prevention and Intervention in the Community, 42*, 31–44. doi:10.1080/10852352.2014.855056

Graham, B., Keys, C. B., McMahon, S. D., & Brubacher, M. (2014). Transportation challenges for urban students with disabilities: Parent perspectives. *Journal of Prevention and Intervention in the Community, 42*, 45–57. doi:10.1080/10852352.2014.855058

Gregory, A., Cornell, D., Fan, X., Sheras, P., Shih, T.-H., & Huang, F. (2010). Authoritative school discipline: High school practices associated with lower bullying and victimization. *Journal of Educational Psychology, 102*, 483–496. doi:10.1037/a0018562

Hansen, D. M., Larson, R. W., & Dworkin, J. B. (2003). What adolescents learn in organized youth activities: A survey of self-reported developmental experiences. *Journal of Research on Adolescence, 13*, 25–55. doi:10.1111/1532-7795.1301006

Huang, L. X., & Der-Hsiang Huang, H. M. (2013). Students' ratings of school climate and school belonging for understanding their effects and relationship of junior high schools in Taiwan. *Global Journal of Human-Social Science Research, 13*(3), 1–7.

Iachini, A. L., Berkowitz, R., Moore, H., Pitner, R., Astor, R. A., & Benbenishty, R. (2017). School climate. In C. Franklin (Ed.), *Encyclopedia of social work*. New York, NY: Oxford University Press. doi:10.1093/acrefore/9780199975839.013.1195

Jia, Y., Way, N., Ling, G., Yoshikawa, H., Chen, X., Hughes, D., & Lu, Z. (2009). The influence of student perceptions of school climate on socio-emotional and academic adjustment: A comparison of Chinese and American adolescents. *Child Development, 80*, 1514–1530. doi:10.1111/j.1467-8624.2009.01348.x

Koth, C. W., Bradshaw, C. P., & Leaf, P. J. (2008). A multilevel study of predictors of student perceptions of school climate: The effect of classroom-level factors. *Journal of Educational Psychology, 100*, 96–104. doi:10.1037/0022-0663.100.1.96

Kraus, N., Slater, J., Thompson, E. C., Hornickel, J., Strait, D. L., Nicol, T., & White-Schwoch, T. (2014). Music enrichment programs improve the neural encoding of speech in at-risk children. *The Journal of Neuroscience, 34*, 11913–11918. doi:10.1523/JNEUROSCI.1881-14.2014

Larson, R. W., Hansen, D. M., & Moneta, G. (2006). Differing profiles of developmental experiences across types of organized youth activities. *Developmental Psychology, 42*, 849–863. doi:10.1037/0012-1649.42.5.849

Lee, T., Cornell, D., Gregory, A., & Fan, X. (2011). High suspension schools and dropout rates for Black and White students. *Education and Treatment of Children, 34*, 167–192. doi:10.1353/etc.2011.0014

Linver, M. R., Roth, J. L., & Brooks-Gunn, J. (2009). Patterns of adolescents' participation in organized activities: Are sports best when combined with other activities? *Developmental Psychology, 45*, 354–367. doi:10.1037/a0014133

Lleras, C. (2008). Do skills and behaviors in high school matter? The contribution of noncognitive factors in explaining differences in educational attainment and earnings. *Social Science Research, 37*, 888–902. doi:10.1016/j.ssresearch.2008.03.004

Mahoney, J. L., Eccles, J. S., & Larson, R. W. (2004). Processes of adjustment in organized out-of-school activities: Opportunities and risks. *New Directions for Youth Development, 101*, 115–144.

Mahoney, J. L., Larson, R. W., Eccles, J. S., & Lord, H. (2005). Organized activities as developmental contexts for children and adolescents. In J. L. Mahoney, R. W. Larson, & J. S. Eccles (Eds.), *Organized activities as contexts of development: Extracurricular activities, after-school and community programs* (pp. 3–22). Mahwah, NJ: Erlbaum.

McNeely, C. A., Nonnemaker, J. M., & Blum, R. W. (2002). Promoting school connectedness: Evidence from the national longitudinal study of adolescent health. *Journal of School Health, 72*, 138–146.

National Center for Education Statistics. (2012). *Table 185. Percentage of high school seniors who participate in various school-sponsored extracurricular activities, by selected student characteristics: 1992 and 2004*. Retrieved April 13, 2014, from http://nces.ed.gov/programs/digest/d12/tables/dt12_185.asp

National School Climate Council. (2007). *The school climate challenge: Narrowing the gap between school climate research and school climate policy, practice guidelines and teacher education policy*. Retrieved from http://www.schoolclimate.org/publications/policy-briefs.php

National School Climate Council. (2015). *School climate and prosocial educational improvement: Essential goals and processes that support student success for all*. Retrieved from https://www.schoolclimate.org/climate/documents/Essential_dimensions_Prosocial_SC_Improvement_P_3-2015.pdf

O'Neill, S. A. (2005). Organized activities as developmental contexts for children and adolescents. In J. L. Mahoney, R. W. Larson, & J. S. Eccles (Eds.), *Organized activities as contexts of development: Extracurricular activities, after-school and community programs* (pp. 3–22). Mahwah, NJ: Erlbaum.

Patrick, H., Ryan, A. M., Alfeld-Liro, C., Fredricks, J. A., Hruda, L. Z., & Eccles, J. S. (1999). Adolescents' commitment to developing talent: The role of peers in continuing motivation for sports and the arts. *Journal of Youth and Adolescence, 28*, 741–763. doi:10.1023/A:1021643718575

Peguero, A. A. (2008). Bullying victimization and extracurricular activity. *Journal of School Violence, 7*, 71–85. doi:10.1080/15388220801955570

Ramey, H. L., & Rose-Krasnor, L. (2012). Contexts of structured youth activities and positive youth development. *Child Development Perspectives, 6*, 85–91. doi:10.1111/j.1750-8606.2011.00219.x

Shakib, S., Veliz, P., Dunbar, M. D., & Sabo, D. (2011). Athletics as a source for social status among youth: Examining variation by gender, race/ethnicity, and socioeconomic status. *Sociology of Sport Journal, 28*, 303–328.

Siperstein, G. N., Glick, G. C., & Parker, R. C. (2009). Social inclusion of children with intellectual disabilities in a recreational setting. *Intellectual and Developmental Disabilities, 47*, 97–107. doi:10.1352/1934-9556-47.2.97

Snellman, K., Silva, J. M., Frederick, C. B., & Putnam, R. D. (2015). The engagement gap: Social mobility and extracurricular participation among American youth. *The ANNALS of the American Academy of Political and Social Science, 657*(1), 194–207.

Thapa, A., Cohen, J., Guffey, S., & Higgins-D'Alessandro, A. (2013). A review of school climate research. *Review of Educational Research, 83*, 357–385. doi:10.3102/0034654313483907

Voight, A. M., Hanson, T., O'Malley, M., & Adekanye, L. (2015). The racial school climate gap: Within-school disparities in students' experiences of safety, support, and connectedness. *American Journal of Community Psychology, 56*, 252–267. doi:10.1007/s10464-015-9751-x

Crystal Coker
DePaul University
Chicago, Illinois, USA

Andrew Martinez
Department of Social Work
Sacred Heart University
Fairfield, Connecticut, USA

Susan D. McMahon
Department of Psychology
DePaul University
Chicago, Illinois, USA

Jonathan Cohen
National School Climate Center
New York City, USA

Amrit Thapa
National School Climate Center
New York City, USA

KATHRYN MOFFA, ERIN DOWDY AND MICHAEL J. FURLONG

5. DOES INCLUDING SCHOOL BELONGING MEASURES ENHANCE COMPLETE MENTAL HEALTH SCREENING IN SCHOOLS?

INTRODUCTION

Approximately one out of every three or four youths worldwide will meet the criteria for a formal mental health disorder in their lifetime (Costello, Mustillo, Keller, & Angold, 2004). Considering that approximately half of all mental disorders have onset by 14 years of age (World Health Organization, 2014), it is important to be mindful of how to identify, treat, and prevent symptoms in early adolescence. Recognizing the barriers to accessing private mental health care (e.g., geographic location, cost, and stigma), and coupled with findings that most youths do not seek help when they experience psychosocial distress (Christina et al., 2000), schools are ideal locations in which to implement efforts to prevent and respond to youths' mental health needs (Manassis et al., 2010). This recommendation for school-based services is aligned with findings that many school associated negative developmental outcomes are linked with psychological distress, including difficulties with social relationships, lack of initiative with schoolwork, and low academic achievement (Fröjd et al., 2008). Robust research findings indicate that youths' feelings of school belonging (a) can mitigate negative developmental outcomes (Lester, Waters, & Cross, 2013), (b) protect against psychological distress (Gratis, 2013; Pittman & Richmond, 2007), and (c) are associated with a range of positive psychological and educational developmental outcomes (Allen & Bowles, 2012). As such, it is possible that considering school belonging as part of schoolwide mental health screening could contribute unique information in support of prevention and intervention strategies to improve adolescents' mental health. Though previous research indicates that school belonging is positively associated with academic achievement (Furrer & Skinner, 2003) and positive mental health indicators (Pittman & Richmond, 2007; Vieno, Perkins, Smith, & Santinello, 2005), the potential additive predictive effects of students' school belonging when included within a school-based, universal complete mental health screening framework has not yet been thoroughly investigated.

DUAL-FACTOR APPROACH TO SCREEN FOR COMPLETE MENTAL HEALTH

Expanding beyond a primarily deficit focused approach, contemporary mental health screening has examined a combination of students' psychological distress

© KONINKLIJKE BRILL NV, LEIDEN, 2018 | DOI:10.1163/9789004386969_005

and subjective wellbeing (Moore et al., 2015). This dual-factor approach, which examines both positive and negative symptoms of mental health (Greenspoon & Saklofske, 2001; Suldo & Schaffer, 2008) is aligned with current definitions of mental health as the state of being

> free of psychopathology and flourishing, with high levels of emotional, psychological, and social wellbeing. (Keyes, 2005, p. 539)

Most school-based studies have first sorted students by symptoms of high and low psychological distress, and then by high and low subjective wellbeing (Greenspoon & Saklofske, 2001; Suldo & Shaffer, 2008; Venning, Wilson, Kettler, & Eliott, 2013), a process that creates four logical mental health groups (Kim et al., in press). By screening students for both positive and negative indicators of mental health, school support teams have an expanded picture of students' functioning, including which strengths might serve as protective factors and improve developmental outcomes (Furlong, Dowdy et al., 2014). It is possible that the addition of other measures beyond those used for dual-factor complete mental health screening could provide an enhanced understanding of students' current and future mental health. Given the known benefits of school belonging to students' mental health (Pittman & Richmond, 2007), this chapter describes a study that examined how information on students' sense of school belonging might enhance complete mental health screening practices.

IMPORTANCE OF SCHOOL BELONGING TO YOUTHS' MENTAL HEALTH

School belonging has been defined in multiple ways, often operationalized by describing the item content of the scale used to measure the construct, and characterized by having overlapping content with similar school belonging domain constructs, such as school connectedness, membership, bonding, engagement, satisfaction, and attachment (Furlong, Froh, Muller, & Gonzalez, 2014). School belonging is defined as

> the extent to which students feel personally accepted, respected, included, and supported by others in the school environment. (Goodenow, 1993, p. 80)

School belonging has also been described as the degree to which students are personally invested in their school, compliant with school rules and expectations, engaged in academic and extracurricular activities, and believe in school values (Kia-Keating & Ellis, 2007). McNeely, Nonemaker, and Blum (2002) asserted that school connectedness, a related term, is defined by feelings of belonging at school and being cared for by members of students' school communities, including other students, families, and school staff. Regardless of the specific definition or terminology employed to describe students' relationships with their schools, what matters most is that schools are addressing these constructs in some way, as students do better when they feel a strong sense of belonging to their school and engage in positive relationships at school (Libbey, 2004).

The importance of school belonging is rooted in multiple theoretical perspectives, including Baumeister and Leary's (1995) assertion that the need to belong drives human motivation, Ryan and Deci's Self-Determination Theory (SDT, 2000), and Bronfenbrenner's Ecological Systems Theory (1986). A strong sense of school belonging is associated with increased academic motivation and performance (Furrer & Skinner, 2003); improved psychological functioning (Pittman & Richmond, 2007); and increased happiness, self-esteem, better coping skills, social skills and social supports, reduced loneliness, and fewer truancies (Vieno et al., 2005). Low levels of school belonging are associated with aggressive and violent behaviours (Chapman et al., 2011), criminal behaviour, gang membership, and substance use (Catalano, Osterle, Fleming, & Hawkins, 2004).

School Belonging and Indicators of Psychological Distress

When examining the impact of school belonging on indicators of internal psychological distress, Resnick and colleagues' (1997) research using the National Longitudinal Study on Adolescent Health (Add Health) was formative in establishing the relations between school connectedness and negative mental health indicators. In a sample of 3,130 adolescents in Grades 7–12, feelings of school connectedness were associated with lower levels of emotional distress, suicidality, involvement in violence, and substance use across age groups. Shochet, Dadds, Ham, and Montague (2006) conducted a study with Australian adolescents and found that one year later a measure of school connectedness (a) negatively predicted depressive symptoms for boys and girls, and anxiety symptoms for girls; and (b) positively predicted general functioning for boys. However, the same study found that mental health status at baseline did not predict later school connectedness, suggesting that students' school belongingness might serve as a protective factor against future mental health concerns.

In a related study, Lester and colleagues (2013) examined the relations between school connectedness, depression, and anxiety among Australian adolescents who were transitioning from primary to secondary schools. Results indicated that symptoms of anxiety and depression increased over time, while feelings of school connectedness decreased. By conducting cross-lagged models to investigate causal direction across time between connectedness, depression, and anxiety, Lester et al. (2013) found that school connectedness in primary school positively predicted connectedness in secondary school. Additionally, higher levels of school connectedness in primary school predicted lower feelings of anxiety and depression in secondary school. As in the Shochet and colleagues' (2006) findings, mental health in primary school did not predict later school connectedness after transitioning from primary to secondary school, reinforcing the hypothesis that early feelings of school connectedness, or belonging, influence later psychological wellbeing (Lester et al., 2013).

In a more recent study, Joyce and Early (2014) examined Waves 1 and 2 of the Add Health study to assess school connectedness as a predictor of depressive symptoms among youth ages 11 to 18. Results of a multilevel regression analysis indicated that school connectedness and teacher-student relationships were significant predictors of depressive symptoms, with school connectedness acting as more of a protective agent against depression for students in the racial majority than minority (Joyce & Early, 2014). Similarly, Shochet, Smith, Furlong, and Homel (2011) found that three factors of school connectedness – *Rejection, Acceptance*, and *Caring Relationships* – predicted negative affect for seventh and eighth graders at three time points across 18 months. As hypothesized, results suggested that less acceptance and fewer caring relationships predicted higher levels of negative affect, while fewer experiences of rejection predicted lower levels of negative affect. The current literature highlights the significant impact school belonging can have in preventing and reducing symptoms of psychosocial distress.

School Belonging and Positive Indicators of Mental Health

When considering mental health using a dual-factor paradigm, it is essential to understand how school belongingness might prevent psychological distress, but also promote robust wellbeing. School belonging is previously linked to youths' subjective wellbeing and mental health throughout development (Pittman & Richmond, 2007; Tian, Zhang, Huebner, Zheng, & Liu, 2016; You et al., 2008). Tian et al. (2016) conducted a study with youth from China, ages 9 to 13, to evaluate the reciprocal relations between school belonging and subjective wellbeing at two times points (T1, T2, six weeks apart). A structural equation modelling (SEM) analysis indicated that school belonging at T1 predicted subjective wellbeing in school at T2 after controlling for age and gender, and that subjective wellbeing at T1 predicted school belonging at T2. The implication of the Tian et al. (2016) study is that by fostering a strong sense of school belonging, schools might be able to enhance students' overall subjective wellbeing.

Using a sample of USA students, You et al. (2008) assessed the role of school connectedness in mediating the relations between hope and life satisfaction for students in Grades 5 through 12 with varying experiences of peer victimization. Results indicated that school connectedness partially mediated the relations between hope and life satisfaction for those individuals who had not experienced peer victimization, but not for those who were victimized by peers and bullies. As hypothesized, bullied victims reported significantly lower levels of school connectedness than peer victims and non-victims. Overall, school connectedness had the influence of a promotive factor for students who were not victimized, but for students who experienced victimization, school connectedness did not promote life satisfaction with the same significance.

Pittman and Richmond (2007) administered surveys to students in their first year of college to assess the relations between school belongingness, peer and family relationships, academic success, self-worth and competence, and social emotional distress. Results suggested that a sense of school belonging both in high school and in college was moderately positively correlated to individuals' perceived academic competence and self-worth. Based on regression analyses, school belonging in high school significantly predicted self-worth and social emotional distress (Pittman & Richmond, 2007), with students reporting a higher sense of school belonging in high school also reporting greater levels of self-worth.

Including School Belonging in School Mental Health Screening

Previous research has focused on the predictive validity of school belonging on future mental health during the transition from primary to secondary school and from Grades 8 to 9 (Lester et al., 2013; Lester & Cross, 2015; Shochet et al., 2006). Results of these studies, however, suggest inconsistencies in the strength of prediction of school belonging on positive and negative indicators of adolescents' future mental health across grade levels, particularly as adolescents near the transition to Grade 9 (Lester et al., 2013; Lester & Cross, 2015; Shochet et al., 2006). Additional research is warranted to investigate how school belonging might be utilized to predict youth's future mental health after the transition to Grade 9 and through high school. Considering that onset of psychological problems typically occurs during late adolescence (Kessler et al., 2009), the present study examined school belonging in youth during high school. By examining students' sense of school belonging in high school, schools might gain information to further inform the scope and context of prevention and intervention strategies. Within the school context, it might be particularly important to assess for variables, such as school belonging, that can be more directly influenced by the school staff and are proximally related to school functioning. However, it is unclear if adolescents' levels of school belonging predicts important outcomes beyond screening measures used in a traditional dual-factor, complete mental health screening context. The current study explored how information on school belonging might enhance the prediction of future psychological distress beyond what is gleaned from complete mental health screening practices. Specifically, the study investigated two questions: (a) Do adolescent dual-factor complete mental health groups differ on their self-reported sense of school belonging? and (b) Does school belonging measured (at Time 1) add to the prediction of adolescents' social emotional wellbeing and internal distress (at Time 2, one year later) net of measures used for universal complete mental health screening?

METHOD

Participants

Students attending a high school in central California completed annual, schoolwide screening surveys at the beginning of the 2014–2015 (Time 1, T1) and 2015–2016 (Time 2, T2) school years. At T2, 1,159 students (62% of the original sample) who completed the T1 survey also completed the survey at T2. At T1, 38% of students were in the ninth grade, 35% in tenth grade, and 27% in eleventh grade. One student did not report grade level. Students' self-reported cultural group/ethnicity was as follows: 46.5% Latino/Hispanic, 38.4% White, 2.8% Asian, 0.9% Black/African American, 0.3% Native Hawaiian or Pacific Islander, 0.4% American Indian or Alaskan Native, and 10.6% Mixed (two or more ethnicities selected). Approximately 51% of students identified as female.

Measures

Complete mental health. Complete mental health was measured using a combination of life satisfaction (Brief Multidimensional Students' Life Satisfaction Scale [BMSLSS], Seligson, Huebner, & Valois, 2003) and psychological distress (selected items from the Strengths and Difficulties Questionnaire [SDQ], Goodman, 1997) instruments.

Global life satisfaction at T1. The BMSLSS is a self-report measure to gauge overall life satisfaction and satisfaction with friends, family, self, school, and living environment (Seligson, Huebner, & Valois, 2003). Previous confirmatory factor analysis supported a one-factor structure. Items were measured using a five-point response option used by Bickman et al. (2007; 1 = *very dissatisfied* to 5 = *very satisfied*), with higher scores indicative of greater global life satisfaction. For the current study, the average of students' scores on the six items was used as the indicator of positive global life satisfaction within the dual-factor complete mental health framework. The measure had good internal consistency (α = .83) in the present sample.

Psychological distress at T1. Negative indicators of students' mental health were measured by using select items from the self-report version of the SDQ (Goodman, 1997). The SDQ is a measure designed for adolescents ages 11–17 that measures five factors: Emotional Problems, Conduct Problems, Hyperactivity, Peer Problems, and Prosocial Behavior. Rushkin and colleagues (2008) conducted a confirmatory factor analysis and found support for a three-factor structure: behavioral reactivity/conduct problems, emotional distress/withdrawal, and prosocial behavior. Drawing from the Rushkin et al. study (2008) and with an interest to maintain survey efficiency, this study used the five items with the highest loadings from the behavioral reactivity/ conduct problems and emotional distress/withdrawal factors. Items are measured on a three-point scale (0 = not true, 1 = *somewhat true*, and 2 = *certainly true*), with higher scores indicating more distress. Within the dual-factor complete mental health model, students' mean scores on these 10 items were used to determine students' psychological distress levels. Cronbach's alpha indicated adequate internal consistency among the 10 items with the present sample (α = .79).

School belonging at T1. Five items from the School Satisfaction subscale of the Multidimensional Students' Life Satisfaction Scale (MSLSS; Huebner, 1994;

Huebner, Laughlin, Ash, & Gilman, 1998) were used to assess students' feelings of belonging to school at T1. The original subscale consists of eight items and was previously used by Antaramian, Huebner, Hills, and Valois (2010) to measure students' feelings of belonging to their school and having strong relationships with teachers and peers. For the current study, the three reverse-keyed items were not used because previous research indicated that students in Grades 7–12 experienced difficulties with the items that were worded negatively (Sawatzky et al., 2009). Items included gauged the emotional and behavioral engagement aspects of school belonging and are similar to item content in the Psychological Sense of School Membership Scale (You, Ritchey, Furlong, Shochet, & Boman, 2011) and the School Connectedness Scale (Furlong, O'Brennan, & You, 2011). Students responded using a Likert scale format indicating how much they agreed or disagreed with each item (1 = *strongly disagree* to 6 = *strongly agree*), with higher scores representing higher levels of self-reported school belonging. The alpha coefficient for the five-item version in this study was .87.

Social emotional wellbeing at T2. The Social Emotional Health Survey–Secondary (SEHS-S) is a 36-item self-report measure that assesses youth's strengths (Furlong, You et al., 2014). Confirmatory factor analyses and invariance testing across multiple groups by You et al. (2015) suggest a higher order-factor structure, with 12 subscales loading onto four second-order traits of Belief-in-Self (self-awareness, persistence, self-efficacy), Belief-in-Others (school support, family coherence, peer support), Emotional Competence (empathy, self-control, behavioral self-control), and Engaged Living (gratitude, zest, and optimism). The second-order traits load onto a higher-order latent trait called Covitality. Other than the gratitude and zest subscales, students report their degree of functioning using a 4-point scale (1 = *not at all true of me* and 4 = *very much true of me*). Students report gratitude and zest on a 5-point scale (1 = *not at all* and 5 = *extremely*). The overall higher-order Covitality score was used in this study as a measure of social emotional wellbeing. For this sample, the internal consistency for the overall Covitality score was .88.

Internal distress at T2. Students' internal symptoms of psychological distress at T2 were measured with the Social Emotional Distress Survey (SEDS), a scale designed for this study that examined symptoms of anxious and depressed emotional experiences. Items were measured using a 5-point response scale (1 = *not at all true of me* to 5 = *very true of me*) and asked students to report on their "past month" experiences. Using the present study's sample, we completed maximum likelihood confirmatory factor analyses using MPlus (Muthén & Muthén, 1998/2013). A one-factor model (labeled Internal Distress) with seven items was supported by parallel analysis, high factor loadings, and adequate fit. To provide additional verification, the one-factor model was also evaluated with an independent sample of students attending a high school in an urban California community located more than 300 kilometers from the present study's primary high school. The internal consistency among the seven internal distress items was high ($\alpha = .90$) for the current sample.

Procedure

Survey administration. Students completed screening surveys in the fall of the 2014–2015 (T1) and 2015–2016 (T2) school years. Measures used at T1 included an assessment of global life satisfaction, psychological distress, and school belonging. T2 included a measure of social emotional wellbeing and internal distress. Surveys were administered in classroom units by regular classroom teachers following a prepared script.

Complete mental health groups. Following the T1 screening, complete mental health groups were created by first categorizing students by low, average, and high levels of life satisfaction (BMSLSS) as suggested by Kim et al. (in press). Consistent with earlier complete mental health research, students were also categorized by normative and elevated levels of psychological distress (using 10 items from the SDQ; Greenspoon & Saklofske, 2001; Suldo & Shaffer, 2008). Similar to Dowdy et al. (2014), z-scores for both overall life satisfaction and psychological distress were utilized to sort students into groups. Standardized scores for BMSLSS mean scores were generated to classify students according to three levels of global life satisfaction: high (z-score greater than 1.0), average (z-score between −1.0 and 1.0), and low (z-score below −1.0). Next, standardized scores for the mean of the 10 SDQ items were generated to classify students according to two levels of distress: elevated (z-score of 1.0 or greater) and normative (z-score below 1.0; we use the term "normative distress" recognizing that many students experience some distress at subsyndromal levels as part of normal life experiences). Following Moore et al.'s (2015) recommendation to consider the number of students to whom a school can realistically provide intervention services, six mental health groups were created by logically crossing life satisfaction and distress scores as shown in Table 5.1. Students traditionally labeled "troubled" in complete mental health research were categorized as 1. low life satisfaction and elevated distress, which is the primary target group of schoolwide mental health screening; that is, students reporting high levels of distress and low levels of personal/social assets. Students that traditionally fall into the "languishing" or "vulnerable" group were categorized as 2. low life satisfaction and normative distress, which is a group of students that is missed by traditional deficit bounded mental health screening surveys.

Data Analysis Plan

Students who participated in screening at T1 and T2 were included in data analysis for the current study. To address the first research question, analysis of variance (ANOVA) with planned contrasts was performed to examine mean levels of school belonging across mental health groups at T1. Students in the counterintuitive group

Table 5.1. Mean school belonging (school satisfaction scale) item scores for complete mental health groups at time 1

Life satisfaction (LS)	Psychological distress	
	>1.0 SD (High) highest 15% of sample	<1.0 SD (Normative) lowest 85% of sample
<−1.0 SD (Low) lowest 15% of sample	**1. Low LS, Elevated Distress** $M = 3.60$, $SD = 1.05$, 3.9%, $n = 45$	**2. Low LS, Normative Distress** $M = 3.65$, $SD = 0.94$, 8.7%, $n = 101$
−1.0 SD to 1.0 SD (average) 16–84% of sample	**3. Average LS, Elevated Distress** $M = 4.00$, $SD = 0.85$, 7.7%, $n = 89$	**4. Average LS, Normative Distress** $M = 4.49$, $SD = 1.05$, 41.6%, $n = 691$
> 1.0 SD (High) Highest 15% of sample	**5. High LS, Elevated Distress**[1] $M = 4.53$, $SD = 1.52$, 0.8%, $n = 9$	**6. High LS, Normative Distress** $M = 5.09$, $SD = 0.63$, 19.4%, $n = 225$

[1] *Not included in data analyses due to small subgroup size*

reporting *high life satisfaction and elevated distress* ($n = 9$) were not included in the analysis due to small sample size. Planned contrasts were utilized to compare the *low life satisfaction and normative distress* group to all other complete mental health groups. Assumptions of normality and homogeneity of variance were considered prior to conducting the ANOVA.

To address the second research question, two hierarchical multiple regressions were performed to evaluate the increase in explained variance of social emotional wellbeing and internal distress at T2 when school belonging at T1 was added as an independent predictor. First, mean scores on the global life satisfaction and the psychological distress measures at T1 were entered as independent predictors in block 1 to predict social emotional wellbeing and internal distress at T2, which were measured by individuals' total scores on the SEHS-S and SEDS, respectively. Next, mean scores on school belonging at T1 were entered in block 2 to examine the added value in screening for school belonging to predict future mental health. Assumptions of linearity, independence of errors, normality of residuals, absence of multicollinearity, absence of univariate and multivariate outliers, and homoscedasticity were considered prior to conducting the hierarchical multiple regressions. With a sample of more than 1,000 students, all analyses conducted for this study had sufficient power to detect a small (d = .30, $f^2 = .02$) effect size.

RESULTS

First, mental health groups were created for students who participated in universal screening at T1. Consistent with prior studies forming complete mental health groups among high school students (e.g., Antaramian et al., 2010; Suldo & Shaffer, 2008),

Table 5.2. *Variable descriptive statistics and correlations among study variables*

Variable	1	2	3	4	5	M	SD
1. BMSLSS (Time 1)	–					4.17	.64
2. SDQ – 10 items (Time 1)	–.49*	–				.50	.37
3. School belonging (Time 1)	.54*	–.32*	–			4.46	.92
4. SEHS-S (Time 2)	.51*	–.33*	.41*	–		116.41	16.92
5. SEDS (Time 2)	–.33*	.47*	–.15*	–.34*	–	1.85	.90

Notes: BMSLSS = Brief Multidimensional Life Satisfaction Scale (range 1–5). SDQ = Strengths and Difficulties Questionnaire (range 0–2). SEHS-S = Social Emotional Health Survey-Secondary (range 26–150). School belonging was measured with the School Satisfaction Subscale of the Multidimensional Students' Life Satisfaction Scale (range 1–6). SEDS = Social Emotional Distress Survey (range 1–5). *p < .01

the two highest proportion of students were categorized as either having *average life satisfaction and normative distress* (41.6%) or *high life satisfaction and normative distress* (19.4%). Both groups would be considered to have "complete mental health" in previous dual-factor research (e.g., Suldo & Shaffer, 2008). Students in the *low satisfaction and normative distress* group, typically labeled as "languishing" in previous dual-factor research (e.g., Suldo & Shaffer, 2008), represented almost 9% of the sample, which is consistent with the rates reported by Antaramian and colleagues (2010). Of interest in this study, at T1, 8.7% of students reported normative distress but also low life satisfaction, a group of students that is missed by traditional deficit focused mental health screeners. Descriptive statistics and correlations among the study variables are presented in Table 5.2.

School Belonging among Complete Mental Health Groups

To answer the first research question, mean level of school belonging was compared across complete mental health groups. The group characterized by *low life satisfaction and elevated distress* had the lowest mean score for school belonging, followed by *low life satisfaction and normative distress* (see Table 5.1). Students who reported *high life satisfaction,* regardless of psychological distress level, reported the highest sense of school belonging. Since previous research indicates that there is a need for schools to address students in the *low life satisfaction and normative distress* group, mean school belonging scores for students in this group were compared to all other groups. Results indicate that there were significant differences between groups with a large effect size, $Eta^2 = .20$. When comparing school belonging of the *low life satisfaction and normative distress* ("languishing") group to all other groups, means were significantly different in all contrasts other than when comparing to the *low life satisfaction and elevated distress* ("troubled") group. Results suggest that students who reported low life satisfaction also reported the lowest sense of school belonging compared to their peers, regardless of psychological distress level.

Predicting Wellbeing and Internal Distress

We next examined if school belonging predicted adolescents' future social emotional wellbeing and internal distress above and beyond measures used for complete mental health screening. T1 life satisfaction and psychological distress (which were used to create mental health groups) were entered as predictors of T2 social emotional wellbeing in a linear regression analysis across the sample. The overall model was statistically significant, accounting for 27% of the variance in T2 social emotional wellbeing. Life satisfaction scores positively predicted social emotional wellbeing scores, while psychological distress scores negatively predicted social emotional wellbeing scores. Next, life satisfaction, psychological distress, and school belonging scores from T1 were entered as predictors of T2 social emotional wellbeing in a hierarchical regression analysis, with school belonging entered in block 2. The overall model was statistically significant, accounting for 29% of the variance in T2 social emotional wellbeing. The addition of T1 school belonging mean item scores significantly contributed to the prediction of social emotional wellbeing one year later with a small effect size, Cohen's $f^2 = .035$.

The same regression procedures were followed for predicting T2 internal distress. The initial model was significant and accounted for 24% of the variance in T2 internal distress. Global life satisfaction scores negatively predicted internal distress, while psychological distress scores positively predicted internal distress. Next, mean item scores of T1 school belonging were added in block 2 of a hierarchical linear regression. The overall model was significant, still accounting for 24% of the variance in T2 internal distress. As expected, life satisfaction at T1 negatively predicted internal distress at T2, and psychological distress at T1 positively predicted internal distress scores at T2. Although school belonging scores positively predicted T2 internal distress, the addition of school belonging to the explained variance in internal distress was not substantial, Cohen's $f^2 = .006$.

DISCUSSION

The aims of the current study were to investigate students' sense of school belonging in a complete mental health, schoolwide screening context, as well as to examine the added contribution that screening for school belonging might provide in predicting social emotional wellbeing and internal distress. The results of this study provide insight into understanding students beyond their level of psychological risk and can aid schools in making more informed decisions about prevention and intervention strategies.

First, the study aimed to identify significant differences in students' sense of school belonging based on complete mental health group categorization. As predicted, students who fell into the *high life satisfaction and normative distress* ("thriving") group reported the highest sense of school belonging, while students categorized by *low life satisfaction and elevated distress* ("troubled") reported the lowest sense of school belonging. However, further analysis found that reported levels of school belonging were not significantly different between the traditionally-labeled "troubled" and "languishing" groups, with these students reporting significantly lower feelings of school belonging than students who reported average and high levels of life satisfaction. Similar results were found by Antaramian and colleagues (2010), in which students identified as "vulnerable" had similar levels of risk for academic and behavioral issues, including low levels of school belonging, as those who were identified as "troubled". Furthermore, differences in school belonging across groups indicated a large practical significance, which suggests that school support teams may consider school belonging to be a differentiating factor among complete mental health groups, especially between students reporting low levels of life satisfaction and those reporting average and high levels. With this knowledge, schools can better address the needs of students reporting low life satisfaction and low distress, a group not typically identified in traditional screening approaches. Considering the negative outcomes associated with low levels of school belonging, including increased externalizing behaviors (Chapman et al., 2011) and internalizing symptoms of psychological distress (Lester et al., 2013), prevention and intervention strategies aimed at bolstering students' belonging and connections to school may be valuable.

The second aim of the current study was to examine the utility of students' school belonging in predicting longitudinal outcomes, particularly social emotional wellbeing and internal distress one year later. Since high levels of school belonging are associated with improved psychological functioning (Pittman & Richmond, 2007), increased happiness and social supports, and reduced loneliness (Vieno et al., 2005), we anticipated that school belonging at T1 would increase the variance explained when predicting social emotional wellbeing and internal distress at T2. When students' school belonging at T1 was added as a predictor of social emotional wellbeing and internal distress, explained variance modestly increased. Despite this, information on the differences in school belonging among students may help inform intervention efforts. A core principle of using a complete mental health screening approach is that the results should potentially have meaning and utility for all students. While the results of this study suggested that a measure of school belonging did not contribute substantially to the prediction of later psychological distress, this does not imply that there are not benefits to schools regularly including school belonging item content in schoolwide screeners, as belonging is an indicator of positive youth development and is associated with positive school climate.

Intervention Strategies to Promote School Belonging

Overall, recommendations for fostering school belonging involve collaboration between families, schools, and students and the development of strong, stable relationships with adults at school (Centers for Disease Control, 2009; Monahan,

Oesterle, & Hawkins, 2010; National Research Council Institute of Medicine, 2004). The United States Centers for Disease Control (CDC) compiled six overarching strategies for schools to promote school belonging, as well as specific recommendations to carry out those strategies (2009). Recommendations are geared toward making classroom spaces inclusive and engaging for all students. Schools were advised to involve parents and community members in decision-making processes while also providing training to teachers so that they can effectively provide academic, social, and emotional skills to students through classroom activities and homework (CDC, 2009).

Chapman, Buckley, Sheehan, and Shochet (2013) compiled a review of school-based prevention and intervention programs to foster school belonging, requiring that the programs be universally implemented in schools for children ages 5 to 18 years. The review identified seven different programs that had been evaluated by pre- and post-test design with a treatment and control group and demonstrated changes to students' attitudes and risk-taking behaviours. The Raising Healthy Children (RHC) program is an example of a comprehensive and effective prevention program aimed at bolstering students' school belongingness (Catalano, 2004; Chapman et al., 2013; Monahan et al., 2010). The program, which has been named an effective program by both the Substance Abuse and Mental Health Services Administration (SAMHSA) and the National Registry of Effective Prevention Programs, involves school staff, students, families, and the community through social skills training, positive classroom management training for teachers, and workshops to help parents engage with their children about school (Monahan et al., 2010). Two longitudinal studies, the Seattle Social Development Project and the RHC program, have compared outcomes of individuals participating in the RHC program to those in a control group (Catalano et al., 2004). Compared to the control group, findings from both studies indicated that students who participated in the RHC program experienced a smaller decline in school connectedness from middle through high school, higher levels of school connectedness and academic success in Grade 12, and fewer school problems, incidents of violence, alcohol use, and risky sexual activity (Catalano et al., 2004). Given findings that school belonging and the domain-related construct, school connectedness, may positively predict later psychological functioning, it is worthwhile to further investigate the relations between belonging and later mental distress.

Limitations and Future Directions

The current study incurred limitations that future research may consider when examining school belonging within a complete mental health screening framework. Significant limitations were found in the measures used to operationalize the variables of interest. As in the Antaramian et al. (2010) investigation, this study operationalized school belonging by employing items from a widely-used school satisfaction scale. However, it is possible that other instruments that explicitly measure other aspects of school belonging and connectedness might prove to be stronger longitudinal predictors of wellbeing and distress. Additional research is needed on the modified version of the SDQ that was used in the current study. Although it was important to include brief measures for use in this schoolwide screening, future research conducted with other measures of similar constructs may yield different results and further examination into the psychometric properties of the measures used in this study is warranted.

Although cut points for complete mental health groups were empirically based, the criteria used were still chosen based on the applicability to the study's sample and school, rather than established criteria that are applied to all complete mental health contexts. Other contemporary approaches to classifying students' mental health status that have employed latent class analysis (e.g., Kim, Dowdy, Furlong, & You, 2016) may provide further insight into how school belonging is meaningfully differentiated among complete mental health groups. Future research should also examine the value of screening for school belonging to predict other outcomes, especially academic achievement.

Further research should investigate differences in school belonging within and between complete mental health groups based on ethnicity, gender, and grade level, as meaningful differences could inform school prevention and intervention practices. Schools can also benefit from future research that examines the added utility of incorporating a measure of school belonging into screening at the primary school level, as results suggest that school belonging may not be associated with changes across time from primary school into high school. Future research may benefit from a focus on interventions that impact students' sense of school belonging to investigate the effect of intervention on stability of complete mental health groups over time. When considering the significant differences in school belonging across groups, as well as previous research that suggests the "languishing" group is the least stable across time (Kelly, Hills, Huebner, & McQuillin, 2012), interventions that target school belonging may foster student strengths, leading to increased life satisfaction and social emotional wellbeing.

ACKNOWLEDGEMENT

This chapter is an adapted version from Moffa, K., Dowdy, E., & Furlong, M. (2016). Exploring the contributions of school belonging to complete mental health screening. *The Educational and Developmental Psychologist, 33*(1), 16–32. doi:10.1017/edp.2016.8

REFERENCES

Allen, K. A., & Bowles, T. (2012). Belonging as guiding principle in the education of adolescents. *Australian Journal of Educational & Developmental Psychology, 12*, 108–119.

Antaramian, S. P., Huebner, E. S., Hills, K. J., & Valois, R. F. (2010). A dual-factor model of mental health: Toward a more comprehensive understanding of youth functioning. *American Journal of Orthopsychiatry, 80*, 462–472. doi:10.1111/j.1939-0025.2010.01049.x

Baumeister, R. F., & Leary, M. R. (1995). The need to belong: Desire for interpersonal attachments as fundamental human motivation. *Psychological Bulletin, 117*(3), 497–529.

Bickman, L., Athay, M. M., Reimer, M., Lambert, E. W., Kelley, S. D., Breda, C., Tempesti, T., Dew-Reeves, S. E., Brannan, A. M., & Vides de Andrade, A. R. (2007). *Manual of the peabody treatment and progress battery* (Electronic version). Nashville, TN: Vanderbilt University. Retrieved from http://peabody.vanderbilt.edu/ptpb/

Bronfenbrenner, U. (1986). Ecology of the family as a context for human development: Research perspectives. *Developmental Psychology, 22*(6), 723–742.

Catalano, R., Oesterle, S., Fleming, C., & Hawkins, D. (2004). The importance of bonding to school for healthy development: Findings from the social development research group. *Journal of School Health, 74*, 252–261. doi:10.1111/j.1746-1561.2004.tb08281

Centers for Disease Control and Prevention. (2009). *School connectedness: Strategies for increasing protective factors among youth.* Atlanta, GA: U.S. Department of Health and Human Services.

Chapman, R. L., Buckley, L., Sheehan, M., & Shochet, I. (2013). School-based programs for increasing connectedness and reducing risk behavior: A systematic review. *Educational Psychology Review, 25*(1), 95–114. Retrieved from http://search.proquest.com/docview/1272268895?accountid=14522

Chapman, R. L., Buckley, L., Sheehan, M., Shochet, I., & Romaniuk, M. (2011). The impact of school connectedness on violent behavior, transport risk-taking behavior, and associated injuries in adolescence. *Journal of School Psychology, 49*, 399–410. doi:10.1016/j.jsp.2011.04.004

Christina, J. M., Gilman, S. E., Guardino, M., Mickelson, K., Morselli, P. L., Olfson, M., & Kessler, R. (2000). Duration between onset and time of obtaining initial treatment among people with anxiety and mood disorders: An international survey of members of mental health patient advocate groups. *Psychological Medicine, 30*, 693–703. doi:10.1017/S0033291799002093

Costello, E. J., Mustillo, S., Keller, G., & Angold, A. (2004). Prevalence of psychiatric disorders in childhood and adolescence. In B. L. Levin, J. Petrila, & K. D. Hennessy (Eds.), *Mental health services: A public health perspective* (2nd ed., pp. 111–128). Oxford: Oxford University Press.

Fröjd, S. A., Nissinen, E. S., Pelkonen, M. U. I., Marttunen, M. J., Koivisoto, A.-M., & Kaltiala-Heino, R. (2008). Depression and school performance in middle adolescent boys and girls. *Journal of Adolescence, 31*, 485–498. doi:10.1016/j.adolescence.2007.08.006

Furlong, M. J., Dowdy, E., Carnazzo, K., Bovery, B., & Kim, E. (2014). Covitality: Fostering the building blocks of complete mental health. *Communique, 42*(8), 28–29.

Furlong, M. J., Froh, J., Muller, M., & Gonzalez, V. (2014). The role of student engagement in engaged living and psychological and social well-being: The centrality of connectedness/relatedness. In D. J. Shernoff & J. Bempechat (Eds.), *National Society for the study of education yearbook – Engaging youth in schools: Empirically-based models to guide future innovations.* New York, NY: Columbia Teachers College.

Furlong, M. J., O'Brennan, L. M., & You, S. (2011). Psychometric properties of the add health school connectedness scale for 18 sociocultural groups. *Psychology in the Schools, 48*, 986–997. doi:10.1002/pits.20609

Furlong, M. J., You, S., Renshaw, T. L., Smith, D. C., & O'Malley, M. D. (2014). Preliminary development and validation of the social and emotional health survey for secondary students. *Social Indicators Research, 117*, 1011–1032. doi:10.1007/s11205-013-0373-0

Furrer, C., & Skinner, E. (2003). Sense of relatedness as a factor in children's academic engagement and performance. *Journal of Educational Psychology, 95*, 148–162. doi:10.1037/0022–0663.95.1.148

Goodenow, C. (1993). The psychological sense of school membership among adolescents: Scale development and educational correlates. *Psychology in the Schools, 30*, 79–90. doi:10.1002/1520-6807(199301)30:1

Goodman, R. (1997). The strengths and difficulties questionnaire: A research note. *Child Psychology & Psychiatry & Allied Disciplines, 38*, 581–586. doi:10.1111/j.1469-7610.1997.tb01545.x

Gratis, M. N. (2013). Are family communication and school belonging protective factors against depressive symptoms in homeless youth in Toronto? *Canadian Journal of Community Mental Health, 32*(4), 75–83. doi:10.7870/cjcmh-2013-034

Greenspoon, P. J., & Saklofske, D. H. (2001). Toward an integration of subjective well-being and psychopathology. *Social Indicators Research, 54*, 81–108. doi:10.1023/A:1007219227883

Huebner, E. S. (1994). Preliminary development and validation of a multidimensional life satisfaction scale for children. *Psychological Assessment, 6*, 149–158. doi:10.1037/1040-3590.6.2.149

Huebner, E. S., Laughlin, J. E., Ash, C., & Gilman, R. (1998). Further validation of the multidimensional students' life satisfaction scale. *Journal of Psychological Assessment, 16*, 118–134. doi:10.1177/073428299801600202

Joyce, H. D., & Early, T. J. (2014). The impact of school connectedness and teacher support on depressive symptoms in adolescents: A multilevel analysis. *Children and Youth Services Review, 39*, 101–107. Retrieved from http://search.proquest.com/docview/1520887659?accountid=14522

Kelly, R. M., Hills, K. J., Huebner, E. S., & McQuillin, S. (2012). The longitudinal stability and dynamics of group membership in the dual-factor model of mental health: Psychosocial predictors of mental health. *Canadian Journal of School Psychology, 27*, 337–355. doi:10.1177/0829573512458505

Kessler, R. C., Aguilar-Gaxiola, S., Alonso, J., Chatterji, S., Lee, S., Ormel, J., Üstün, T. B., & Wang, P. S. (2009). The global burden of mental disorders: An update from the WHO World Mental Health (WMH) surveys. *Epidemiology Psichiatria Sociale, 18*(1), 23–33. doi:10.1017/S1121189X00001421

Keyes, C. L. M. (2005). Mental illness and/or mental health? Investigating axioms of the complete state model of health. *Journal of Consulting and Clinical Psychology, 73*, 539–548. doi:10.1037/0022-006X.73.3.539

Kia-Keating, M., & Ellis, B. H. (2007). Belonging and connection to school in resettlement: Young refugees, school belonging, and psychosocial adjustment. *Clinical Child Psychology and Psychiatry, 12*, 29–43. doi:10.1177/1359104507071052

Kim, E. K., Dowdy, E., Furlong, M. J., & You, S. (2016). Mental health profiles and quality of life outcomes among Korean adolescents. *School Psychology International, 38*(1), 98–116.

Kim, E. K., Furlong, M. J., Ng, Z. J., & Huebner, E. S. (in press). Child well-being and children's rights: Balancing positive and negative indicators in assessments. In S. Hart & B. Nastasi (Eds.), *International handbook on child rights in school psychology.* New York, NY: Springer.

Lester, L., & Cross, D. (2015). The relationship between school climate and mental and emotional well-being over the transition from primary to secondary school. *Psychology of Well-being, 5*(1), 1–15. doi:10.1186/s13612-015-0037-8

Lester, L., Waters, S., & Cross, D. (2013). The relationship between school connectedness and mental health during the transition to secondary school: A path analysis. *Australian Journal of Guidance and Counseling, 23*, 157–171. doi:10.1017/jgc.2013.20

Libbey, H. P. (2004). Measuring students' relationship to school: Attachment, bonding, connectedness, and engagement. *Journal of School Health, 74*, 274–283. doi:10.1111/j.1746-1561.2004.tb08284.x

Monahan, K. C., Oesterle, S., & Hawkins, J. D. (2010). Predictors and consequences for school connectedness: The case for prevention. *The Prevention Researcher, 17*(3), 3–7.

Manassis, K., Wilansky-Traynor, P., Farzan, N., Kleiman, V., Parker, K., & Sanford, M. (2010). The feelings club: Randomized controlled evaluation of school-based CBT for anxious or depressive symptoms. *Depression and Anxiety, 27*, 945–952. doi:10.1002/da.20724

McNeely, C., Nonnemaker, J., & Blum, J. (2002). Promoting school connectedness: Evidence from the national longitudinal study of adolescent health. *Journal of School Health, 72*, 138–147. doi:10.1111/j.1746-1561.2002.tb06533.x

Moore, S. A., Widales-Benitez, O., Carnazzo, K. W., Kim, E. K., Moffa, K., & Dowdy, E. (2015). Conducting universal complete mental health screening via student self-report. *Contemporary School Psychology, 19*, 253–267. doi:10.1007/s40688-015-0062-x

Muthén, L. K., & Muthén, B. O. (1998/2013). *Mplus user's guide* (6th ed.). Los Angeles, CA: Muthén & Muthén.

National Research Council and Institute of Medicine. (2004). *Engaging schools: Fostering high school students' motivation to learn.* Washington, DC: The National Academic Press.

Pittman, L. D., & Richmond, A. (2007). Academic and psychological functioning in late adolescence: The importance of school belonging. *The Journal of Experimental Education, 75*, 270–290. doi:10.3200/JEXE.75.4.270-292

Resnick, M. D., Bearman, P. S., Blum, R. W., Bauman, K. E., Harris, K. M., Jones, J., Tabor, J., Beuhring, T., Sieving, R. E., Shew, M., Ireland, M., Bearinger, L. H., & Udry, J. R. (1997). Protecting adolescents from harm: Findings from the national longitudinal study on adolescent health. *Journal of American Medical Association, 278*(10), 823–832. doi:10.1001/jama.278.10.823

Rushkin, V., Jones, S., Vermeiren, R., & Schwab-Stone, M. (2008). The strengths and difficulties questionnaire: The self-report version in American urban and suburban youth. *Psychological Assessment, 20*, 175–182. doi:10.1037/1040-3590.20.2.175

Ryan, R. M., & Deci, E. L. (2000). Self-determination theory and the facilitation of intrinsic motivation, social development, and wellbeing. *American Psychologist, 55*(1), 68–78. doi:10.1037/0003-066X.55.1.68

Sawatzky, R., Ratner, P. A., Johnson, J. L., Kopec, J. A., & Zumbo, B. D. (2009). Sample heterogeneity and the measurement structure of the multidimensional students' life satisfaction scale. *Social Indicators Research, 94*, 273–296. doi:10.1007/s11205-008-9423-4

Seligson, J., Huebner, E. S., & Valois, R. F. (2003). Preliminary validation of the Brief Multidimensional Students' Life Satisfaction Scale (BMSLSS). *Social Indicators Research, 61*, 121–145. doi:10.1023/A:1021326822957

Shochet, I. M., Dadds, M., Ham, D., & Montague, R. (2006). School connectedness is an underemphasized parameter in adolescent mental health: Results of a community prediction study. *Journal of Clinical Child & Adolescent Psychology, 35*, 170–179. doi:10.1207/s15374424jccp35

Shochet, I. M., Smith, C. L., Furlong, M. J., & Homel, R. (2011). A prospective study investigating the impact of school belonging factors on negative affect in adolescents. *Journal of Clinical Child & Adolescent Psychology, 40*(4), 586–595. doi:10.1080/15374416.2011.581616

Suldo, S. M., & Shaffer, E. J. (2008). Looking beyond psychopathology: The dual-factor model of mental health in youth. *School Psychology Review, 37*, 52–68.

Tian, L., Zhang, L., Huebner, E. S., Zheng, X., & Liu, W. (2016). The longitudinal relationship between school belonging and subjective well-being in school among elementary school students. *Applied Research in Quality of Life, 11*, 1269–1285. doi:10.1007/s11482-015-9436-5

Venning, A., Wilson, A., Kettler, L., & Eliott, J. (2013). Mental health among youth in South Australia: A survey of flourishing, languishing, struggling, and floundering. *Australian Psychologist, 48*, 299–310. doi:10.1111/j.1742-9544.2012.00068.x

Vieno, A., Perkins, D., Smith, T., & Santinello, M. (2005). Democratic school climate and sense of community in school: A multilevel analysis. *American Journal of Community Psychology, 36*, 327–341. doi:10.1007/s10464-005-8629-8

World Health Organization. (2014). *Young people: Health risks and solutions* (Fact sheet No. 345). Geneva: Author.

You, S., Furlong, M. J., Felix, E., & O'Malley, M. (2015). Validation of the social and emotional health survey for five sociocultural groups: Multigroup invariance and latent mean analyses. *Psychology in the Schools, 52*, 349–362. doi:10.1002/pits.21828

You, S., Furlong, M. J., Felix, E., Sharkey, J. D., Tanigaay, D., & Green, J. G. (2008). Relations among school connectedness, hope, life satisfaction, and bully victimization. *Psychology in the Schools, 45*, 446–460. doi:10.1002/pits.20308

You, S., Ritchey, K., Furlong, M. J., Shochet, I., & Boman, P. (2011). Examination of the latent structure of the psychological sense of school membership scale. *Journal of Psychoeducational Assessment, 29*, 225–237. doi:10.1177/0734282910379968

Kathryn Moffa
Department of Counseling, Clinical, and School Psychology
University of California, Santa Barbara
USA

Erin Dowdy
Department of Counseling, Clinical, and School Psychology
University of California, Santa Barbara
USA

Michael J. Furlong
International Center for School Based Youth Development
University of California, Santa Barbara
USA

CLEMENCE DUE, DAMIEN W. RIGGS AND
MARTHA AUGOUSTINOS

6. "THIS REMINDS ME OF MY COUNTRY"

*Exploring Experiences of Belonging at School for
Young Children with Refugee Backgrounds*

INTRODUCTION

In 2015, the office for the United National High Commissioner for Refugees (UNHCR) reported that there were nearly 20 million refugees[1] world-wide, over half of whom were under 18. This is the highest number of refugees since World War II (UNHCR, 2015). While only a proportion of these young people and their families will be moved to a resettlement country, it is nevertheless vitally important that resettlement countries have an evidence base upon which to draw from when providing settlement services and support to young people with refugee backgrounds.

In resettlement countries such as Australia, school is one of the primary places where newly arrived refugee students will connect with their community, build relationships, and establish a sense of belonging in their new country (Correa-Velez, Gifford, & Barnett, 2010; de Heer, Due, & Riggs, 2016; Mace, Mulheron, Jones, & Cherian, 2014; Matthews, 2008; Woods, 2009). As such, school belonging plays a crucial role in establishing a sense of social inclusion, positive wellbeing and the development of peer relationships for refugee young people from the beginning of their resettlement (Correa-Velez et al., 2010; de Heer et al., 2016; Woods, 2009).

However, while there is a body of research that has explored school belonging in adolescents in general (Anderman, 2002; Goodenow, 1993; Shochet & Smith 2014; Van Ryzin, Gravely, & Roseth, 2006) and in adolescents with refugee backgrounds in particular (Gifford, Correa-Velez, & Sampson, 2009; Kia-Keating & Ellis, 2007; Trickett & Birman, 2005) very little research has explored experiences of school belonging for young people (aged under 13) with refugee backgrounds. As such, the aim of this chapter was to consider experiences of school belonging in a sample of young students with refugee backgrounds in Intensive English Language Centres (IELCs) in South Australia. In considering these experiences, the study also aimed to explore the role of schools in providing support to newly arrived refugee young people and their families.

© KONINKLIJKE BRILL NV, LEIDEN, 2018 | DOI:10.1163/9789004386969_006

School Belonging

School belonging is typically defined as a multi-dimensional concept, incorporating a student's level of attachment, commitment, involvement and belief in their school (Wehlage, Rutter, Smith, Lesko, & Fernandez, 1989). As such, definitions of school belonging mirror definitions of belonging more broadly (e.g., Baumeister & Leary, 1995). Specifically, attachment to school refers to attachment to the broader school and students' investment in the school itself, including in relation to both environmental aspects and interpersonal relationships (Baumeister & Leary, 1995; Goodenow, 1993). Commitment refers to issues such as how happy students are to comply with the rules and expectations of their school, and has been shown to influence decisions about school in adolescents, such as whether to remain at school or leave. Involvement at school includes a focus on student engagement (both in relation to academic work, as well as any extracurricular activities which are school-related). Finally, belief in school refers to the extent to which students feel that their school values have significance for them. Taken together, higher levels of school belonging have been shown to be related to a number of positive outcomes for adolescents, including improved self-esteem and motivation, and lower levels of depression and peer rejection (Anderman, 2002; Battistich, Solomon, Watson, & Schaps, 1997; Goodenow, 1993; Kia-Keating & Ellis, 2007; Sujoldzic, Peternel, Kulenovic, & Terzic, 2006).

Correspondingly, understanding experiences of school belonging in students from refugee backgrounds is critically important. Indeed, ensuring that schools and other educational institutions understand how to promote school belonging for refugee students is vital to providing students with the opportunity to feel a sense of connection to their school environment (Kia-Keating & Ellis, 2007). Moreover, such an understanding must take into account refugee students' own identities and knowledge rather than assuming that refugee students can simply "fit in" to existing school environments and school cultures (Matthews, 2008; Woods, 2009). In other words, understandings of school belonging for students with refugee backgrounds must lead to a two way interaction which takes into account existing power relationships, and ensures that refugee students can feel belonging in all of the domains on their own terms as well as those of the school (Matthews, 2008; Riggs & Due, 2011; Woods, 2009). Examples of such two-way interaction seen in existing research include translating documentation for students into languages of families in the community, supporting friendship development through shared interests such as art and sport, and sharing elements of all students' cultural backgrounds in the classroom (e.g., see Block, Cross, Riggs, & Gibbs, 2014; Due, Riggs, & Augoustinos, 2016; Pugh, Every, & Hattam, 2012).

Despite the importance of focusing on belonging for refugee students, there is currently very little research outlining how such students experience school belonging in resettlement countries such as Australia – with most of the educational literature focusing on either English language acquisition (e.g., Oliff & Couch, 2005), social inclusion (e.g., Block, Cross, Riggs, & Gibbs, 2014; de Heer et al., 2016), issues of social justice (e.g., Keddie, 2012; Taylor & Sidhu, 2012), or promoting whole-school approaches (e.g., Pugh, Every, & Hattam, 2012). While each of these areas are important, our aim in this chapter is to provide an overview of how refugee students experience school belonging specifically, and to consider how these experiences can be used in policies for refugee education in resettlement countries.

School Belonging in Refugee Students

Kia-Keating and Ellis (2007) argue that schools have a "unique and influential impact on the lives of adolescents" (p. 30), and that this impact is particularly important for newly arrived refugee students as they learn to navigate their new environments. In their study of 76 Somalian refugees aged between 12 and 19 in the United States, Kia-Keating and Ellis found that higher levels of school belonging were related to lower levels of depression and higher levels of self-efficacy, reflecting the broader studies noted above. Importantly, Kia-Keating and Ellis note that studies considering the experiences of refugee students at school –and the impact of these experiences on school belonging – are important given the relationship between school belonging and some wellbeing domains. The protective role of school belonging in relation to positive wellbeing outcomes has also been found in other studies (e.g., Fazel, Reed, Panter-Brick, & Stein, 2012; Rousseau, Drapeau, & Platt, 2004; Sujoldzic et al., 2006).

In a second study undertaken in the United States, Trickett and Birman (2005) found a positive relationship between overall support at school and school belonging in a sample of 110 adolescents with refugee backgrounds from the former Soviet Union. Interestingly, they found different results for support from American peers as compared to support from Russian peers, and conclude that "… substantively, these findings suggest the importance of ethnic peer support in creating an alternative sense of belonging for adolescents who did not feel that they fit into the school" (p. 36). In other words, they found that while support from American peers was positively related to school belonging, not all students experienced this support. When this support was not available, support from Russian peers provided an important avenue for experiencing belonging. However, Trickett and Birman found that Russian peer support was related to higher levels of disciplinary infraction in their sample of refugee students, although they did not explore the extent to which this was due to the fact that students who felt they did not "fit in" to school may be more likely to behave in ways perceived to be outside the rules of the school. They also found a positive relationship between parental support and school belonging, highlighting the importance of involving parents in the school community in addition to students.

In the Australian context, the *Good Starts* study (Gifford et al., 2009) found that school belonging was an important factor in the wellbeing of newly arrived adolescents with refugee backgrounds (aged 12 to 18) enrolled in English Language Schools (ELS) in Melbourne. Gifford, Correa-Velez and Sampson found that the students in their study valued their time at school, and had high aspirations in relation to their education. Specifically, their findings indicate that students reported valuing, amongst other things: the cultural diversity of their intensive language school, the presence of other students who spoke their own language, having a sense of safety and belonging, and a curriculum which allowed them to experience some success in their education. These findings indicate the importance of ensuring that the facilitation of school belonging is collaborative and reciprocal. This can be achieved particularly by providing opportunities for refugee students to contribute their own knowledge and aspirations, rather than focusing school experiences around existing school values and culture (Matthews, 2008; Woods, 2009).

Finally, the literature exploring school belonging for refugee students has also found that school belonging is negatively impacted by experiences of discrimination (e.g., Brown & Chu, 2012; Trickett & Birman, 2005). Specifically, experiences of discrimination lead to a range of negative outcomes, including difficulties developing peer relationships at school, lower levels of school belonging and engagement, and decreased mental health and wellbeing (Priest et al., 2014).

Taken together, these findings indicate that, as with young people in general, school belonging plays an important role in a range of areas of young people with refugee backgrounds, including mental health and wellbeing. In addition, it is important to note that positive experiences of school belonging play a particularly important role for young refugee students not only because of the outcomes of school belonging outlined above, but also because trauma and mental health interventions for refugees are increasingly being administered through schools (Ehntholt & Yule, 2006). It is plausible to suggest that if levels of school belonging are not high, such interventions risk being less effective from the very beginning. As such, understanding how to promote school belonging in refugee students is extremely important to their health and wellbeing in a broad range of areas.

METHOD

This chapter forms part of a broader project which aimed to explore experiences of education for students from both migrant and refugee backgrounds in South Australia. Some details of this broader study are provided here by way of providing contextual information to the current study.

Setting

In South Australia, the Intensive English Language Program (IELP) involves 15 Intensive English Language Centres (IELCs), located at the same sites as mainstream government-run primary schools. As such, newly arrived children – including both those with refugee backgrounds and those with migrant[2] backgrounds – begin their education on a mainstream education site, but spend their time in specialised intensive English language classes. Students are typically enrolled in an IELC for six to 12 months (with special provisions for refugee students, who are eligible for extended time in the program), whereupon they transition from their IELC into mainstream education, either at the same school or at a different site (DECD, 2012). Students enter the program on a continuous, rolling basis, soon after their arrival in Australia rather than only in one intake at the beginning of the school year. Students are eligible to be enrolled in an IELC if they have been in Australia for less than 12 months.

It should be noted that this system of the provision of education for students with refugee backgrounds at primary school level differs around Australia, with some states enrolling students into intensive English programs that are not at the same site as *mainstream* primary schools. In South Australia, the sites are relatively consistent in their approach to education and their support for transition into mainstream classes or schools, however it should be noted that the sites do differ somewhat in the composition of the class – that is, some sites will have higher numbers of students with refugee backgrounds, and others will have higher numbers of students with migrant backgrounds.

Participants

The sample included in the broader study consisted of 63 children (15 with refugee backgrounds, and 48 with migrant backgrounds) from three separate schools with IELCs. This chapter focuses on the 15 children with refugee backgrounds. This sample of children was aged between five and 13, with seven male and eight female participants. Participants came from eight countries of origin: the Democratic Republic of the Congo, Iraq, Mongolia, Nepal, Pakistan, Papua New Guinea, Syria, and Zambia. Many spoke multiple languages, reflecting a number of moves prior to coming to Australia. The three sites included in the study were close (within 15km) to the city centre of Adelaide.

Procedure

Ethics approval was granted by The University of Adelaide's Human Research Ethics Committee, and the Department for Education and Child Development (DECD) in South Australia. It is important to note that the authors are aware of the ethical issues of working with this vulnerable group of young people, including issues such as gaining ongoing assent from children in addition to informed consent for parents and caregivers (Due, Riggs, & Augoustinos, 2014; Gifford et al., 2007; Crivello, Camfield, & Woodhead, 2009). As such, the first author (who undertook the data collection) spent a term at each school involved in the study in order to build rapport with participants, to let them know about the aims of the study, and to gain ongoing assent from them for their participation (see Due et al., 2014; Gifford et al., 2007; Crivello et al., 2009).

In terms of participant recruitment, information sheets and consent forms (translated into first languages by professional translators) were sent home to the parents or caregivers of most students with refugee backgrounds enrolled in the IELC. On two occasions, teachers chose not to send home information sheets and consent forms due to high levels of trauma in families who were very newly arrived.

The data collection relevant to this chapter consisted of a photo elicitation methodology, with accompanying interviews. Photo elicitation, or PhotoVoice, is a research technique which has been identified as a child-focussed, flexible approach to research that allows children's views to be communicated on their own terms in the research process (Darbyshire, MacDougall, & Schiller, 2005; Newman, Woodcock, Dunham, 2006; Due et al., 2014). Photo elicitation involves participants being provided with a camera (in this case, a digital camera) and asked to take photos according to a particular theme that relates to the research aims.

For the purposes of our research, students were asked to take photographs that represented their experiences at school. The students were then shown their photographs on a laptop, and invited to discuss their images in either a focus group of up to three children or in an individual interview. Whether discussions took place in focus groups or individual interviews was determined by external factors, such as what was happening in the classroom at the time, whether or not an interpreter was needed, and ensuring that the discussion did not disrupt the child's lessons. All conversations took place at the child's school. Focus groups and interviews relating to the photographs were audio recorded and transcribed, with student's names changed for anonymity.

Analytic Approach

Given that the aim of this chapter was to explore experiences of school belonging, a deductive thematic analysis of the interviews and focus groups where the photographs were discussed was undertaken. Specifically, the six stages outlined by Braun and Clarke (2013) including: reading and familiarisation, coding, searching for themes, reviewing themes and producing a thematic map, naming and defining themes and finalising the analysis through writing. The final thematic structure received consensus from all authors. The final themes are presented here – under each of the areas of school belonging – together with accompanying photographs. In all instances, attempts have been made to provide representative photographs, however due to ethical reasons, we cannot provide photographs which identify either individuals or specific schools.

RESULTS

The themes are presented here, under each of the main domains of school belonging identified in previous research (e.g., Kia-Keating & Ellis, 2007; Wehlage et al., 1989; Goodenow, 1993). In particular, the Kia-Keating and Ellis domains are used as a deductive framework due to the fact that they have been used previously in research with students with refugee backgrounds, and found to be a useful framework for school belonging (Kia-Kating & Ellis, 2007). Three themes were seen under the domain of attachment (*Specific spaces and activities in the school help build school attachment; Friendships with children from similar cultural, ethnic or linguistic backgrounds help build attachments to the school;* and *Relationships with teachers help build attachments to the school*), two under the domain of commitment (*Commitment to the school is seen through school rules* and *The requirement to learn English may impact school commitment*), one under involvement (*Involvement in the school is seen through school activities, not extracurricular activities*), and one under belief (*Students believe in their school when it reflects their identities and values*). These are outlined further below.

Attachment to the School

The domain of attachment to school refers to personal investment in the school, and attachment to the school community and space (e.g., Kia-Keating & Ellis, 2007; Wehlage et al., 1989; Goodenow, 1993). In general, students displayed high levels of attachment to their school, and indicated that they enjoyed coming to school and participating in school activities. Specific ways in which students created or displayed this attachment are discussed in this section, under the subheadings below.

Specific Spaces and Activities in the School Help Build School Attachment

Attachment to the school was often displayed through students' attachment to spaces in the school ground, leading to investment in particular aspects of school life (defined by particular spaces). These spaces were generally places where students frequently went for their classes (such as their own classroom, the school library, the school gym or the art room), but also included playground spaces where the students typically spent their breaks. It is noteworthy that, as found in previous research (de Heer et al., 2016), such spaces and activities frequently revolved around activities which did not rely on knowledge of English – such as art and sport. Indeed, all of the 15 students in this study photographed spaces in the school that involved learning in areas that did not rely on English. Examples of photographs and extracts are seen in Figures 6.1, 6.2 and 6.3.

As the photographs and excerpts in Figures 6.1, 6.2 and 6.3 indicate, students frequently drew upon spaces or activities that did not rely on English language skills. Indeed, in the last excerpt (Figure 6.3), the students discussing the photograph either actively avoided, or were excluded from, activities that did rely specifically on English language competency (that is, sitting and talking). Correspondingly, the students often spoke about forming friendships specifically with students with whom they could identify, and this is discussed in the following section.

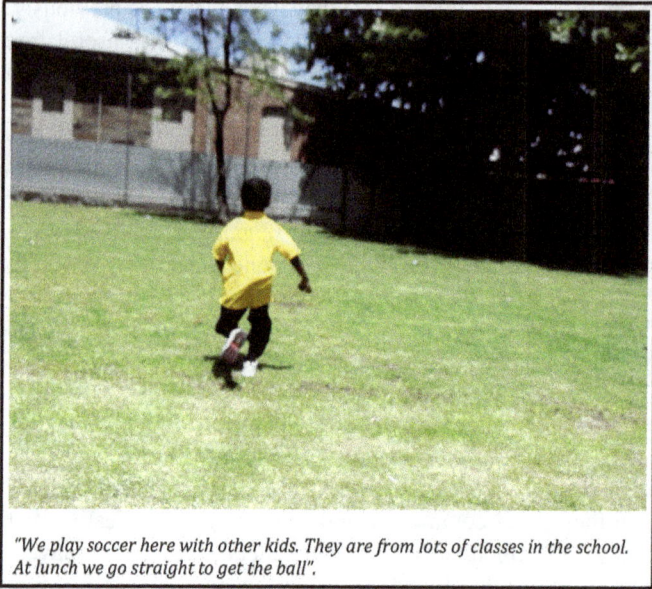

"We play soccer here with other kids. They are from lots of classes in the school. At lunch we go straight to get the ball".

Figure 6.1. A child running on an oval

"This is the art room. It's my favourite room."

Figure 6.2. Inside an art room

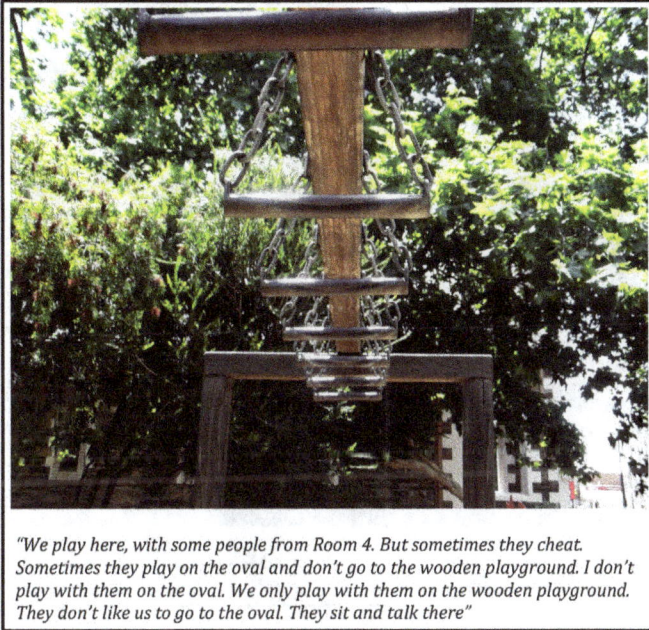

"We play here, with some people from Room 4. But sometimes they cheat. Sometimes they play on the oval and don't go to the wooden playground. I don't play with them on the oval. We only play with them on the wooden playground. They don't like us to go to the oval. They sit and talk there"

Figure 6.3. A playground

Friendships with children from similar cultural, ethnic or linguistic backgrounds help build attachments to the school. The children frequently took photographs of their friends, and discussed their peer relationships. Indeed, as in the previous theme, all students photographed other students, and stated in interviews that this is because they were their friends. When asked *why* particular children in photographs were their friends, 10 of the 15 students indicated that they sought friendships with children from similar cultural, ethnic or linguistic backgrounds to themselves, and that these relationships increased their sense of school belonging. Examples of photographs and excerpts discussing friendships can be seen in Figures 6.4 and 6.5.

Relationships with teachers help build attachments to the school. All the students in the study discussed their relationship with their teachers, and it is notable that all students took photographs of at least one of their teachers (usually either their classroom teacher, or a school support officer). An example of this type of photograph is seen in Figure 6.6.

Students displayed excitement when talking about their teachers, generally indicating that their sense of school belonging was improved by these relationships. Again, this supports previous research concerning the importance of relationships with teachers (Crouch, Keys, & McMahon, 2014), and is elaborated further in the Discussion.

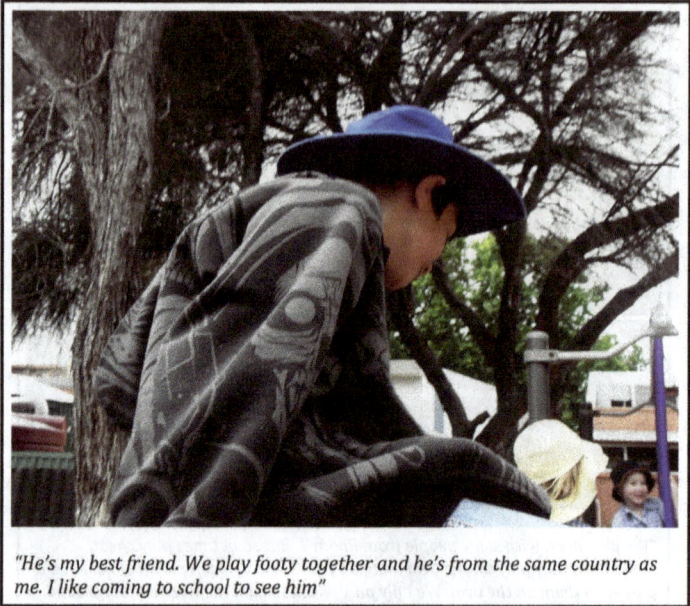

"He's my best friend. We play footy together and he's from the same country as me. I like coming to school to see him"

Figure 6.4. A friend sitting on some play equipment

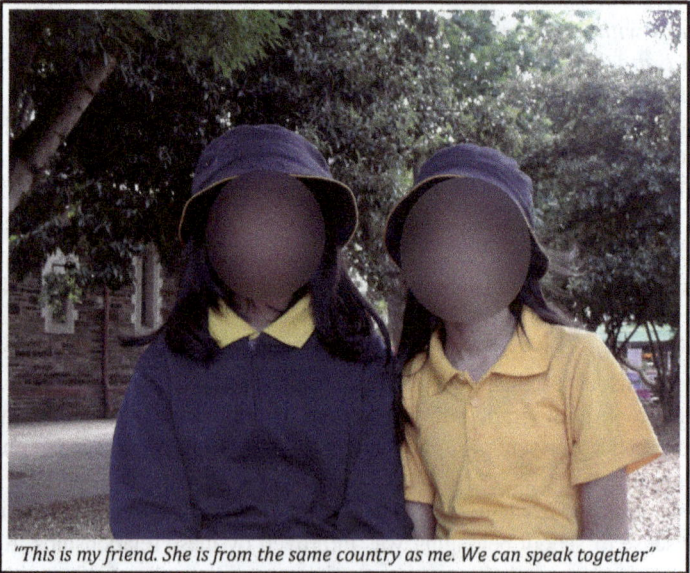

"This is my friend. She is from the same country as me. We can speak together"

Figure 6.5. Two friends sitting together

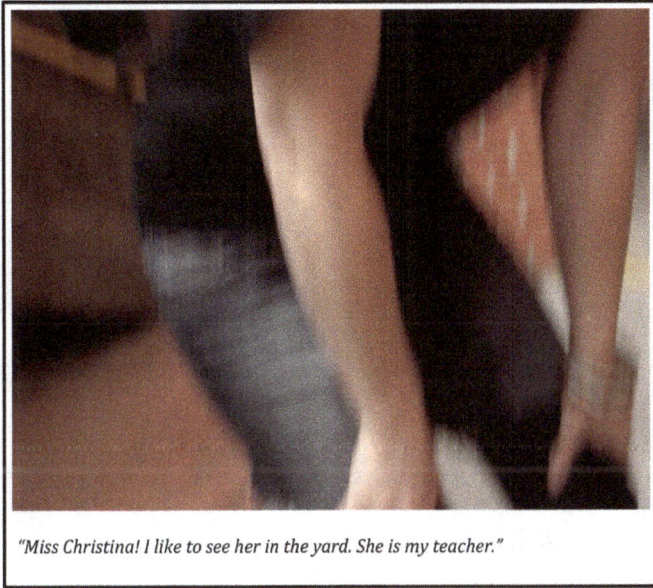

"Miss Christina! I like to see her in the yard. She is my teacher."

Figure 6.6. A classroom teacher

Commitment to the School

The school commitment domain of school belonging refers to areas such as valuing and adhering to school rules and expectations (e.g., Kia-Keating & Ellis, 2007; Wehlage et al., 1989; Goodenow, 1993). Commitment to the school was less evident in the photographs than the previous domain of attachment to school. However, it is worth noting that the fact that students took so many photographs of their teachers, as discussed above, could indicate an element of commitment to the school in terms of their enjoyment of participating at school.

Commitment to the school is seen through school rules. Students did sometimes discuss school rules in the photograph, with four of the 15 students noting at least one school rule or expectation in their interviews. These rules or expectations were typically discussed in relation to certain areas of the school grounds that were "out of bounds", as seen in Figure 6.7.

Here, a student outlines a place in the schoolyard where the students are not meant to play alone. However, photographs and discussions such as this were rare, and this photograph illustrates one of the few times where students discussed school rules in this research.

The requirement to learn English may impact school commitment. Notably, commitment to the school also came up in relation to learning English, and the

"This is my favourite place to play. We should not go close to the wall.
Sometimes at lunch we go with a teacher to the wall."

Figure 6.7. Some play equipment near an "out of bounds" area

"...no, he doesn't like coming to this school! All of the time he just speak Korean!!
English. We should speak English."

Figure 6.8. A friend sitting near some play equipment

expectation that students were at school in order to learn English first and foremost. Indeed, 8 of the students in this study discussed English in their interviews. An example of this is in Figure 6.8.

The extract seen in Figure 6.8 indicates the impact of the focus on learning English on school belonging for the students – in particular, the fact that speaking English was seen as an important element of the school's identity, and that not wishing to speak English was likely to lead to a dislike of school in Australia. This is perhaps particularly noticeable in the students' expression of *"this* school" rather than school in general, suggesting that the student may otherwise have a positive relationship with school and education.

Involvement in the School

The domain of involvement in the school generally concerns both students' engagement with their academic work, as well as their involvement in school-related extracurricular activities (Kia-Keating & Ellis, 2007; Wehlage et al., 1989). While students showed high levels of engagement with their academic work, they did not appear to be involved in many extracurricular activities associated with the school. In this domain, all of the students in the study took photographs of inside their classrooms, and displayed high levels of engagement with their academic work

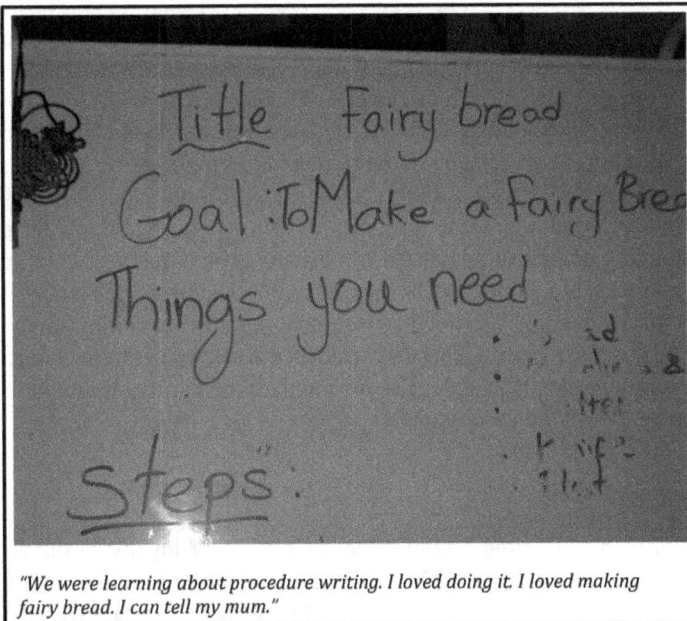

"We were learning about procedure writing. I loved doing it. I loved making fairy bread. I can tell my mum."

Figure 6.9. A classroom activity for learning English

95

"A skeleton! We learnt about the body. That is my favourite thing to learn about. I also go to the library at lunch. So that is why I took the photo."

Figure 6.10. Inside a library

at the school, leading to the theme of: 'Involvement in the school is seen through school activities, not extracurricular activities'. See Figures 6.9 and 6.10.

While students displayed high levels of engagement with school activities conducted during school hours, very few students were engaged with extracurricular activities outside school. This could be indicative of their newly arrived status (in that they had not had the opportunity to engage with activities out of school as yet), but this could also indicate an issue for this group of students in relation to school belonging. Indeed, only one student discussed participating in extracurricular activities related to the school (in this case, attending a sport session on the weekend). It is worth noting that this was not due to students simply not talking about activities outside school, since other students discussed their weekend or after-school activities, including religious events, language school, and seeing family. Again, this is a point we take up further in the Discussion.

Belief in the School

The domain of belief in the school refers to a sense of loyalty to the school and its values (Kia-Keating & Ellis, 2007). Students displayed a quite high degree of loyalty to some aspects of their school, most noticeably in relation to their IELC. Ten of the 15 students discussed their IELC as being very important to their sense

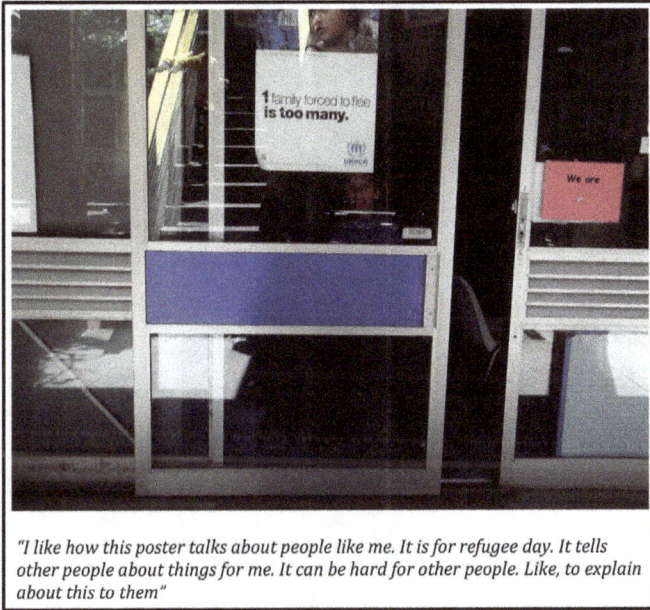

"I like how this poster talks about people like me. It is for refugee day. It tells other people about things for me. It can be hard for other people. Like, to explain about this to them"

Figure 6.11. A UNHCR poster on the door to a library

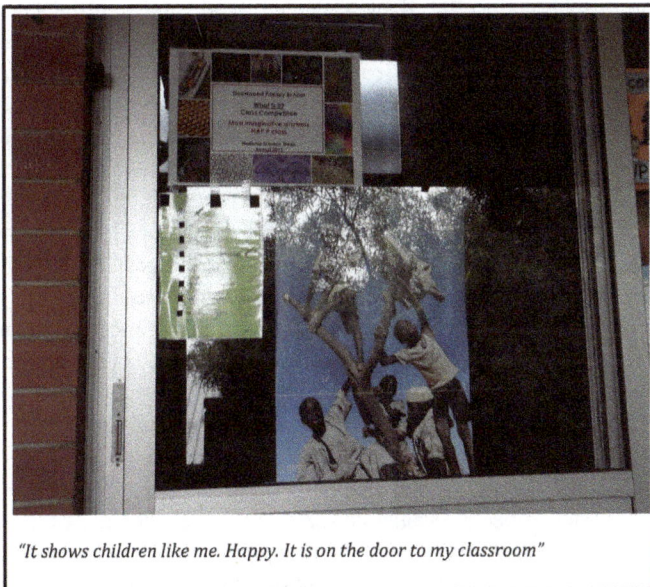

"It shows children like me. Happy. It is on the door to my classroom"

Figure 6.12. A World Refugee Day poster on the door to a classroom

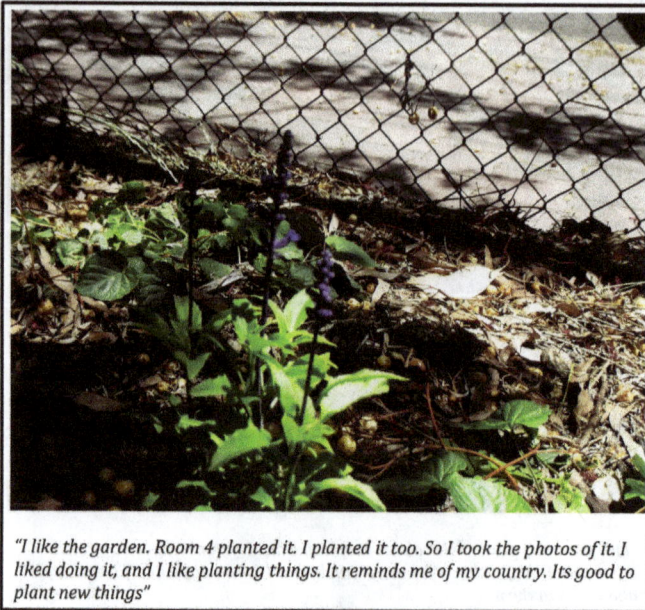

"I like the garden. Room 4 planted it. I planted it too. So I took the photos of it. I liked doing it, and I like planting things. It reminds me of my country. Its good to plant new things"

Figure 6.13. A flower planted during a gardening activity

of belonging in school since the IELC reflected the diversity of the students in the classroom, leading to the theme of: 'Students believe in their school when it reflects their identities and values'. In particular, students frequently took photographs of school spaces that reflected their experiences as refugees, and told us that they felt that these spaces reflected their own identities in ways that "mainstream" classrooms did not. Figures 6.11, 6.12 and 6.13 provide examples of these photographs.

As can be seen in the excerpt relating to this photograph, the students frequently articulated that they valued aspects of the school that reflected some of their experiences as refugees. Here, the student states that the poster "tells other people about things for me", with the implication that there were challenges explaining these experiences to other students in the school at other times. It is plausible that the poster allowed the student to see how the values of the school aligned with her own experiences, thereby increasing school belonging. In this sense, posters such as this one and the one displayed in Figure 6.12, may play an important role in that they reflect refugee students' experiences and identities in the school, rather than reflecting only non-refugee or mainstream identities.

Apart from posters reflecting values consistent with their experiences and identities, refugee students also discussed some activities as consistent with their own values. Earlier, we noted that subjects that do not rely on English, such as art and sport, were important for attachment to school. Here, students discuss other school activities as reflecting the activities that they enjoyed and had participated in prior to coming to Australia. An example of this is seen in Figure 6.13.

Here, the student discusses how participating in a school activity – planting – reminded her of her country prior to coming to Australia, and that she enjoyed the activity for this reason. Again, this indicates the importance of ensuring that school activities also reflect the identities and values of students from refugee backgrounds, and incorporates these into school curriculum and daily activities.

DISCUSSION

One of the most important findings of the present study relates to the fact that the refugee students appeared to forge their own sense of school belonging in ways which may differ from that of other groups of students. This was particularly seen in relation to the domain of "belief in the school", whereby students discussed how important posters and activities depicting refugee-like experiences were to their sense of belonging to the school. This finding is important since previous research indicates that school belonging is likely to be improved where students see themselves and their families reflected in the beliefs of the school, and this may be difficult for students newly arrived to Australia (Block et al., 2014; Kia-Keating & Ellis, 2006). In this sense, the IELCs included in this study appeared to offer students some reflection of their experiences as refugees (as seen in this chapter, by promoting organisations such as the UNHCR and initiatives such as world refugee day).

However, it is important to note that such a reflection may not carry through to mainstream classes, and that studies which investigate school belonging in children outside IELCs are therefore important (de Heer et al., 2016). It is also of note that, while students identified some aspects of the school as consistent with their beliefs, they rarely discussed aspects of the broader school environment which may lead to a wider sense of school belonging – that is, a sense of belonging in the whole school rather than only the IELC. For example, students didn't discuss areas such as the broader values of the school, or initiatives such as sports day. Again, it is beyond the scope of this study to ascertain whether this reflects the students' status as newly arrived (and therefore still forging a connection to and understanding of the schools' values), or whether this represents a limited sense of belonging in this domain.

As noted above, attachment to the school appeared to be high amongst the students. In terms of building school attachment, the study found that students frequently drew upon particular spaces to increase their sense of belonging at school, and discussed their relationships with teachers and peers. The finding concerning the importance of spaces reflects the results of previous research (e.g. Due & Riggs, 2011), and highlights the importance of ensuring that students with refugee backgrounds feel they belong in all aspects of the school, and not just areas where English language is not a priority (Matthews, 2008; Trickett & Birman, 2005; Woods, 2009). The finding concerning teachers is particularly important, given the fact that previous research highlights that good student-teacher relationships predict a range of positive outcomes, including ongoing school engagement and belonging (Crouch et al., 2014). Here, we would suggest that teaching staff's specific experience in working with students with refugee and migrant backgrounds played an important role in ensuring cultural competency and positive student-teacher relationships. Our study also demonstrates that refugee students were keen to develop relationships with teachers, and that this is one useful way of immediately building school belonging when students arrive at a school in their resettlement country.

While students showed high levels of attachment to their school (or at least their IELC), the photographs taken by students did not highlight high levels of commitment or involvement in the school. In relation to commitment to the school, and as noted above, students rarely discussed school rules, although one student did note that the requirement to speak English was problematic for some students. We acknowledge here that our findings may reflect limitations with the photo elicitation approach as it may have been difficult for students to capture this domain of school belonging through photographs. As such, the fact that students did not discuss school rules or other aspects of school commitment may not reflect low levels of school belonging on this domain, perhaps with the exception of the potential challenge of being required to speak in English. This exception is noteworthy and relates to the findings of previous research in regards to the potentially detrimental impact that a strict focus on English-language acquisition may have on refugee students at school (Matthews, 2008; Woods, 2009).

In relation to involvement at school, students displayed high levels of involvement in the academic aspect of school, and displayed high levels of educational aspiration, supporting the work of Gifford and colleagues (2009). However, only one student discussed participating in extra-curricular activities related to school. This finding is important due to previous research highlighting that elements of school belonging may be increased where participation in extra-curricular activities is higher (McNeely, Nonnemaker, & Blum, 2002). As noted above, our findings may reflect students' newly arrived status, however it is worth noting that increasingly the ability of refugee students and their families to participate in such activities may play an important role in increasing school belonging (see a wider discussion on the benefits of extra-curricular activity in Chapter 4 of this book). We would also suggest that expanding the school's extra-curricular activities to include events important to refugee students and their families would offer a very useful pathway for schools to assist students to develop a strong sense of school belonging. In this sense, schools could invest more time identifying activities which young people or children with refugee backgrounds may be interested in. Examples of such activities include the school hosting culturally important festivals on the weekend, holding activities for days such as Harmony Day (in which refugees' families can be involved in planning and development should they wish to do so), and ensuring the sporting activities are deliberately inclusive of newly arrived students and their families (for example, by facilitating transport, or ensuring that information is translated so that families can be included).

Taken together, our research indicates the students in the study generally showed high levels of school belonging in most areas, but that this was frequently facilitated by the specific policies of the IELC they were in. This was seen through the focus on global issues, including awareness of the situation of refugees (as seen in the posters), and in strong relationships with teaching staff at the school. The study showed that, by reflecting the identities of newly arrived students (at least to a degree), the students were able to build on what the school offered to create their own spaces in the broader school community. In this sense, it would appear that the IELCs were able to successfully open up a two-way dialogue with refugee students to promote their sense of belonging. Within this space, then, the students themselves were able to develop relationships and make meaning in the school in order to form attachments. The question remains as to whether such positive experiences of school belonging continue after students have left their IELC and transitioned into mainstream schools, where such initiatives and staff training may not be present. This is a useful area for future research.

It is important to note that this study is not without its limitations. In particular, the study includes a focus on only three schools with a total of 15 participants. Given the diverse nature of refugee experiences, the study may not represent the experiences of all students in all IELCs, particularly those that are further from the city centre, or have higher numbers of refugee students. In addition, the IELCs themselves are specific to South Australia, and in this sense, the findings may not extend to other intensive English language programs. Furthermore, and as seen perhaps specifically in the domain of commitment, the methodology of photo elicitation may have provided some limited data concerning school belonging. Nevertheless, the study highlights some important aspects of school belonging for young, newly arrived, students with refugee backgrounds – and does so on their own terms. The findings highlight the importance of ensuring that schools develop activities which are of interest to students with refugee backgrounds, and which reflect their skills, identities and values. If they do so, our findings suggest that newly arrived refugees will find spaces and relationships within the school through which to form a sense of belonging in their new community.

ACKNOWLEDGEMENTS

We would like to acknowledge all the children and schools who participated in this research. We could not have done it without them, and we are very grateful for their generosity in participating. We would also like to acknowledge the Australian Research Council for funding the research.

This chapter is an adapted version from Due, C., Riggs, D., & Augoustinos, M. (2016). Experiences of school belonging for young children with refugee backgrounds. *The Educational and Developmental Psychologist, 33*(1), 33–53. doi:10.1017/edp.2016.9

NOTES

[1] The term "refugee" refers to those who have met either the United Nations High Commissioner for Refugees (UNHCR) definition according to the 1951 Convention, or meet the criteria for refugee status according to a particular resettlement country.

[2] The term "migrant" here refers to those who arrived in Australia voluntarily. Most children with migrant backgrounds in the study arrived with their parents as part of Australia's skilled migration program.

REFERENCES

Anderman, E. M. (2002). School effects on psychological outcomes during adolescence. *Journal of Educational Psychology, 94*, 795–809. doi:10.1037//0022-0663.94.4.795

Battistich, V., Solomon, D., Watson, M., & Schaps, E. (1997). Caring school communities. *Educational Psychologist, 32*, 137–151.

Baumeister, R. F., & Leary, M. R. (1995). The need to belong: Desire for interpersonal attachments as a fundamental human motivation. *Psychological Bulletin, 117*, 497–529.

Block, K., Cross, S., Riggs, E., & Gibbs, L. (2014). Supporting schools to create an inclusive environment for refugee students. *International Journal of Inclusive Education, 18*(12), 1337–1355. doi:10.1080/13603116.2014.899636

Braun, V., & Clarke, V. (2013). *Successful qualitative research: A practical guide for beginners.* London: Sage Publications.

Brown, C. S., & Chu, H. (2012). Discrimination, ethnic identity and academic outcomes of Mexican immigrant children: The importance of school context. *Child Development, 83*, 1477–1485. doi:10.1111/j.1467-8624.2012.01786.x

Correa-Velez, I., Gifford, S., & Barnett, A. (2010). Longing to belong: Social inclusion and wellbeing among youth with refugee backgrounds in the first three years in Melbourne, Australia. *Social Science and Medicine, 71*, 1399–1408. doi:10.1016/j.socscimed.2010.07.018

Crivello, G., Camfield, L., & Woodhead, M. (2009). How can children tell us about their wellbeing? Exploring the potential of participatory research approaches within young lives. *Social Indicators Research, 90*, 51–72. doi:10.1007/s11205-008-9312-x

Crouch, R., Keys, C. B., McMahon, S. (2014). Student-teacher relationships matter for school inclusion: School belonging, disability, and school transitions. *Journal of Prevention and Intervention in the Community, 42*(1), 20–30. doi:10.1080/10852352.2014.855054

Darbyshire, P., MacDougall, C., & Schiller, W. (2005). Multiple methods in qualitative research with children: More research or just more? *Qualitative Research, 5*, 417–436. doi:10.1177/1468794105056921

de Heer, N., Due, C., & Riggs, D. W. (2016). "It will be hard because I will have to learn lots of English": Experiences of education for children with migrant backgrounds in Australia. *The International Journal of Qualitative Studies in Education, 29*(3), 297–319. doi:10.1080/09518398.2015.1023232

Department for Education and Child Development (DECD). (2012). *Effective transition.* Retrieved from http://www.decd.sa.gov.au/literacy/files/links/Effective_Transition.pdf

Due, C., & Riggs, D. W. (2011). Freedom to roam? Space use in primary schools with new arrivals programs. *Online Journal of International Research in Early Childhood Education, 2*, 1–16. Retrieved from http://arrow.monash.edu.au/hdl/1959.1/1048518

Due, C., Riggs, D. W., & Augoustinos, M. (2014). Research with children of migrant and refugee background: A review of child-centered research. *Child Indicators Research, 7*, 209–227. doi:10.1007/s12187-013-9214-6

Due, C., Riggs, D. W., & Augoustinos, M. (2016). Diversity in intensive English language centres in South Australia: Sociocultural approaches to education for students with migrant or refugee backgrounds. *International Journal of Inclusive Education, 20*(12), 1286–1296. doi:10.1080/09518398.2015.1023232

Ehntholt, K., & Yule, W. (2006). Practitioner review: Assessment and treatment of refugee children and adolescents who have experienced war-related trauma. *Journal of Child Psychology and Psychiatry, 47*(12), 1197–1210. doi:10.1111/j.1469-7610.2006.01638.x

Fazel, M., Reed, R. V., Panter-Brick, C., & Stein, A. (2012). Mental health of displaced and refugee children resettled in high-income countries: Risk and protective factors. *The Lancet, 379*(9812), 266–282. doi:10.1016/S0140-6736(11)60051-2

Gifford, S., Bakopanos, C., Kaplan, I., & Correa-Velez, I. (2007). Meaning or measurement? Researching the social contexts of health and settlement among newly-arrived refugee youth in Melbourne, Australia. *Journal of Refugee Studies, 20*(3), 414–440. doi:10.1093/jrs/fem004

Gifford, S., Correa-Velez, I., Sampson, R. (2009). *Good starts for recently arrived youth with refugee backgrounds: Promoting wellbeing in the first three years of settlement in Melbourne, Australia.* Melbourne: La Trobe Refugee Research Centre.

Goodenow, C. (1993). Classroom belonging among early adolescent students: Relationships to motivation and achievement. *Journal of Early Adolescence, 13*, 21–43.

Keddie, A. (2012). Refugee education and justice issues of representation, redistribution and recognition. *Cambridge Journal of Education, 42*(2), 197–212. doi:10.1080/0305764X.2012.676624

Kia-Keating, M., & Ellis, B. H. (2007). Belonging and connection to school in resettlement: Young refugees, school belonging and psychosocial adjustment. *Clinical Child Psychology and Psychiatry, 12*(1), 29–43. doi:10.1177/1359104507071052

Mace, A. O., Mulheron, S., Jones, C., & Cherian, S. (2014). Educational, developmental and psychological outcomes of resettled refugee children in Western Australia: A review of school of special educational needs: Medical and mental health input. *Journal of Paediatrics and Child Health, 50*, 985–992. doi:10.1111/jpc.12674

Matthews, J. (2008). Schooling and settlement: Refugee education in Australia. *International Studies in Sociology of Education, 18*(1), 31–45. doi:10.1080/09620210802195947

McNeely, C., Nonnemaker, J., & Blum, R. (2002). Promoting school connectedness: Evidence from the national longitudinal study of adolescent health. *The Journal of School Health, 72*, 138–146. doi:10.1111/j.1746-1561.2002.tb06533.x

Newman, M., Woodcock, A., & Dunham, P. (2006). 'Playtime in the borderlands': Children's representations of school, gender and bullying through photographs and interviews. *Children's Geographies, 4*(3), 289–302. doi:10.1080/14733280601005617

Priest, N., Walton, J., White, F., Kowal, E., Baker, A., & Paradies, Y. (2014). Understanding the complexities of ethnic-racial socialization processes for minority and majority groups: A 30-year systematic review. *International Journal of Intercultural Relations, 43*, 139–155. doi:10.1016/j.ijintrel.2014.08.003

Pugh, K., Every, D., & Hattam, R. (2012). Inclusive education for students with refugee experience: Whole school reform in a South Australian primary school. *The Australian Educational Researcher, 39*(2), 125–141. doi:10.1007/s13384-011-0048-2

Riggs, D. W., & Due, C. (2011). (Un)common ground? English language acquisition and experiences of exclusion amongst new arrival students in Australian primary schools. *Identities: Global Studies in Culture and Power, 18*, 273–290. doi:10.1080/1070289X.2011.635373

Rousseau, C., Drapeau, A., & Platt, R. (2004). Family environment and emotional and behavioural symptoms in adolescent Cambodian refugees: Influence of time, gender, and acculturation. *Medicine, Conflict and Survival, 20*, 151–65. doi:10.1080/1362369042000234735

Shochet, I. M., & Smith, C. L. (2014). A prospective study investigating the links among classroom environment, school connectedness, and depressive symptoms in adolescents. *Psychology in the Schools, 51*(5), 480–492. doi:10.1002/pits

Sujoldzic, A., Peternel, L., Kulenovic, T., & Terzic, R. (2006). Social determinants of health: A comparative study of Bosnian adolescents in different cultural contexts. *Collegium Antropologicum, 30*, 703–711.

Taylor, S., & Sidhu, R. K. (2012). Supporting refugee students in schools: What constitutes inclusive education? *International Journal of Inclusive Education, 16*(1), 39–56. doi:10.1080/13603110903560085

Trickett, E. J., & Birman, N. (2005). Acculturation, school context, and school outcomes: Adaptation of refugee adolescents from the former Soviet Union. *Psychology in the Schools, 42*(1), 27–39. doi:10.1002/pits.20024

UNHCR. (2015). *Worldwide displacement hits all time high as was and persecution increase.* Retrieved from http://www.unhcr.org/558193896.html

Van Ryzin, M., Gravely, A., & Roseth, C. (2009). Autonomy, belongingness, and engagement in school as contributors to adolescent psychological well-being. *Journal of Youth and Adolescence, 38,* 1–12. doi:10.1007/s10964-007-9257-4

Wehlage, G. G., Rutter, R. A., Smith, G. A., Lesko, N., & Fernandez, R. R. (1989). *Reducing the risk: Schools as communities of support.* Philadelphia, PA: Falmer.

Woods, A. (2009). Learning to be literate: Issues of pedagogy for recently arrived refugee youth in Australia. *Critical Inquiry in Language Studies, 6,* 81–101. doi:10.1080/15427580802679468

Clemence Due
School of Psychology
The University of Adelaide
Australia

Damien W. Riggs
School of Social Sciences
Flinders University
Adelaide, Australia

Martha Augoustinos
School of Psychology
The University of Adelaide
Australia

VICTORIA L. MCKENZIE AND JESSICA J. E. SMEAD

7. THE RELATIONSHIP BETWEEN SCHOOL CONNECTEDNESS, FAMILY FUNCTIONING, AND RESILIENCE

INTRODUCTION

Increasing community concern about the level of anxiety and depression in the Australian population has led to calls for the implementation of resilience training in schools, with parents being encouraged to focus on their children's resilience (Allen & McKenzie, 2015; Lawrence et al., 2015). Resilience is defined variously, but its essence is captured in the following definition: 'Resilience is the ability to cope and thrive in the face of negative events, challenges or adversity' (DET, 2017).

In general, it is assumed that resilience is a set of attitudes and skills that are learned, based on the constructivist view that it is possible for individuals to act on their life experience and build a positive and successful self. The process of developing resilience is complex and multifaceted (Garmezy, 1985; Rutter, 1987), and, following the ecological model of development posed by Bronfenbrenner (1977, 1979) has been shown to relate to a range of contributing factors: individual microsystemic factors including the attitudes and skills of the individual (Prince-Embury, 2007; Schwarzer & Warner, 2013), and meso- and exosystemic factors such as family, school and community (Epstein, Bishop, & Levin, 1978; Lemerle & Hardie, 2004; Phillipson & McFarland, 2016; Ross, Shochet, & Bellair, 2010). Ecological systems theory, in demonstrating that individuals exist within multiple complex systems, identified that protective factors come from three broad areas: first, an individual's personality factors, or mechanisms within the individual; second, family factors; and finally the availability of external support systems such as friends and school community (Garmezy, 1985).

Robust adjustment can be seen as an outcome of the capacity of the individual to utilize their assets and minimize the impact of adverse circumstances. Protective factors decrease the saliency of risk factors in determining adverse outcomes (Garmezy, 1985).

Resilience, as an asset, has been identified as a capacity which helps to protect the individual from negative outcomes (Fergus & Zimmerman, 2005; Prince-Embury, 2007). External factors or resources may also influence a child's development of resilience. Research studies have shown that influences such as peer relationships and connectedness to school can reduce the impact of adversity on the individual

© KONINKLIJKE BRILL NV, LEIDEN, 2018 | DOI:10.1163/9789004386969_007

(Goodenow, 1993). The study reported herein addresses two of the contextual elements that have been established as important protective factors in supporting young people when in difficult situations – the family and the school.

FAMILY

Family is the foundation arena for healthy psychological development alongside providing for children's basic needs. It is the centre for learning about dealing with others and dealing with life's challenges. Throughout development, transitions challenge young people and can raise stress and anxiety. Although there is a keen focus in research on the adjustment needs of adolescents, prepubescent children have also been found to experience challenging changes and health risks (Eccles & Midgley, 1990; Shochet, Homel, Cockshaw, & Montgomery, 2008). Family support can provide a sense of security, self value, and comfort. The way in which the family functions can impact on the degree to which it can provide these supports. Family factors that have been shown to influence child development are parenting approach, interest in education, and family relationships (Tollitt et al., 2015). Negative outcomes associated with dysfunctional family patterns have been noted in academic achievement, low prosocial skills, bullying, disordered eating patterns, anxiety and behavioral difficulties (Berge, Wall, Larson, Loth, & Neumark-Sztainer, 2013; Renzaho, Mellor, McCabe, & Powell, 2013; White et al., 2014). The impact of socioeconomic status demonstrates that family circumstance can also be a factor in children's academic achievement, which is integral to their wellbeing (Tollit et al., 2015).

The McMaster Model of Family Functioning (Epstein, Bishop, & Levin, 1978) provides a useful model in the study of family practices. Using its accompanying survey tool, The Family Assessment Device (FAD), the model allows the researcher to locate family practices on a spectrum from healthy and well-functioning to poor and unhealthy functioning.

Resilience and Family Functioning

A number of studies have demonstrated that healthy family functioning plays an important role in positive developmental outcomes for children. Lester and colleagues (2013) applied the McMaster Model of Family Functioning to improving resiliency outcomes for children living on military bases. The study examined the effect of a family-centered prevention program aimed at resilience training with 280 families. The training provided information about stress reactions, communication, identifying and utilising family strengths, and on child development and stress reactions, as well as education in cognitive behavioural skills that promote resilience including emotion regulation, goal setting, and, problem solving and communication. Positive changes in the FAD, particularly in relation to affective involvement, problem solving and communication were associated with reductions in child distress.

Berge, Wall, Larson, Loth, and Neumark-Sztainer (2013) investigated weight, eating and exercising habits with a sample of 2,793 adolescents (M = 14.4 years) in Minnesota. Family functioning was assessed with items from the general functioning scale of the FAD and 229 self-report items measuring family meals, fast-food intake, nutrition, physical activity, and other covariates such as race, socioeconomic status (SES) and age. Results of this study indicated that higher family functioning was significantly associated with more frequent family meals and more frequent breakfast consumption for females after adjusting for age, socioeconomic status and race. Higher functioning was associated with more frequent family meals for males after adjusting for the same variables as the females. At the extreme ends of the family functioning spectrum (5th and 95th percentiles) family functioning was strongly associated with weight and weight-related health behaviours. Although this study had small effect sizes, the results suggest that in poorly functioning families defined by fewer rules, reduced warmth, difficulties with communication and low problem-solving skills, adolescents are more vulnerable to developing health-related risk behaviours. There was a statistically significant difference between family functioning scores for gender, and SES. Males rated overall family functioning higher than females. Students from low and low middle SES rated their average level of family functioning significantly lower than middle and high-middle SES. High SES students gained the highest mean family functioning score.

A third study in Australia, linking family functioning and child development was conducted by Renzaho, Mellor, McCabe, and Powell (2013) who examined secondary data from primary caregivers of 3,370 children aged between 4–12 years, collected in the Victorian Child Health and Wellbeing Study (VCHWS). Data. Poor family functioning predicted emotional problems, conduct problems, peer relationship problems and lower levels of prosocial skills in children. These three studies highlight the association between positive family functioning, health, developmental issues, and resilience.

SCHOOL CONNECTEDNESS

After family, the second significant and influential environment for a young person is school (Roffey, 2013; Shochet, Dadds, Ham, & Montague, 2006). The degree to which students engage with their school becomes a factor in the capacity of the school to support a student's wellbeing and to teach the necessary skills for managing difficulties both educationally and personally (Goodenow, 1993; Wigfield, Byrnes, & Eccles, 2006). For early and mid-adolescents the need to be accepted, valued, respected and feel like they belong is a strong priority (Goodenow, 1993). Baumeister and Leary (1995) suggest that belonging can be considered as a primary human need, as essential as nutrition and safety. As children develop, being accepted in the social group, including at school and by peers, is also a powerful need (Roffey, 2013).

There has been extensive research using multiple definitions and foci on the construct of 'belonging', which in this study has been labeled school connectedness.

107

Numerous terms operationalising school connectedness appear in the literature, such as school belonging, school bonding, student engagement, and commitment to school (Frydenberg, Care, Freeman, & Chan, 2009; Tollit et al., 2015). In this chapter, school connectedness is defined as the belief held by students that their school, peers, and teachers accept, include, respect, and support their academic and personal needs (Frydenberg, Care, Freeman, & Chan, 2009; Goodenow, 1993; Murphy & McKenzie, 2015). It reflects qualities of the student experience at school, the degree to which students feel that they belong in the school community, and the sense that they matter to other students and staff in the school (McNeely, Nonnemaker, & Blum, 2002; Rowe, Stewart, & Patterson, 2007).

Failure to feel connected to school has been associated with negative outcomes such as conduct problems (Loukas, Roalson, & Herrera, 2010), depressive and anxious symptoms (Ross et al., 2010), and a reduction in motivation, effort, participation and achievement (Goodenow, 1993), involvement in antisocial behaviours (Chapman, Buckley, Sheehan, Shochet, & Romaniuk, 2011), unlawful behaviour and substance use (Catalano et al., 2004; Resnick et al., 1997), and risk taking and injury (Chapman et al., 2011). Gaete, Rojas-Barahona, Olivares, and Araya (2016) found that having a stronger sense of school connectedness reduced the likelihood of mental health issues such as emotional, conduct, hyperactivity, and peer problems. Connectedness has also been shown to be associated with a more positive attitude towards others, better psychological adjustment, lower emotional distress, and reduced suicide risk (Resnick et al., 1997). In a study of over 4,000 adolescents, Vieno, Perkins, Smith, and Santinello (2005) found school connectedness, was positively associated with increased happiness, self-esteem, improved coping skills, social skills, social supports and reduced loneliness. School connectedness has been shown to increase with academic competence and achievement (Catalano, Oesterle, Fleming, & Hawkins, 2004; Libbey, 2004).

FAMILY FUNCTIONING AND SCHOOL CONNECTEDNESS

There is growing evidence that interactions between school connectedness and family functioning are related to positive adjustment. The Social Connectedness Model, developed by Law, Cuskelly, and Carroll (2013) proposed relationships between student views of family-related factors including parenting, functioning and structure, and school-related factors such as peer group, peer connectedness and school connectedness, and their combined impact on adjustment. Using two measures that are also used in the present study, the Sense of School Membership scale and the Family Assessment Device, and others, the model was tested in eight schools in Queensland, Australia, with 563 students from 9 to 16 years. All independent variables, beside peer group, made a unique contribution to adjustment; students who reported a strong sense of family connectedness also reported a strong sense of school connectedness.

Basing their study on the Social Connectedness Model (2015), the Longitudinal Study of Australian Children (LSAC study) examined the mediating effect of adolescent perceptions of parenting and school connectedness on the relationship between particular parenting behaviours (warmth, anger, consistency and self-efficacy), and student academic performance and self-efficacy. Data were collected from 3,956 complete cases of wave five of the LSAC study. Self-report and parent-rated data were collected, with the mean age of the participants being 12.41 years. Having a positive perception of parenting styles was found to be associated with a greater sense of school connectedness. Adolescent's sense of school connectedness and perception of their parents' approach to parenting, mediated the relationship between parent self-reported parenting style and academic performance. Girls reported a higher sense of school connectedness than boys, and parental roles had a greater impact on girls. An association was found between perceptions of parenting style, school connectedness, gender and academic performance, with children from high functioning families likely to be high in connectedness and attainment.

RESILIENCE AND SCHOOL CONNECTEDNESS

There is evidence that schools that promote positive health programs (HPS) are able to increase levels of protective factors through school connectedness, which in turn fosters and builds resilience in students. These programs have been associated with significantly higher student resilience as measured by communication, cooperation, self-esteem, empathy and goals, compared with schools with an average or low emphasis on health promotion (Stewart, Sun, Patterson, Lemerle, & Hardie, 2004). Significant protective factors identified by high HPS students included feeling connected to adults at home, feeling autonomous, and belonging to a prosocial group when compared to average and low HPS schools. The benefit of school connectedness in improving resilience in disadvantaged areas was also demonstrated in this study.

In an Indian study, Kapoor and Tomar (2016), using the Psychological Sense of School Membership (Goodenow, 1993) to measure school connectedness, found a high positive correlation between school connectedness, resilience, and self-efficacy. School membership was significantly related to all subscales of resilience and self-efficacy measures. In an Australian study, school connectedness was shown to partially mediate the relationship between social skills and depression in preadolescence in a sample of 127 students aged 10 to 13 years, using the Psychological Sense of School Membership (PSSM) (Ross, Shochet, & Bellair, 2010). Importantly, this study highlighted the importance of including children in the preadolescent stage in resilience studies.

RESILIENCE

Typically resilience definitions reflect a general resourcefulness and flexibility in the person's ability to respond to positive and negative influences (Prince-Embury, 2007).

Self-efficacy has been identified as a core factor of resiliency in children and adults and can be defined as an individual's self-belief in their ability to perform tasks successfully and overcome difficulties to achieve desired outcomes (Prince-Embury, 2011; Rutter, 1985). Resilience is represented as a set of measureable internal factors, described by Prince-Embury as sense of relatedness, sense of mastery, and emotional reactivity. Prince-Embury (2007) has identified conceptualized sense of mastery as a critical internal mechanism with two key facets: self-efficacy and optimism (Prince-Embury, 2007).

Self-efficacy beliefs play an essential role in resilience because of their ability to motivate, encourage perseverance and activate behavioural processes in challenging situations (Schwarzer & Warner, 2013). In contrast to self-efficacy being attributable to one's own *ability* to control and manipulate one's future, optimism refers to a *belief* that the future will be positive and can be attributable to internal or external forces, and chance (Schwarzer & Warner, 2013). Optimism has been identified as a key factor in increasing resilience and coping in children (Cunningham, Brandon, & Frydenberg, 2002). Furthermore, parenting books focus on increasing resilience in children though teaching optimism (Brooks & Goldstein, 2001). The value of optimism is evident in a study by Chang and Sanna (2003), who examined the moderating effect of optimism-pessimism on the relationship between life hassles and psychological maladjustment in adolescents. Participants included 263 American high school students aged 14–19 years. Self-report measures were used to gain information about optimism-pessimism, life hassles (hassles experienced by high school students such as low grades), depressive symptoms, and hopelessness. Higher optimism scores were significantly associated with less depressive symptoms and less hopelessness. The relationship between life hassles and depressive symptoms was significantly stronger for pessimistic adolescents, than for optimistic adolescents. Similar results were identified for hopelessness.

The Australian Child and Adolescent Survey of Mental Health and Wellbeing (Lawrence et al., 2015) reported almost one in seven 4–17 year-olds were assessed as having a mental disorder in the past twelve months. Anxiety disorders were experienced by 6.9% of the sample (sample was 6,310 households). Furthermore, 12–17 year-olds were three times more likely to experience a severe mental disorder than 4–11 year olds. These results suggest a growing need for research into prevention strategies to reduce the burden of mental health issues in children and adolescents. Whilst research has examined the factors that protect young people from negative outcomes, further investigation into the best time for intervention is necessary. The time that children transition from primary school to secondary school is a time of adjustment and stress. Furthermore, the onset of puberty during this time has its own set of biological, psychological and emotional implications (Buchanan, Eccles, & Becker, 1992). Compounding these physiological changes are the stressors of changing school including social changes in friendships and expectations, and increased workload and demand on cognitive abilities (Eccles & Midgley, 1990). Cumulative Stress Theory suggests that the combination of a major school transition and a varied amount of stressors related to the onset of puberty leads to a decline in academic and intrinsic motivation, self-perception, and reduced confidence in intellectual abilities (Eccles & Midgley, 1990). In line with this theory, Tollit et al. (2015) found that the majority of research on resilience factors contributed by the family and school was completed with adolescents. However importantly, research shows intervention programs should begin before adolescence to help prepare students and increase the likelihood of positive outcomes in the future (Ross, Shochet, & Bellair, 2010).

AIM

This study aimed to examine the proposition that school connectedness is a mediating factor which can support students from low functioning families by giving them a sense of mastery involving a purpose, selfhood and value which supports them in addressing problems and encouraging perseverance based on an optimistic view of the future.

The following hypotheses were addressed:

- Reported levels of mastery will be significantly associated with perceived family functioning and school connectedness.
- Perceived family functioning will be significantly associated with reported levels of mastery.
- School connectedness will mediate the relationship between family functioning and sense of mastery in preadolescent children.
- Gender differences will be evident between ratings of sense of mastery including self-efficacy and optimism, school connectedness and family functioning.
- Socio economic status will be reflected in reported levels of sense of mastery, school connectedness, and family functioning.

METHOD

Participants

One-hundred and twenty six participants (68 females, 58 males) were recruited from four primary schools across Melbourne, Australia. Schools from Catholic and government systems were located in the north-western, eastern, inner eastern and northern rural suburbs. All 526 students in Grade 5 and 6 at each school were invited to participate. Parent consent forms were returned for 139 students. A total of 130 students participated in the study, a consent rate of 24.7%. Four questionnaires were omitted from the dataset as three children appeared to have misunderstood the questions due to language barriers or disability.

Data were viable and entered for 126 students, with 31.7% of the sample in Grade 5 and 68.3% in Grade 6. The students ranged in age from 10–13 years ($M = 11.37$, $SD = .71$). The majority the students, 73.8%, lived in two-parent households.

Measures

Family functioning. Family Functioning was assessed using the McMaster Family Assessment Device (FAD; Epstein, Baldwin, & Bishop, 1983). The FAD is based on the McMaster Model of Family Functioning and has been used to distinguish well-functioning and poorly functioning families (Epstein, Baldwin, & Bishop, 1983; Epstein et al., 1978). The FAD is designed to reflect the six dimensions outlined in the McMaster model: problem solving, communication, roles, affective responsiveness, affective involvement and behaviour control. The FAD also provides a seventh scale which provides an overall score for the general functioning of the family. Research has demonstrated that adolescent's self-reported perceptions of parenting have provided better information towards outcome measures than parent self-reports examining family functioning (Phillipson & McFarland, 2016).

The FAD is a 60-item self-report questionnaire in which participants rate their agreement and disagreement to the statements using a 4-point Likert scale: 1 = Strongly Agree, 2 = Agree, 3 = Disagree, and 4 = Strongly Disagree. The FAD takes approximately 15–20 minutes to complete. Items negatively worded which reflect unhealthy functioning such as "we often don't say what we mean" are reverse scored. An average score, ranging from one to four, is provided as a mean for each of the subscales. Scores above two are indicative of poor family functioning.

The FAD has demonstrated acceptable reliability and internal consistency with Cronbach's alphas ranging from .72 to .92 across the seven subscales (Epstein et al., 1983). One hundred and twelve clinical and typically developing families were used in the norming of the instrument. The original questionnaire was designed to be used with all family members including children aged 12 and above (Epstein et al., 1983), however Bihun, Wamboldt, Gavin, and Wamblodt (2002) found it is acceptable to use with children aged between 7 and 12, and is endorsed with modification (APA, 2014). In keeping with previous research (Law et al., 2013; Murphy & McKenzie, 2015), items 11 and 13 were deleted to improve internal consistency. Furthermore, in accordance with Murphy and McKenzie (2015) minor alterations to the language of a number of items to ensure accessibility to children aged 10 to 12 years, was retained for consistency in the questionnaires and data.

Cronbach's alpha scores in the current study ranged from .55 to .91. Contrary with the findings of Law et al. (2013) and Murphy and McKenzie (2015), behavioural control demonstrated acceptable reliability and was therefore included in the analysis. Affective responsiveness however, was found to have unacceptable reliability and was therefore not included in the analysis. As general functioning was the only subscale used in the main analyses of this study, all remaining subscales were determined to demonstrate acceptable reliability except for exploratory analysis (Hair, Black, Babin, & Anderson, 2010; Robinson, Shaver, & Wrightsman, 1991). The reliability scores (Cronbach's Alpha) were General Functioning .91, Problem Solving .77, Communication .77, Roles .62, Affective Responsiveness .55, Affective involvement .69, and Behavioural control .69.

School connectedness. School Connectedness was measured using the Psychological, Sense of School Membership Scale (PSSM; Goodenow, 1993). The PSSM is an 18 item self-report questionnaire in which participants rate their agreement or disagreement with statements relating to areas of school connectedness including belonging, respect, encouragement, acceptance and inclusion in the school environment. Examples of statements include "Most teachers at my school are interested in me" and "I can really be myself at my school". Items are rated on a five point Likert scale ranging from 1 = *not at all true*, to 5 = *completely true.*

Goodenow (1993) reported a strong internal consistency of the PSSM with Cronbach's alpha measuring .88 in two studies with suburban students. The PSSM was originally designed to be used with students aged 12 to 18 years, however use with students aged 10 to 13 years in an Australian study yielded strong internal consistency (α = .89). Similarly, strong internal consistency of the PSSM was demonstrated in the current study (α = .94). The PSSM has been found to have good construct validity as it significantly correlated with teacher-rated social standing, self-reported student motivations, academic grades, and teacher-rated student effort (Goodenow, 1993). After reverse scoring negatively worded items, ratings on the PSSM are summed. A higher score indicates increased school connectedness.

Resilience Scales for Children and Adolescents

Sense of mastery: Self-efficacy and optimism. Sense of mastery was assessed using the Sense of Mastery Scale (MAS) a component of the Resiliency Scales for Children and Adolescents (RSCA; Prince-Embury, 2007). The MAS is a 20-item self-report questionnaire designed to measure internal factors of resiliency. Items are rated on a 5-point Likert scale ranging from 0 = *Never*, to 4 = *Almost Always*. The scale has strong internal consistency for children aged 9 to 11 years (α = .85) and 12 to 14 years (α = .89). Strong internal consistency was also found in the current study (α = .94). As the MAS is written at a grade three reading level it was appropriate to use with the current sample. Completion time is between 5 to 10 minutes.

The MAS can be further subdivided into three related subscales: optimism, self-efficacy and adaptability. Optimism is defined as a positive attitude about life in general and one's life specifically. This subscale obtained strong internal consistency in the current study (α = .88). An example of a statement from the optimism subscale is "Good things will happen to me". Self-efficacy is associated with problem solving attitude and approach to obstacles. This subscale also obtained a strong internal consistency in the current study (α = .87). An example of a statement from the self-efficacy subscale is "I am good at figuring things out". The Adaptability subscale was not used in the current study because of poor internal consistency for children aged 9 to 11 years (Prince-Embury, 2007). Items on the MAS are summed and the total raw score is converted into a *T*-score. Furthermore, items pertaining to each subscale are summed for a raw score which is then converted into scale scores. *T*-scores for the MAS range from 1 to 74, with scores between 46 and 55 in the average range.

113

Table 7.1. Index of Community Socio-Educational
Advantage (ICSEA) in each location

School locations	ICSEA Value
Western Suburbs	1,018
Eastern Suburbs	1,111
North Western Suburbs	1,052
Inner Eastern Suburbs	1,146
Rural Northern Suburbs	1,051

Socio-economic status. The school's socio-economic status was determined using the Index of Community Socio-Educational Advantage (ICSEA) provided by the Australian Curriculum, Assessment and Reporting Authority (ACARA, 2015) (Table 7.1). The ISCEA represents the relative magnitude of influence of a student's family background, which includes parent occupation, parent education, geographical location and proportion of indigenous students. The average of the ICSEA is 1,000 with a standard deviation of 100 (values typically range from 500 to 1300). The higher the ICSEA value, the higher the level of educational advantage of the students at the school.

Demographic information. Brief demographic information was collected from the participants regarding their age, sex, grade, and family structure (including one or two parent family, and other family members living in the home).

PROCEDURE

This study received ethical clearance from the University of Melbourne Human Ethics Committee (Ethics identification number 1646471), approval from the Department of Catholic Education (project number 2196), from the Department of Education and Training (project number 2016_003088), and written consent from the school principals of two Catholic and two Government schools. Consent forms and information regarding the study were sent home to all parents of students in Grade 5 and 6. Students who returned parent consent forms consenting for participation were included in the study. Most students completed all the questionnaires in 25 to 45 minutes. The student researcher was present and facilitated each session to provide assistance and clarification when necessary. All questionnaires were scored and entered into a data file and reverse score items were completed according to instructions on the PSSM and the FAD.

Data Analysis

Data were analysed using SPSS version 20. The associations between the independent variables of family functioning, school connectedness, and the dependent variables of sense of mastery, optimism, and self-efficacy were examined using Pearson product-moment correlation coefficients. To test whether school connectedness mediated the relationship between family functioning and sense of mastery, a mediation analysis was performed using a computations tool for path analysis based mediation called PROCESS (Hayes, 2013). A standard multiple regression was performed between sense of mastery as the dependent variable and problem solving, communication, roles, and affective involvement and behavioural control as the independent variables.

Assumption testing was completed to assess whether data met the requirements for multiple regression. Multicollinearity was examined across the five independent variables used in the multiple regression analysis. All correlations between independent variables were between .3 and .7 showing variables were all correlated but not to concerning levels (Pallant, 2013). All Tolerance statistics were over .10 (ranging from .41 to .70), and all VIF statistics were below 10 (ranging from 1.43 to 2.45). Therefore, multicollinearity was not violated (Pallant, 2013).

RESULTS

Family Functioning and Sense of Mastery

Table 7.2 presents the descriptive information for the final sample used in the analysis (123 participants). The relationship between family functioning and sense of mastery was investigated using Pearson product-moment correlation coefficient. As shown in Table 7.3, there was a strong, statistically significant, negative relationship between the two variables. Higher scores on the FAD were associated with lower scores on the MAS. The more poorly the participants perceived their family to function, the lower their sense of mastery. Further examination was completed with family functioning

Table 7.2. Mean, standard deviation and ranges of the study variables

Variable	M	SD	Possible	Actual
Sense of Mastery	52.06	10.81	1–74	21–74
Optimism	10.66	3.09	1–16	3–16
Self-Efficacy	10.63	3.12	1–17	1–17
General Family Functioning	1.77	.46	1–4	1–3.27
Problem Solving	1.97	.44	1–4	1–3.33
Communication	2.12	.43	1–4	1–3.56
Roles	2.17	.39	1–4	1.27–3.31
Affective Involvement	2.18	.49	1–4	1–3.34
Behaviour Control	1.83	.39	1–4	1.11–2.78
School Connectedness	71.85	11.50	18–90	40–90

Table 7.3. Correlations between variables

Measures	1	2	3	4	5	6	7	8	9	10
1. General family functioning	1.0									
2. Problem solving	.73**	1.0								
3. Communication	.73**	.60**	1.0							
4. Roles	.71**	.58**	.69**	1.0						
5. Behaviour control	.47**	.46**	.38**	.50**	1.0					
6. Affective involvement	.60**	.35**	.44**	.52**	.38**	1.0				
7. School connectedness	-.56**	-.38**	-.40**	-.54**	-.32**	-.36**	1.0			
8. Sense of mastery	-.67**	-.56**	-.49**	-.59**	-.39**	-.41**	.72**	1.0		
9. Optimism	-.65**	-.54**	-.49**	-.58**	-.36**	-.40**	.68**	.92**	1.0	
10. Self-efficacy	-.60**	-.52**	-.40**	-.54**	-.35**	-.39**	.65**	.94**	.79**	1.0

$**p < .01$ (two tailed), $*p < .05$ (two-tailed)

and factors of mastery; optimism and self-efficacy. Strong, negative relationships were found between family functioning and both self-efficacy and optimism. Poor family functioning was significantly associated with low optimism and low self-efficacy. This association was stronger for optimism. The relationship between school connectedness and sense of mastery was also investigated using Pearson product-moment correlation coefficient. Table 7.3 shows a strong, significant, positive relationship between school connectedness and sense of mastery. Therefore, the more connected participants reported feeling towards their school, the greater their sense of mastery. Strong, positive and significant relationships were also found between school connectedness and mastery factors; optimism and self-efficacy. Similar to family functioning, this association was stronger for optimism.

Mediation Effect of School Connectedness

As all correlations between the variables in the analysis were significant (Table 7.3), the data were able to be used in mediation analysis. This was completed using a bootstrap method investigating the role of school connectedness in the relationship between family functioning and sense of mastery, using Hayes' (2013) macro for SPSS called PROCESS (Hayes, 2013).

The relationship between family functioning and school connectedness was significant, as was the relationship between school connectedness and sense of mastery (Figure 7.1). After controlling for the impact of school connectedness, family functioning continued to have a significant effect on mastery. The indirect (mediating) effect (= −6.68) was significantly different from zero, as indicated by the 95% bias-corrected bootstrap CI [−9.69, −4.17] based on 10,000 bootstrap samples. These results suggest that the connectedness a student has with their school may reduce the impact, and partially mediate the effect, of poor family functioning on their sense of mastery.

Figure 7.2 illustrates results when data from the current study were integrated with data from a previous study by Murphy and McKenzie (2015). The mediation

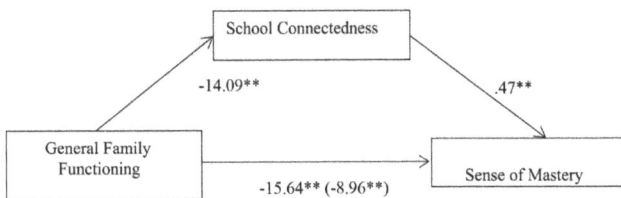

Figure 7.1. Unstandardised regression coefficients for the relationship between family functioning, sense of mastery as partially mediated by school connectedness. The unstandardised regression coefficient between family functioning and sense of mastery, controlling for school connectedness is in parentheses.
$**p < .01, n = 123$

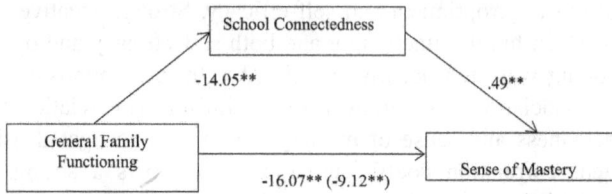

Figure 7.2. Unstandardised regression coefficients for the relationship between family functioning, sense of mastery as partially mediated by school connectedness. The unstandardised regression coefficient between family functioning and sense of mastery, controlling for school connectedness is in parentheses.
**p < .01, n = 198*

analysis was repeated and showed the indirect (mediating) effect (= −6.94) was significantly different from zero, as indicated by the 95% bias-corrected bootstrap CI [−9.35, −4.89] based on 10,000 bootstrap samples, confirming and replicating the previously found relationship.

Factors of Family Functioning and Sense of Mastery

To further explore the impact of the different components of family functioning on sense of mastery, a standard multiple regression was completed. Problem solving, communication, roles, affective responsiveness, and behaviour control were entered as independent variables, with sense of mastery as the dependent variable.

Results are presented in Table 7.4 and indicate that R was significantly different from zero, $F(6,116) = 18.28$, $p < .001$. Furthermore, 48% of the variability in preadolescent sense of mastery is accounted for by family factors such as problem solving, communication, roles, affective responsiveness, and behaviour control. Roles made the largest and only significant unique contribution to the regression model accounting for 2.3% of the variance in sense of mastery. The size and direction of the relationship suggests that preadolescents from families which lack clear accountability and allocations of responsibilities and roles, have a lower sense of mastery.

Furthermore, results in the current study were similar to those found previously by Murphy and McKenzie (2015). The model posited in Murphy and McKenzie (2015) was supported by results in this study, confirming the importance of roles in the family and their influence on mastery.

Gender Effects

ANOVA results indicated that there was no significant difference between males and females on their ratings of school connectedness, sense of mastery and family functioning.

Table 7.4. Standard multiple regression of FAD components on mastery

Variable	B	SE B	β	sr² (unique)
Problem Solving	−3.28	2.49	−.13	−.09
Communication	2.90	2.64	.12	.07
Roles	−6.86*	2.98	−.25	−.15
Affective Involvement	.32	1.91	.01	.01
Behaviour Control	−.92	2.19	−.03	−.03
				$R^2 = .47$
				Adjusted $R^2 = .46$
				$R = .70**$

**p< 0.01, *p<0.05*

Socioeconomic Status Effects

School and differences in scores on sense of mastery, school connectedness and family functioning were examined using one-way analyses of variance (ANOVA). Examination of a medium effect size (.06) using G*Power version 3.0.10 indicated a required sample size of 52 participants (Field, 2013). Therefore, before analysis, data from the north western school ($n = 9$) were combined with data from the rural north school ($n = 46$), as these localities had very nearly identical school SES values (ICSEA = 1,052 and 1,051 respectively), and came from large hierarchical school systems (both catholic and government). Similarly, both of the eastern suburbs schools were collapsed into set of results as the inner eastern and eastern school had similar SES values (1,146 and 1,111 respectively) and similar school systems.

Levene's Statistic was examined and found for school connectedness and sense of mastery the statistic was above .05, therefore not violating the assumption of homogeneity. Levene's statistic for family functioning was .008, which violated the assumption of homogeneity therefore, the Welch test was used as an F score replacement as it reduces the probability of a Type One error.

ANOVA results (Table 7.5) indicated a significant difference between school locations on school connectedness, $F(2,195) = 10.15$, $p < .001$, sense of mastery $F(2, 195) = 13.44$, $p < .001$, and family functioning $F(2, 124.20) = 8.03$, $p = .001$. Post Hoc tests determined the rural sample was statistically significantly different to the eastern region for each independent variable at the .05 level, and the western region at $p < .001$ level. Sense of mastery was the only scale with a significant difference between all three regions. The difference between the eastern and western regions was significant at $p < .05$.

Students in the rural region school rated their school connectedness, sense of mastery and family functioning significantly lower than students in the other regions. Effect sizes, calculated using eta squared ranged from .08 (family functioning) to .12 (sense of mastery) indicating medium to large effects (Field, 2013).

Table 7.5. Regional comparisons

Variable	Western n = 75		Eastern n = 68		Rural n = 55	
	M	SD	M	SD	M	SD
School Connectedness	76.95	8.84	74.38	10.63	68.73	11.86
General Family Functioning	1.58	.43	1.67	.44	1.90	.46
Sense of Mastery	58.71	10.39	54.47	9.80	49.07	11.34

DISCUSSION

This study examined the influence of school connectedness and family functioning on the resilience factor of mastery in preadolescent children. School connectedness was found to partially mediate the relationship between family functioning and sense of mastery. The first two hypotheses, which proposed a relationship between school connectedness, family functioning, and sense of mastery, were supported by the findings. Lower scores on family functioning were associated with lower sense of mastery scores and higher school connectedness was associated with a higher sense of mastery scores. The third hypothesis was supported, confirming that school connectedness partially mediated the relationship between family functioning and sense of mastery. There were no significant differences between male and female results; however, results indicated that there were significant differences in scores on all three variables according to local area. Medium to large effect sizes were found for students from different socio-economic areas, and were significantly related to poorer family functioning, lower school connectedness, and lower sense of mastery in the rural region. Children in the rural northern area had lower feelings of school connectedness, a lower sense of mastery and rated their families significantly less well functioning than other regions.

The results supported the findings of previous studies (Murphy & McKenzie, 2015; Mutimer, Reece, & Matthews, 2007; Renzaho et al., 2013). A significant relationship was found between family functioning and sense of mastery. Poorly perceived family functioning was associated with lower sense of mastery. The greater the students felt connected to their school, the higher their sense of mastery. The relationship between family functioning and sense of mastery was partially mediated by school connectedness, as was found in Murphy and McKenzie (2015). This encourages educators to develop interventions to enhance school connectedness, particularly in lower socio-economic areas and for families which are not functioning well.

Students who perceived their families to be functioning poorly also reported a lower sense of mastery, whereas students from families that were functioning more positively with clearly established boundaries and expectations had greater scores on mastery (Mutimer, Reece, & Matthews, 2007; Renzaho et al., 2013). The research is in line with studies undertaken by Lester and colleagues (2013) and Renzaho and colleagues (2013), reporting on the FAD, who found that family functioning operated as a protective buffer against negative developmental outcomes. The present study's results suggest that optimism and self-efficacy may play key roles in mastery, and hence in resilience. Preadolescents from positively functioning families may have more positive attitudes and perceptions of present and future outcomes, which are likely to be considered helpful in bouncing back from negative events and influences that may arise.

These results support other findings highlighting the link between school connectedness and positive attitudes (Kapoor & Tomar, 2016; Stewart et al., 2004). Kapoor and Tomar (2016), using an Indian version of the PSSM and the SEQ-Cefficacy, the SEQ-C to measure resiliency, found a strong positive correlation between school connectedness, resiliency and self-efficacy for year 10 and 11 students. Correlations between self-efficacy and school connectedness were similar for the current study ($r = .65$) and the SEQ study ($r = .57$). Stewart and colleagues (2004) found that implementing a universal level program within a school to promote school connectedness related positively to students' scores on resilience, in keeping with the results of the current study.

Findings from the current study underline the role of school connectedness in resiliency, and support the use of mastery to measure resilience. Furthermore, the findings support the shift of emphasis of research in this area to include preadolescents and promoting school connectedness in primary school (Berge et al., 2013; Tollit et al., 2015; Renzaho et al., 2013). Previous research has revealed the mediating effect of school connectedness on the relationship between social skills and depression in preadolescence (Ross et al., 2010). Students who felt connected to their school reported a higher sense of mastery, suggesting that enhancing school connectedness can benefit students by increasing their sense of competency, positive outlook, and problem solving ability (Prince-Embury, 2007). Furthermore, the impact of school connectedness on positive development may be further enhanced by providing opportunities to develop a sense of mastery.

Previous research has identified that the core components of mastery, optimism and self-efficacy, impact mental health measures in young people (Gaete et al., 2016; Hamill, 2003; Ross et al., 2010). Self-efficacy and optimism have been explored, mostly with adolescents and adults (Chang & Sanna, 2003; Hamill, 2003; Jackson et al., 2005; Rodriguez & Loos-Sant'Ana, 2015). The current study results, correlating optimism and self-efficacy with family functioning and school connectedness, reflect those found by Jackson et al. (2005) who found that optimism mediated the relationship between authoritative parenting and adolescents adjustment (self-esteem and depression). This suggests that for students in Grade 5 and 6, beliefs that their future will be positive are similarly important as the sense of their ability to manipulate and control their future (Schwarzer & Warner, 2013).

The current study identified a stronger correlation between family functioning and school connectedness than Law et al. (2013). Law et al. identified the correlation as −.43, Murphy and McKenzie (2015) found it to be −.61 and the current study found it to be −.56. This discrepancy may be due to sample size (563, 75, and

123 respectively), or may reflect aspects specific to a community or geographic location. The findings are also consistent with Phillipson and McFarland (2016) who, in examining the Social Connectedness Model, found adolescents' perceptions of parenting and school connectedness partially mediated the effect of parenting behaviours and academic performance (including academic mastery). Whilst the 2016 study also used a large Australian sample of early adolescent students (3,956 participants, Mage = 12.41 years), it was unclear what measures were used to measure mastery. Furthermore, the mastery variable appeared to be related to goal orientations and preparing for school (e.g., "Goal to get better grades than other students", Phillipson & McFarland, 2016, p. 5) rather than the sense of mastery that explores psychological attitudes such as optimism and self-efficacy definition in the current study (Prince-Embury, 2007). Nevertheless, the finding that school connectedness may have the ability to counterbalance negative developmental outcomes in poorly functioning families was consistent with results from Phillipson and McFarland (2016) and Law et al. (2013).

Previous studies have found that the factor of family functioning that had the greatest influence on sense of mastery was roles, the repetitive patterns of behavior that structure family patterns (Murphy & McKenzie, 2015). Similar results were found in the current study with roles having the largest influence on sense of mastery, indicating preadolescents who perceive their family having difficulty assigning roles and completing assigned tasks had a lower sense of mastery. This may be addressed for example by providing information and support to parents about the beneficial outcome of affirming consistent rules and expectations with their children which is likely to help them to navigate and thrive in the face of adversity.

Some studies have found that gender and socioeconomic status variables were influential in levels of connectedness, family functioning, and mastery (Berge et al., 2013; Phillipson & McFarland, 2016). The current study found no gender differences in preadolescent children in their levels of school connectedness, family functioning or sense of mastery, however differences in socio-economic status (SES) influence were identified. Data collapsed from five areas into three similar SES areas, indicated significant differences between ratings of school connectedness, sense of mastery, and family functioning in preadolescent children. The rural sample was found to be significantly different to the metropolitan areas. Students in the rural region rated their school connectedness and sense of mastery significantly lower and family functioning significantly poorer, than the other regions. All three regions significantly differed on their sense of mastery. Berge and colleagues (2013) separated participants into five SES categories ranging from low SES to high SES using parental variables (i.e., parent education level, eligibility for reduced meals). Results indicated the two lower SES groups rated their level of family functioning significantly lower than middle to high-middle SES. Students with high SES also had the highest family functioning score. Results from the current study were in contradiction to those found by Berge and colleagues as analysis of means in the current study found the western region, which had the lowest SES level, perceived their families to be functioning best when compared to other regions. However as there was a limited number of schools in the study, this result needs to be considered with caution. Furthermore, comparison with the Berge et al. study can be confusing due to the use of a brief version of the general functioning scale of the FAD (6-items) and their description of higher scores as representing more effective functioning, although the original scale used higher scores to indicate poor family functioning (Epstein et al., 1983). Further investigation of a socioeconomically varied sample may be valuable to examine the relationship between SES and sense of mastery and strengthen the results found in the current study.

Enhancing School Belonging

The important role of school connectedness in preadolescent resilience has been revisited and confirmed in the current study. Results support previous findings, and with a larger sample from varied locations, the current study confirmed the role of school connectedness as a partial mediator in the association between family functioning and sense of mastery. Comparable to conclusions acknowledged in earlier studies, current results support the recognition of school connectedness as a target for intervention especially with students from poorly functioning families. Links have been found between low school connectedness and low sense of mastery, which highlights for schools the importance of sustaining interventions that promote opportunities to build school connectedness.

Families play a crucial role in early development, however as the child grows and seeks external supports, settings beyond the family can become influential in guiding and fostering resilience in children. School creates a unique environment in which programs can be targeted to increase school connectedness and in turn, resilience in young people. Working with the whole school offers the opportunity to offer interventions that target the entire school community (Stewart et al. 2004; Roffey, 2008). Successful initiatives such as the Australian program KidsMatter (Slee et al., 2009) demonstrate the value of a positive school community which promotes inclusion and belonging alongside family friendly environments, social and emotional learning for students, parenting support and education, and early intervention for students experiencing mental health difficulties. They conclude that connectedness is essential to resilience and achievement and well being. The evaluation of the effectiveness of the KidsMatter initiative in 100 schools indicated that there were significant and positive changes in the schools, teachers, parents/caregivers, and students over the two-year evaluation period. KidsMatter promotes a systemic approach to developing school connectedness, addressing the school philosophy, policy, and implementation. At the microsystem level, schools might involve parents in school activities and education programs to help foster parent-adolescent relationships, encourage support and engagement between students in activities and peer support programs, and finally encourage teachers to support students emotionally, respectfully and academically. Results from the current study identified when the student feels more connected to their family they also feel more connected to their school.

Limitations and Future Studies

The current cross-sectional research design provides correlational results; hence inferences cannot be made about the causal relationships between variables. Whilst the current study showed the importance of school connectedness in resilience, future studies could also examine school programs that build school connectedness and improve outcomes for students. In addition to examining school connectedness, further research could examine the benefit of enhancing sense of mastery.

Whilst the current study extended the results of Murphy and McKenzie (2015) by providing a larger sample from varied school settings, a more diverse sample could be examined in a future study to ensure the greater power of the results. Participants from the current study were sampled from different geographic locations in Melbourne, however the SES of the schools were within 1.5 standard deviations above the mean. The Index of Community Socio-Educational Advantage (ICSEA) has a mean of 1,000 and a standard deviation of 100. ICSEA values in the current study ranged from 1,018 to 1,146. Although results indicated the rural sample was significantly different from the other three regions, further support and information could be gained by using a stratified sample ensuring information was gathered from students well below the average and above it. This may extend the current results and provide information about the compensatory role of school connectedness in resilience in areas of disadvantage.

In further review of the sample, it should be highlighted that only 26% of all Grade 5 and 6 parents consented to their children participating out of 526 information packs sent home. This raises questions about any defining characteristics that may have differed between the students who participated and those who did not. Furthermore, these unknown characteristics may limit the generalisability of the results. It could be possible that the families who participated had a more positive relationship with the school (Murphy & McKenzie, 2015). The average school connectedness found in the current study was higher ($M = 71.55$) than those found by previous studies with large sample sizes ($M = 65.03$; Law et al, 2013), however lower than Murphy and McKenzie ($M = 76.95$) who had a smaller sample. This may indicate that Murphy and McKenzie (2015) had a more biased sample, and with increased participation a more accurate representation of the population can be observed.

Further assessment of the generalisability of the results suggests the sample may have been more representative of Grade 6 students, as one school restricted their participation to that grade group. The average age of the students in the study, 11.37 years suggests the sample is representative of preadolescents (Ross et al., 2010). One specific variable that warrants more attention is the family structure component. Because of consistency, the current study split this variable into one or two parent households. Observations of students answering questions during data collection sessions provided information that would be very interesting to examine in the future. Participants identified issues such as spending 50% of their time in divorced parents' houses (one may have had a step-parent, and the other was a sole-parent), which house should they answer questions in relation to, and issues such as siblings having disabilities which was self-reported to affect the functioning of the family. Research has indicated children with divorced parents are more likely to have emotional, behavioural, social and academic problems (Amato & Keith, 1991). Research has identified that rather than just divorce, multiple life events and transitions may be related to negative childhood outcomes (Amato, 2010). Future research could collect additional information from families such as a parent reported version of the FAD and a stress scale such as the social readjustment rating scale (Holmes & Rahe, 1967). This would provide more information about family functioning from multiple sources. This information may provide further support for the role school connectedness plays in resiliency outcomes for children from poorly functioning families compounded by life stressors. Results may further inform practices for children who are known to the school as members of families in difficulty, to provide opportunities for positive outcomes despite adversity.

The final limitation of the current study to be acknowledged is the possibility that mediation may oversimplify the relationship between variables (Hayes, 2013). There may have been other factors beyond school connectedness influencing the relationship between family functioning and sense of mastery given the partial mediation effect. Future studies may wish to further control for other variables such as family structure and SES to further unpack the complexity of this relationship. Analysis of the specific components of family functioning which strongly influence outcomes, offers a rich area for further examination. The current study, consistent with Murphy and McKenzie (2015), found family roles to be significantly linked to positive outcomes however inconsistencies of other family factors in their reliabilities and correlations with sense of mastery (e.g. communication and problem solving) suggests this is also an area to be further investigated.

CONCLUSION

The current study explored the complex structure of resiliency in preadolescent children. Student's perceptions of their family functioning played an important role in their feelings of connectedness to their school and sense of mastery. Further support for the importance of school connectedness in its relationship with resilience was highlighted through a partial mediation effect. Lower scores on mastery were associated with lower scores on family functioning, and higher mastery scores were associated with stronger scores on school connectedness. For both family functioning and school connectedness, the mastery subscale of optimism was slightly better able to predict scores on these variables than self-efficacy, however both factors were significant. The study provided support for, and extended, the results previously found by Murphy and McKenzie (2015) and indicates potential for further exploration in subsequent studies of factors of SES and family structure. The results from the current study suggest important implications for school programs aimed at enhancing school connectedness and which encourage and work towards positive outcomes for their students; especially those experiencing less effective family functioning.

REFERENCES

Allen, K., & McKenzie, V. (2015). Mental health in an Australian context and future interventions from a school belonging perspective. *Special Issue on Mental Health in Australia for the International Journal of Mental Health, 44*, 80–93. doi:10.1080/00207411.2015

Amato, P. R. (2010). Research on divorce: Continuing trends and new developments. *Journal of Marriage and Family, 72*(3), 650–666.

Amato, P. R., & Keith, B. (1991). Parental divorce and the well-being of children: A meta-analysis. *Psychological Bulletin, 110*(1), 26.

Australian Curriculum, Assessment and Reporting Authority (ACARA). (2015). *Guide to understanding ICSEA (Index of Community Socio Educational Advantage) values my school – Fact sheet*. ACARA. Retrieved July 16, 2018, from http:\\\\www.Docs.acara.edu.au/resources/ Guide to understanding icsea values.pdf

Baumeister, R. F., & Leary, M. R. (1995). The need to belong: Desire for interpersonal attachments as a fundamental human motivation. *Psychological Bulletin, 117*(3), 497.

Berge, J. M., Wall, M., Larson, N., Loth, K. A., & Neumark-Sztainer, D. (2013). Family functioning: Associations with weight status, eating behaviors, and physical activity in adolescents. *Journal of Adolescent Health, 52*(3), 351–357.

Bihun, J. T., Wamboldt, M. Z., Gavin, L. A., & Wamblodt, F. S. (2002). Can the Family Assessment Device (FAD) be used with school aged children? *Family Process, 41*(4), 723.

Block, J. H., & Block, J. (1980). The role of ego-control and ego-resiliency in the organization of behavior. In W. A. Collins (Ed.), *Development of cognition, affect, and social relations: The Minnesota symposia on child psychology* (Vol. 13, pp. 39–101). Hillsdale, NJ: Lawrence Erlbaum Associates.

Bronfenbrenner, U. (1977). Toward an experimental ecology of human development. *American Psychologist, 32*(7), 513–531.

Bronfenbrenner, U. (1979). *The ecology of human development: Experiments by nature and design*. Cambridge, MA: Harvard University Press.

Brooks, R., & Goldstein, S. (2001). *Raising resilient children: Fostering strength, hope, and optimism in your child*. New York, NY: McGraw-Hill.

Buchanan, C. M., Eccles, J. S., & Becker, J. B. (1992). Are adolescents the victims of raging hormones? Evidence for activational effects of hormones on moods and behavior at adolescence. *Psychological Bulletin, 111*(1), 62.

Chang, E. C., & Sanna, L. J. (2003). Experience of life hassles and psychological adjustment among adolescents: Does it make a difference if one is optimistic or pessimistic? *Personality & Individual Differences, 34*(5), 867. doi:10.1016/S0191-8869(02)00077-6

Cunningham, E. G., Brandon, C. M., & Frydenberg, E. (2002). Enhancing coping resources in early adolescence through a school-based program teaching optimistic thinking skills. *Anxiety, Stress & Coping, 15*(4), 369. doi:10.1080/1061580021000056528

Department of Education and Training, Victorian Government (DET). (2017). *Building resilience in children and young people*. Retrieved August 20, 2017, from http://www.education.vic.gov.au/ Documents/about/department/resiliencelitreview.pdf

Eccles, J. S., & Midgley, C. (1990). Changes in academic motivation and self-perception during early adolescence. In R. Montemayor, G. R. Adams, & T. Gullotta (Eds.), *From childhood to adolescence: A transitional period?* (pp. 134–155). Newbury Park, CA: Sage Publications.

Epstein, N. B., Baldwin, L. M., & Bishop, D. S. (1983). The McMaster family assessment device. *Journal of Marital and Family Therapy, 9*(2), 171–180.

Epstein, N. B., Bishop, D. S., & Levin, S. (1978). The McMaster model of family functioning. *Journal of Marriage & Family Counseling, 4*(4), 19–31.

Fergus, S., & Zimmerman, M. A. (2005). Adolescent resilience: A framework for understanding healthy development in the face of risk. *Annual Review of Public Health, 26*, 399–419.

Field, A. (2013). *Discovering statistics using IBM SPSS statistics* (4th ed.). Sussex: Sage Publications.

Frydenberg, E., Care, E., Freeman, E., & Chan, E. (2009). Interrelationships between coping, school connectedness and wellbeing. *Australian Journal of Education, 53*(3), 261–276. doi:10.1177/000494410905300305

Garmezy, N. (1985). Stress-resistant children: The search for protective factors. In J. E. Stevenson (Ed.), *Recent research in developmental psychopathology: Journal od child psychology and psychiatry book supplement 4* (pp. 213–233). Oxford: Pergamon Press.

Goodenow, C. (1993). The psychological sense of school membership among adolescents: Scale development and educational correlates. *Psychology in Schools, 30*(1), 79–90.

Hair, J. F., Black, W. C., Babin, B. J., & Anderson, R. E. (2010). *Multivariate data analysis: A global perspective* (7th ed.). Upper Saddle River, NJ: Pearson Prentice Hall.

Hamill, S. K. (2003). Resilience and self-efficacy: The importance of efficacy beliefs and coping mechanisms in resilient adolescents. *Colgate University Journal of the Sciences, 35*(1), 115–146.

Hayes, A. F. (2013). *Introduction to mediation, moderation, and conditional process analysis: A regression-based approach.* New York, NY: The Guilford Press.

Holmes, T. H., & Rahe, R. H. (1967). The social readjustment rating scale. *Journal of Psychosomatic Research, 11*(2), 213–218.

Jackson, L. M., Pratt, M. W., Hunsberger, B., & Pancer, S. M. (2005). Optimism as a mediator of the relation between perceived parental authoritativeness and adjustment among adolescents: Finding the sunny side of the street. *Social Development, 14*(2), 273–304. doi:10.1111/j.1467-9507.2005.00302.x

Kapoor, B., & Tomar, A. (2016). Exploring connections between students' psychological sense of school membership and their resilience, self-efficacy, and leadership skills. *Indian Journal of Positive Psychology, 7*(1), 55.

Law, P. C., Cuskelly, M., & Carroll, A. (2013). Young people's perceptions of family, peer, and school connectedness and their impact on adjustment. *Australian Journal of Guidance and Counselling, 23*(1), 115–140. doi:10.1017/jgc.2012.19

Lawrence, D., Johnson, S., Hafekost, J., Boterhoven de Haan, K., Sawyer, M., Ainley, J., & Zubrick, S. R. (2015). *The mental health of children and adolescents: Report on the second Australian child and adolescent survey of mental health and wellbeing.* Canberra: Department of Health.

Lester, P., Stein, J. A., Saltzman, W., Woodward, K., MacDermid, S. W., Milburn, N., Mogil, C., Beardslee, W. (2013). Psychological health of military children: Longitudinal evaluation of a family-centered prevention program to enhance family resilience. *Military Medicine, 178*(8), 838–845. doi:10.7205/MILMED-D-12-00502

Loukas, A., Roalson, L. A., & Herrera, D. E. (2010). School connectedness buffers the effects of negative family relations and poor effortful control on early adolescent conduct problems. *Journal of Research on Adolescence, 20*(1), 13–22. doi:10.1111/j.1532-7795.2009.00632.x

Murphy, E. L., & McKenzie, V. L. (2015). The impact of family functioning and school connectedness on preadolescent sense of mastery. *Journal of Psychologists and Counsellors in Schools, 26*(1), 35–51. doi:10.1017/jgc.2015.17

Mutimer, A., Reece, J., & Matthews, J. (2007). Child resilience: Relationship between stress, adaptation and family functioning. *Journal of Applied Psychology, 3*(1), 16–25. doi:10.7790/ejap.v3i1.76

Pallant, J. (2013). *SPSS survival manual: A step by step guide to data analysis using IBM SPSS* (5th ed.). Maidenhead: McGraw-Hill.

Phillipson, S., & McFarland, L. (2016). Australian parenting and adolescent boys' and girls' academic performance and mastery: The mediating effect of perceptions of parenting and sense of school membership. *Journal of Child and Family Studies, 25*(6), 2021–2033.

Prince-Embury, S. (2007). *Resiliency scale for children and adolescents: Profiles of personal strengths.* San Antonio, TX: Harcourt Assessments.

Prince-Embury, S. (2011). Assessing personal resiliency in the context of school settings: Using the resiliency scales for children and adolescents. *Psychology in Schools, 48*(7), 672–685. doi:10.1002/pits.20581

Renzaho, A., Mellor, D., McCabe, M., & Powell, M. (2013). Family functioning, parental psychological distress and child behaviours: Evidence from the Victorian child health and wellbeing study. *Australian Psychologist, 48*(3), 217–225. doi:10.1111/j.1742-9544.2011.00059.x

Robinson, J. P., Shaver, P. R., & Wrightsman, L. S. (1991). Criteria for scale selection and evaluation. In J. P. Robinson, P. R. Shaver, & L. S. Wrightsman (Eds.), *Measures of personality and social psychological attitudes* (pp. 1–16). San Diego, CA: Academic Press.

Rodriguez, S. N., & Loos-Sant'Ana, H. (2015). Self-concept, self-esteem and self-efficacy: The role of self-beliefs in the coping process of socially vulnerable adolescents. *Journal of Latino-Latin American Studies, 7*(1), 33–44.

Roffey, S. (2008). Emotional literacy and the ecology of school wellbeing. *Educational and Child Psychology, 25*(2), 29–39.

Roffey, S. (2013). Inclusive and exclusive belonging: The impact on individual and community well-being. *Educational and Child Psychology, 30*(1), 38–49.

Ross, A. G., Shochet, I. M., & Bellair, R. (2010). The role of social skills and school connectedness in preadolescent depressive symptoms. *Journal of Clinical Child and Adolescent Psychology, 39*(2), 269–275. doi:10.1080/15374410903532692

Rutter, M. (1985). Resilience in the face of adversity. Protective factors and resistance to psychiatric disorder. *The British Journal of Psychiatry, 147*, 598–611.

Rutter, M. (1987). Psychosocial resilience and protective mechanisms. *The American Journal of Orthopsychiatry, 57*(3), 316–331. doi:10.1111/j.1939-0025.1987.tb03541.x

Ryan, C. E., Epstein, N. B., & Keitner, G. I. (2005). *Evaluating and treating families: The McMaster approach.* New York, NY: Taylor & Francis.

Schwarzer, R., & Warner, L. M. (2013). Perceived self-efficacy and its relationship to resilience. In S. Prince Embury & D. H. Saklofske (Eds.), *Resilience in children, adolescents, and adults* (pp. 139–150). New York, NY: Springer.

Shochet, I. M., Dadds, M. R., Ham, D., & Montague, R. (2006). School connectedness is an underemphasized parameter in adolescent mental health: Results of a community prediction study. *Journal of Clinical Child and Adolescent Psychology, 35*(2), 170–179.

Shochet, I. M., Homel, R., Cockshaw, W. D., & Montgomery, D. T. (2008). How do school connectedness and attachment to parents interrelate in predicting adolescent depressive symptoms? *Journal of Clinical Child and Adolescent Psychology, 37*(3), 676–681.

Slee, P. T., Lawson, M. J., Russell, A., Askell-Williams, H., Dix, K. L., Owens, L., Skrzypiec, G., & Spears, B. (2009). *Kidsmatter primary evaluation final report.* Adelaide: Centre for Analysis of Educational Futures, Flinders University of South Australia.

Stewart, D., Jing, S., Patterson, C., Lemerle, K., & Hardie, M. (2004). Promoting and building resilience in primary school communities: Evidence from a comprehensive 'health promoting school' approach. *International Journal of Mental Health Promotion, 6*(3), 26–33. doi:10.1080/14623730.2004.9721936

Tabachnick, B. G., & Fidell, L. S. (2013). *Using multivariate statistics.* Boston, MA: Pearson Education.

Tollit, M., McDonald, M., Borschmann, R., Bennett, K., von Sabler, M., & Patton, G. (2015). *Epidemiological evidence relating to resilience and young people: A literature review.* Melbourne: Victorian Health Promotion Foundation.

Wigfield, A., Byrnes, J. P., & Eccles, J. S. (2006). Development during early and middle adolescence. *Handbook of Educational Psychology, 2*, 87–113.

Vicki L. McKenzie
Educational Psychology Unit
Melbourne Graduate School of Education
University of Melbourne
Australia

Jessica J. E. Smead
Educational Psychology Unit
Melbourne Graduate School of Education
University of Melbourne
Australia

PART 3

CONTEMPORARY ISSUES FOR SCHOOL BELONGING

BINI SEBASTIAN AND CHRISTOPHER D. SLATEN

8. THE ROLE OF BELONGINGNESS IN INTERNATIONAL STUDENTS' ACCULTURATION PROCESS

INTRODUCTION

The Institute of International Education® (IIE, 2016) reported that 1,043,839 international students enrolled in United States colleges and universities in 2015–2016. These students travel across the world to America in hopes of receiving quality education they may not have access to in their home countries. The majority of these students come from Asia, making up 65% of the total international student population; Chinese students comprise 31.5% of the total Asian student population (IIE, 2016). International students continue to enroll in U.S. universities at steadily increasing numbers (Healey, 2008), bringing their diverse perspectives and knowledge to American classrooms. Through international students' efforts to achieve academic and professional success, they may encounter a number of challenges that hinder their abilities to prosper in a new country, particularly comparted to their domestic US peers. International students may find it especially difficult to adjust to a new culture (Mori, 2000; Poyrazli, Kavanaugh, Baker, & Al-Timimi, 2004) while trying to succeed academically and socially (Frey & Roysircar, 2004). These may include: acquiring a new language, forming new relationships, and adhering to different cultural values (Telbis, Helgeson, & Kingsbury, 2014), which are all modes of acculturating. Acculturation has been described as the process of adapting to a new cultural environment or the process of cultural change through intercultural contact (Berry, 2003).

Berry (1999) has categorized acculturation into four different categories: assimilation, marginalization, integration, separation. International students have typically adapted to the American culture through integration while trying to maintain ties with their home (Charles & Stewart, 1991). As previous research has found the quality of international students' social context to be highly indicative of the impact of their acculturation orientation on their wellbeing, we will be focusing primarily on the students' sense of belonging on campus. The sense of social connectedness may set a foundation for the way they communicate, relate to, and bond with others, which impacts their academic engagement and ability to cope during the acculturation process. The purpose of this chapter is to examine the influence of international students' sense of belongingness on campus on their acculturation process. Additionally, this chapter explores potential barriers to adopting a sense of belongingness for international students on campus.

© KONINKLIJKE BRILL NV, LEIDEN, 2018 | DOI:10.1163/9789004386969_008

ACCULTURATIVE STRESS

Berry (2006) describes acculturative stress as the negative psychological impact of environmental stressors that are specifically associated with the acculturation process. Previous research has shown that international students experience acculturative stress that impacts their ability to fulfil their original endeavors to obtain knowledge (Berry, 2006). Adhering to new cultural norms and adopting different cultural values presents difficulties that both members of the international student community and the host country have to navigate through, complicating the cross-cultural transition. Because many students experience psychological distress due to their acculturation process (Du & Wei, 2015; Iwamoto & Liu, 2010; Rice et al., 2012; Swagler & Elis, 2003), they may experience a number of personal and social challenges that influence their academic endeavors.

Sociocultural Factors

As the number of international students in the U.S. rises, it is imperative that specific factors are identified to aid in international students' acculturation experiences. Sociocultural factors influence students' overall psychological wellbeing as well as their willingness to engage with others and their academics. Research has shown that social support is directly related to cross-cultural adjustment (Baba & Hosoda, 2014). Students are not only forced to adhere to new educational systems, but they are also immersed in new social situations that may lead to psychological discomfort or distress. Jackson, Ray, and Bybell (2013) examined the role of self-esteem, hope, optimism, coping, acculturative stress, and social support on international students' psychological wellbeing and sociocultural adjustment. This study found that the international students utilized adaptive and maladaptive coping mechanisms at similar rates to deal with stress, and their coping strategies were related to their acculturative stress and sociocultural adjustment. International students in Ireland who do not have strong social support systems tend to experience higher levels of loneliness and distress (O'Reilly, Ryan, & Hickey, 2010).

Students may find that certain differences in values or culture may be too arduous of a challenge to take on, possibly leading them to avoid establishing relationships with members of the host culture altogether. For example, a recent study showed the differences in cultural values between Chinese international students and students from Canada (Kenyon, Frohard-Dourlent, & Roth, 2012). The partying, drinking, and clubbing are very alluring and a part of many western cultures, but many international students who come from Asia may not find this appealing; thus, they may not be curious about or engage in these activities. This study also showed that international students tended to experience higher quality relationships when they spent more time with domestic peers and engaged in open dialogue to foster language learning skills. Research has also shown that the role of the host culture influences the negative impact of acculturative stressors including academic tasks, building relationship with domestic peers, and discrimination (Smith & Khawaja, 2011). Sociocultural factors may influence international students' psychological and academic adjustment, affecting their overall wellbeing and ability to succeed.

Academic Adjustment

International students' sociocultural experiences also contribute to their overall academic adjustment; many of these academic challenges are related social interactions as well as individual self-efficacy. A student may integrate themselves into various academic situations by learning how to communicate outside of the academic institution, especially since language acquisition is a factor that hinders many students in this population. Students may not feel confident in their language proficiency, so they may avoid social experiences and academic engagement. Furthermore, individuals may not engage with their peers within the classroom, which may exacerbate feelings of loneliness and impacting their educational development (Sawir, Marginson, & Deumert, 2008). Additionally, Gong and Fan (2006) found that standardized English test scores and social support both contributed positively to social adjustment. This further highlights the important role of social factors in international students' acculturative process. Gu and Maley (2005) conducted a study that explained the impact of culture shock experiences on academic adjustment. Culture shock is the unfamiliarity, uneasiness, or unacceptance that marginalized students may experience when they come in contact with a culture that is not their own (Torres, 2009). Culture shock was found to influence classroom behavior and level of engagement with other students on coursework. International students may feel discouraged in a learning environment that they are not at all acquainted with, which may inhibit them from acquiring knowledge effectively. It has been reported that the greater the difference between the home and host culture, the more likely it is for students to experience culture shock (Ramsay, Jones, & Barker, 2007). Other studies have indicated that the extent of culture shock experienced by a student relates to not only the degree of cultural differences, but also to one's ability to cope and adapt to new circumstances (Khawaja & Stallman, 2011). Furthermore, these students' self-efficacy may be negatively impacted by their sense of discomfort, preventing them from even attempting to participate fully in academic endeavors. As sociocultural and academic adjustment factors influence overall levels of psychological wellbeing, international students' sense of belonging may not only act as a buffer against the negative impacts of acculturation related to academic achievement, but it may also be the groundwork for which these students build resiliency and confidence in themselves and their relationships in order to grow, learn, and contribute to the greater society.

BELONGINGNESS

Colleges have acknowledged the importance of the sense of belonging on campus as a critical component of overall wellbeing (Hoffman, Richmond, Morrow, & Salomone, 2002; Hurtado & Carter, 1997; Hurtado & Ponjuan, 2005; Strayhorn, 2012). The human need to belong has been examined by Freud (drives; 1930), Bowlby (attachment theory; 1973), and Maslow (1970). They contend that every human desires to care for others and feel cared for through consistent interaction. Baumeister and Leary (1995) presupposed that humans long for positive interpersonal relationships. The need to belong can be traced back to evolutionary origins as an adaptive mechanism. When individuals are deprived of the sense of belonging, they may experience negative health effects such as chronic stress, lower quality of health, and maladaptive emotions (Baumeister & Leary, 1995). Furthermore, human beings naturally desire to feel like they fit in or belong, and they often contemplate their place in the world and in their community. Individuals may be a part of many different social circles, but still feel a lack of belongingness.

Individuals' connection to their academic institution has been referred to as school belonging at the K-12 level (Goodenow, 1993) or university belonging (Slaten et al., 2014) at the university level. Since the dissemination of research on belongingness, a handful of scholars have examined its role in psychological wellbeing in academic settings (Hoffman, Richmond, Marrow, & Salomone, 2002; Hurtado & Carter, 1997; Pittman & Richmond, 2008; Slaten et al., 2014). Using the Student Experience in the Research University survey administered to students at 12 large, public research universities in 2010, it was discovered that general participation in service and becoming involved in service through student organizations, fraternities or sororities, and university departments are positively associated with students' sense of belonging (Soria, Troisi, & Stebleton, 2012). Slaten et al. (2014) further elaborated on the experiences of belongingness in universities and observed four overarching themes: Feeling Valued by Others in Group Settings, Sustaining Meaningful Personal Relationships, Being Aware of the Campus Culture, and Feeling Supported by the University Environment. The commonalities among these themes highlight the significance of sociocultural and interpersonal factors in international students' process of acculturation. It is imperative that these students make an effort to build authentic, meaningful relationships to foster a strong sense of belongingness. Moreover, campus environments also influence students' sense of belonging. Institutions that have strengthened their messages of inclusivity and tolerance typically do so by providing resources that could help international students specifically.

International Students' Sense of Belonging

International students desire to feel valued in meaningful friendships and involved in different activities and much of this building of relationships is formed in academic settings. The field of counseling psychology has contributed to an abundance of research on international students' wellbeing in relation to acculturative stress, social engagement, and academic adjustment (Lin & Betz, 2009; Rice et al., 2012; Smart & Smart, 1995; K. T. Wang et al., 2015). In a study conducted by Hechanova-Alampay et al. (2002), it was reported that the more frequently international students interacted with Americans, the greater their adjustment. This emphasis on the positive psychological impact of social connectedness is also reflected in a study conducted by Slaten et al. (2016) that utilized a qualitative methodology to investigate international Asian students' understanding of what it means to belong, sense of belongingness, and motivation to satisfy their potential need to belong. The qualitative nature of this study provided a unique and detailed evaluation of the role of Asian international students' sense of belonging in the context of acculturation. The findings of this study revealed that international students are more likely to feel a sense of belonging if they establish and build relationships with those from similar backgrounds than those from the host culture. Additionally, belongingness increased cross-cultural interaction for international and domestic students and boosted grade point averages. It is evident that students' academic success is at least partially dependent on the quality of their social interactions. Furthermore, a different study found that leadership programs, cultural events, and community service strengthened the sense of belongingness for students (Glass & Westmont, 2013). Rajapaksa and Dundes (2002) found that international students' level of loneliness and home-sickness was influenced by their contentment with their social networks, and that domestic and international seniors reported less belongingness than their first-year counterparts.

Other factors related to belongingness on campus, especially in relation to international students, may include relationships with mentors or faculty, an openly tolerant climate on campus, and participation in social activities. Mentors may serve as an excellent resource for students to refer to when they have questions about coursework or larger cultural issues that influence their knowledge acquisition in general. Moreover, mentors of the same ethnic background as the international students they interact with may help provide a sense of security or comfort for international students, as they may be more able to relate to those that resemble them physically (Lewthwaite, 1996). These students may receive reassurance in ways that positively impacts on their sense of belonging and education. International students are also influenced by the larger campus culture in that they may seek multicultural initiatives that impact their academic development (Jackson & Heggins, 2003). The more resourceful international students perceive the university to be, the more likely they are to feel as if the university was also created for them to thrive as well. Nadelson et al. (2013) found that international students who perceived their university to be providing resources specifically to them were more likely to enroll again. Furthermore, Slaten et al. (2014) found that students valued social support as well as accessibility of resources to their sense of belonging. These resources may include mentors who represent a similar ethnic background, the availability of various cultural events, and the accessibility to language-learning programs. Students' sense of social connectedness may also depend on their experience in social activities (Rienties et al., 2012). Individuals may gain a sense of belongingness through a variety of means, including joining different organizations or groups on campus. Hurtado and Carter (1997) conducted a study on Latino college students and discovered affiliation with religious clubs and sororities/fraternities to play a role in their sense of belonging. Many international students join different organizations, clubs, or groups that may provide a foundation for them to find others with similar values. If international students are proactive in their fathering of knowledge about the new world around them, they may comprehend cultural conflicts more acceptingly, openly, and curiously, rather than closemindedly and judgmentally. This perception on behalf of the international student influences their actions in how they participate in the host culture. Their level of openness is also likely to influence feelings of belongingness directly and indirectly, as belongingness involves consistent interaction and care.

Belongingness on campus seems to encompass not only the motivation to interact with others and feel a sense of care, but also environmental factors on campus that influence whether or not they feel like they have a place at the university through access to resources and likelihood of academic achievement. Educational pursuits and academic commitment require students to be mentally capable of acquiring and retaining new knowledge, and feelings of isolation or disconnectedness with others may impede these efforts. Feelings of belongingness may reduce stress by providing students with the feeling of comfort associated with social support, allowing them to experience distress to a lesser extent.

The Need to Belong throughout the Acculturation Process

International students' sense of belonging may determine how they experience stress, succeed academically, and contribute to society. Interpersonal interactions are a critical component of the acculturation process. Belongingness is a factor that may actually buffer the psychological distress that results from a stressful acculturation process. College students experience growth due to different pressures, experiences, and social circles, but international students experience these same pressures with an added layer of acculturation. Multiple studies have observed a strong relationship between acculturation and social connectedness in international students (Du & Wei, 2015; K. T. Wang et al., 2015; Wei et al., 2012). Previous research has also shown that international students experience social connectedness through members of their own culture and through members of the host country; international students' subjective wellbeing was partially explained by acculturation, social connectedness in the ethnic community, and social connectedness in mainstream society (Yoon & Lee, 2008). The sense of belonging has been shown to increase when international students had meaningful relationships with those from the host culture and those with similar ethnic identities (Slaten et al., 2014). International students' perception of campus tolerance may also influence their sense of belongingness and acculturative process. International students experience challenges related to cultural expectations and the environment (Suarez-Morales et al., 2007). International students' cultural expectations may influence the way in which they choose to adopt certain cultural values of the host culture, and this may vary among the subcultures within the population of international students.

As sociocultural factors influence many aspects of international students' acculturation process, it is imperative that these students are able to identify specific factors that contribute to their distress or overall wellbeing. The factors related to acculturation are complex and multifaceted, but common themes among experiences may illuminate the sense of belonging as a key component in successful acculturation. International students may or may not desire to identify themselves with an institution, and the intensity of this drive will likely impact social and academic participation. Pittman and Richmond (2008) investigated the associations among feelings of pride toward an academic institution, student stress, and academic focus. This study found that the degree to which international students identify with their academic institution or feel proud to be a part of it, the more able they are to combat stress and concentrate on their coursework. The results of this study emphasize the idea that international students' sense of belonging or pride for their school may affect their motivation or drive to engage socially or succeed academically. Students who have positive acculturation experiences tend to form social networks early, participate in activities outside of the university, and feel that their time spent as an international student has made them more independent and confident in themselves (McLachlan & Justice, 2009).

International students' sense of belongingness may also influence personal development in that their persistence may be dependent on whether or not they feel as if they belong (Hausmann, Schofield, & Woods, 2007). Strayhorn (2012) described belonging as the influence of one's personal development on their academic pursuits. International students might contemplate their own values, abilities, and interests outside of or within their ethnic experiences, and the way in which they identify themselves as a part of a group, may influence how and how much they choose to contribute to that group. This process of self-exploration may introduce new cultural challenges that hinder students from focusing mainly on coursework or establishing relationships, which may influence their educational achievements. The acculturation process presents many challenges that require reflection, attention, energy, and time. In order for international students to maintain their psychological wellbeing, they will attempt to cope in a variety of ways. These efforts demand energy to alleviate acculturative stress, which may be exhaustive, time-consuming, and likely to take time away from other undertakings, such as academic interests. As international students take steps pursue their academic goals, their attention and energy may be divided in a way that harms or discourages them.

POTENTIAL BARRIERS TO CULTIVATING A SENSE OF BELONGINGNESS

Discrimination

Among negative acculturation experiences that international students encounter, perceived discrimination is one of the most common sources of stress in international students (Sandhu & Asrabadi, 1994). Racism or discrimination may include harmful, negative, or damaging views or actions towards a specific group of people. Not only may international students receive discriminatory threats, they also may not have a sufficient social support system to help them cope with discrimination, which exacerbates their levels of distress (Brown & Jones, 2013). This further creates distance and possible harm between members of the host culture and the international students, making it very difficult for these students to form relationships and stay academically engaged. Socially connected individuals who reported lower levels of discrimination were more likely to stay in the host culture versus those who experienced higher levels of discrimination and felt less socially connected (Duru & Poyrazli, 2011). Slightly outside of discrimination, neo-racism is a phenomenon that is described as the "discrimination on the basis of cultural difference or national origin rather than by physical characteristics alone and appeals to 'natural' tendencies to pre-serve group cultural identity" (Spears, 1999). With regards to international students, experiences of racism may be derived from stereotypes or preconceived notions rather than skin color. Unfortunately, many international students simply "get used to" different discriminatory remarks or behaviors against them (Lee & Rice, 2007). This widens the gap between themselves and the host culture, especially since the discrimination is simply accepted. Social connectedness with those who come from similar backgrounds has been found to buffer the negative impacts of discrimination (Wei et al., 2012).

Language Acquisition

Research has shown that language acquisition is among the most difficult barriers that international students face while acculturating to the host culture. Their English proficiency and confidence in their ability to communicate, comprehend, and interact on both an academic and social levels, influences their wellbeing and academic pursuits (Telbis, Helgeson, & Kingsbury, 2014). Linguistic challenges seemed to be the base on which all other issues (sociocultural, college adjustment, etc.) build upon. Not only do these challenges influence these students' academic performance directly and indirectly, they also interfere with their willingness to engage in dialogue with their domestic peers (Aune, Hendreickson, & Rosen, 2011; Jacob & Greggo, 2001). Discrimination is also another issue that is presented with the challenge of acquiring a new language; individuals may be stereotyped or experience hostility from host members because of the unnatural communication (Smith & Khawaja, 2011). For other individuals, feelings of embarrassment or shyness may take over their willingness to interact with those from the host culture, possibly leading to feelings of avoidance or isolation. Foreign language anxiety is a phenomenon that impacts the way one acquires a language. Students may stiffen up in fear when called on to participate during class due to their lack of confidence in their ability to speak the language adequately. Furthermore, because learning a new language is a cognitive skill as well as a social skill, anxiety may blunt the development in multiple ways (MacIntyre, 1995). This reflects the importance of intercultural interaction in language acquisition; quality communication and in-depth comprehension influences international students' ability to form meaningful relationships and their sense of belonging. Tompson and Tompson (1996) are two business professors whose research suggested that international students' most unproductive behaviors were clinging to those of similar backgrounds, lack of class participation, and not speaking up if they had questions about an assignment. Interestingly, this study also found that international students highly prioritized building social networks, acquiring proficient language skills, and becoming familiar with cultural norms. Although international students seem to want to engage socially with their peers of different backgrounds, their contradictory actions may reveal a feature about the environment's impact on self-efficacy. Additionally, there may be many programs set in place to aid international students with language acquisition; however, many are not adequate to help students foster language skills. This highlights the important role that the host culture may play in international students' acculturation process.

IMPLICATIONS FOR HIGHER EDUCATION

Future Directions

Research on belongingness in international students may provide suggestions for how higher education administration can support these students. As the differences between independent (individualistic) and interdependent (collectivistic) cultures may influence the acculturation experiences of international students, researchers may investigate the differential impact of sociocultural factors on domestic and international students. Although there is a growing body of literature on belonging among international students, future research should investigate different sources and aspects of social support available to Asian international students specifically, as the Asian populations makes up 65% of all international students in the United States (IIE, 2016). The Asian population is among the most understudied populations in American colleges, which has created a dearth of research regarding their psychological wellbeing and factors that may be harmful. Future researchers may consider studying subcultures of international student populations as within group differences may reveal unique characteristics that help buffer or exacerbate the negative influences of acculturative stress. In fact, Chinese students comprise 31.5% of the total Asian student population, therefore it may be helpful to examine unique characteristics of the Chinese culture in the context of belongingness and acculturation. Because there are many subgroups within international students, the distinctions among groups in the international student community are important to consider; this may include their cultural values, and how they relate to their acculturation process and distress. Secondly, international students' acculturation orientation and process may differ depending on location in the U.S. Cultural climates may vary widely depending on the geographic metrics of a particular university, possibly influencing international students' ability to adopt new values in a healthy manner and to cope. Thirdly, researchers may consider examining specific sources of social support and where they perceive the highest sense of belonging and in what context (Chavajay, 2013). Additionally, college attendance involves many stressful experiences that vary between undergraduate and graduate students; therefore, it is important to distinguish any characteristics between these two groups to help their population more effectively. Undergraduates may experience what it is like to live alone for the first time and fulfill new obligations. Graduate students, on the other hand, may need to learn how to fit their personal and cultural values in with the mainstream society while facing the other pressures that come with a highly competitive environment. International students are burdened with the same academic stresses that undergraduate and graduate students experience; however, their experiences are layered with acquiring a new language, living in a country with different sets of values, and not being in close proximity with their loved ones (Misra, Crist, & Burant, 2003; Searle & Ward, 1990). Examining the multifaceted nature of international students' acculturation experiences with these suggestions in mind may allow for a more comprehensive evaluation of their adaptation processes.

The Host Culture

Although there are many steps international students can take to assimilate or adopt cultural values of the host culture in a way that is most comfortable, the host culture may also be a part of a healthy, smooth transition. Institutions may modify the services they provide or how systems are set up that may hinder international students from succeeding or getting promoted. According to Rose-Redwood and Rose-Redwood (2013) colleges continue to struggle with fostering communication between the international and American students. Both American and international students experience some level of difficulty when it comes to establishing relationships. The "American experience" is one that may emphasize freedom, assertiveness, and egalitarian values. Even the method of communication may be a hindrance; American teachers or professors expect participation from students versus other Asian countries where students typically let their teachers lecture for the majority of class. Western teaching methods may lead international students to feel like they do not belong or as if they have not acquired the necessary skills to participate (Wong, 2004). Additionally, the various subcultures within the international student population may hold different cultural values; therefore, unique cultural differences should be taken into consideration.

Institutions may consider prioritizing actions to create an environment for international students to flourish socially and academically due to the strong research support behind the relationship between social and academic wellbeing. Diversity initiatives may set the groundwork for fostering authentic relationships, which has been supported by research to serve as a foundation for acculturation (Jang & Kim, 2010). Intensive English as a Second Language courses may also provide international students with a boost in confidence to engage with others from the mainstream culture. Sparking an interaction may come easier for international students through repeated trials and attempts, as long as they are supported throughout. Members of the host culture may encourage students to undertake additional language acquisition programs. The members of the mainstream culture may also try to make a conscious effort to try to understand the background and values of immigrants. Additionally, many Americans may lack the awareness needed to cater to these international students' psychosocial wellbeing. As international students continue to seek ways to feel connected, the institutions that are open to their presence should provide services to aid in the acculturation transition. Through awareness and curiosity, international students' domestic peers may also lend out a hand or simply engage in dialogue with them to help with their acculturation process.

Counseling Implications

Counselors may collaborate with the client to identify cultural differences in values, beliefs, and behaviors and encourage them to seek out opportunities in which they would feel most comfortable and open to new social and academic experiences. One study described several ways in which counselors can help international students adjust to a new cultural environment; counselors may focus with their client on developing more diverse social networks, learning how to adapt to local academic norms, rules, and regulations, and networking with others on the larger college campus (Sullivan & Kashubeck-West, 2015). As social support has been shown to act as a buffer against acculturative stress, international students may prioritize forming new bonds and friends with those in diverse circles. Previous research has shown that frequency of contact between international students and domestic peers was imperative to maintaining friendships and level of engagement with the institution as a whole. Furthermore, students were more likely to participate in various campus activities and explore additional opportunity to engage if they were in frequent contact with their domestic peers. Counselors may explain the benefits of intercultural contact and elaborate on how it increases multicultural competence, language proficiency, and overall better adjustment (de Wit, 1995; Gudykunst, 2004; Huntington & Bender, 1993).

As international students' cultural experiences play an important role in their process of adopting different values, counselors may choose to inquire about these issues and collaborate with faculty and staff to help international students adjust (Glazer, 2016). For example, one study showed that students who valued clear

143

rules and regulations for behavior had a harder time making friends and attending social gatherings. Counselors may encourage their clients to seek support from their faculty members in order to understand and engage in the academic and social systems. International students need a robust social support system in order to stay academically motivated and accomplish goals. This may further increase the possibility of engagement on the students' part (Mallinckrodt & Leong, 1992). Because diversity is said to be a critical part of personal and academic growth for all students, it is important that education is being delivered in a way that is comprehensible to all students (Simmons, 2011), and counselors may be able to play a part in giving their clients the verbal tools they need in order to modify their learning approaches. International students supplement the academic institutions in the United States in unique ways (Orchowski, 2008), it is essential that colleges are committed to providing the necessary resources for international students appropriately and that students are able to ask for them. Studies have also found that networking and building authentic friendships contributes to positive change for international students (Sawir, Marginson, & Deumert, 2008).

Previous research has shown that intercultural contact enhances thoughtful understanding and open-mindedness towards different cultures, thereby, reducing discrimination and prejudice. (Allport, 1954; Berry, 2006; Li & Gasser, 2005). It may be a social responsibility of and benefit to both the international students and the members of the host culture to engage in quality interaction. These relationships are a critical part of helping the client acculturate with a smooth transition. Over time, the bridging of these gaps will lead to a more inclusive, diverse society in which belongingness is more perceived rather than desired. Intercultural contact and care can create the opportunity to help all students adjust to or accept a new way of living, leading to a stronger sense of belongingness through the acceptance of cultural differences.

REFERENCES

Baba, Y., & Hosoda, M. (2014). Home away home: Better understanding of the role of social support in predicting cross-cultural adjustment among international students. *College Student Journal, 48*(1), 1–15.

Baumeister, R. F., & Leary, M. R. (1995). The need to belong: Desire for interpersonal attachments as a fundamental human motivation. *Psychological Bulletin, 117*(3), 497.

Berry, J. W. (2006). Acculturation: Living successfully in two cultures. *International Journal of Intercultural Relations, 29*(6), 697–712.

Berry, J. W. (2003). *Conceptual approaches to acculturation.* Washington, DC: American Psychological Association.

Berry, J. W. (1999). Intercultural relations in plural societies. *Canadian Psychology/Psychologie Canadienne, 40*(1), 12.

Bowlby, J. (1973). *Attachment and loss, vol. II: Separation.* New York, NY: Basic Books.

Campbell, N. (2011). Promoting intercultural contact on campus: A project to connect and engage international and host students. *Journal of Studies in International Education, 16*(3), 205–227.

Charles, H., & Stewart, M. A. (1991). Academic advising of international students. *Journal of Multicultural Counseling and Development, 19*(4), 173–181.

Chavajay, P. (2013). Perceived social support among international students at a US university. *Psychological Reports, 112*(2), 667–677.

Chuah, J. S., & Singh, M. K. M. (2016). International students' perspectives on the importance of obtaining social support from host national students. *International Education Studies, 9*(4), 132.

de Wit, H. (1995). *Strategies for the internationalisation of higher education: A comparative study of Australia, Canada, Europe and the United States of America*. Amsterdam: European Association for International Education.

Du, Y., & Wei, M. (2015). Acculturation, enculturation, social connectedness, and subjective well-being among Chinese international students. *The Counseling Psychologist, 43*(2), 299–325.

Duru, E., & Poyrazli, S. (2011). Perceived discrimination, social connectedness, and other predictors of adjustment difficulties among Turkish international students. *International Journal of Psychology, 46*(6), 446–454.

Freud, S. (1930). *Civilization and its discontents* (J. Strachey, Trans.). London: Hogarth Press.

Frey, L. L., & Roysircar, G. (2004). Effects of acculturation and worldview for white American, South American, South Asian, and Southeast Asian students. *International Journal for the Advancement of Counselling, 26*(3), 229–248.

Glass, C. R., & Westmont, C. M. (2013). Comparative effects of belongingness on the academic success and cross-cultural interactions of domestic and international students. *International Journal of Intercultural Relations, 38*, 106–119.

Gong, Y., & Fan, J. (2006). Longitudinal examination of the role of goal orientation in cross-cultural adjustment. *Journal of Applied Psychology, 91*(1), 176.

Goodenow, C. (1993). The psychological sense of school membership among adolescents: Scale development and educational correlates. *Psychology in the Schools, 30*(1), 79–90.

Gu, Q., & Maley, A. (2008). Changing places: A study of Chinese students in the UK. *Language and Intercultural Communication, 8*(4), 224–245.

Gudykunst, W. B. (2004). *Bridging differences: Effective intergroup communication*. London: Sage Publications.

Hausmann, L. R., Schofield, J. W., & Woods, R. L. (2007). Sense of belonging as a predictor of intentions to persist among African American and White first-year college students. *Research in Higher Education, 48*(7), 803–839.

Healey, N. M. (2008). Is higher education in really 'internationalising'? *Higher Education, 55*(3), 333–355.

Hoffman, M., Richmond, J., Morrow, J., & Salomone, K. (2002). Investigating "sense of belonging" in first-year college students. *Journal of College Student Retention: Research, Theory & Practice, 4*(3), 227–256.

Huntington, D. D., & Bender, W. N. (1993). Adolescents with learning disabilities at risk? Emotional well-being, depression, suicide. *Journal of Learning Disabilities, 26*(3), 159–166.

Hurtado, S., & Carter, D. F. (1997). Effects of college transition and perceptions of the campus racial climate on Latino college students' sense of belonging. *Sociology of Education, 70*(4), 324–345.

Hurtado, S., Han, J. C., Sáenz, V. B., Espinosa, L. L., Cabrera, N. L., & Cerna, O. S. (2007). Predicting transition and adjustment to college: Biomedical and behavioral science aspirants' and minority students' first year of college. *Research in Higher Education, 48*(7), 841–887.

Hurtado, S., & Ponjuan, L. (2005). Latino educational outcomes and the campus climate. *Journal of Hispanic Higher Education, 4*(3), 235–251.

Institute of International Education. (2016). *Open doors data: Community college data resource*. Retrieved from http://www.iie.org/en/Research-and-Insights/Open-Doors/Data/Community-College-Data-Resource

Iwamoto, D. K., & Liu, W. M. (2010). The impact of racial identity, ethnic identity, Asian values, and race-related stress on Asian Americans and Asian international college students' psychological well-being. *Journal of Counseling Psychology, 57*(1), 79.

Jackson, J. F., & Heggins III, W. J. (2003). Understanding the collegiate experience for Asian international students at a Midwestern research university. *College Student Journal, 37*(3), 379–391.

Jackson, M., Ray, S., & Bybell, D. (2013). International students in the US: Social and psychological adjustment. *Journal of International Students, 3*(1), 17–28.

Jacob, E. J., & Greggo, J. W. (2001). Using counselor training and collaborative programming strategies in working with international students. *Journal of Multicultural Counseling and Development, 29*(1), 73–88.

Jang, D., & Kim, D. Y. (2010). The influence of host cultures on the role of personality in the acculturation of exchange students. *International Journal of Intercultural Relations, 34*(4), 363–367.

Kenyon, K., Frohard-Dourlent, H., & Roth, W. D. (2012). Falling between the cracks: Ambiguities of international student status in Canada. *The Canadian Journal of Higher Education, 42*(1), 1.

Khawaja, N. G., & Stallman, H. M. (2011). Understanding the coping strategies of international students: A qualitative approach. *Australian Journal of Guidance and Counselling, 21*(2), 203.

Kim, G. S., Suyemoto, K. L., & Turner, C. B. (2010). Sense of belonging, sense of exclusion, and racial and ethnic identities in Korean transracial adoptees. *Cultural Diversity and Ethnic Minority Psychology, 16*(2), 179.

Lewthwaite, M. (1996). A study of international students' perspectives on cross-cultural adaptation. *International Journal for the Advancement of Counselling, 19*(2), 167–185.

Li, A., & Gasser, M. B. (2005). Predicting Asian international students' sociocultural adjustment: A test of two mediation models. *International Journal of Intercultural Relations, 29*(5), 561–576.

Lin, S. P., & Betz, N. E. (2009). Factors related to the social self-efficacy of Chinese international students. *The Counseling Psychologist, 37*(3), 451–471.

Maslow, A. H. (1970). *Motivation and personality.* New York, NY: Harper.

McIntyre, T. (1996b). Guidelines for providing appropriate services to culturally diverse students with emotional and/or behavioral disorders. *Behavioral Disorders, 21*(2), 137–144.

McLachlan, D. A., & Justice, J. (2009). A grounded theory of international student wellbeing. *Journal of Theory Construction & Testing, 13*(1), 27.

Misra, R., Crist, M., & Burant, C. J. (2003). Relationships among life stress, social support, academic stressors, and reactions to stressors of international students in the United States. *International Journal of Stress Management, 10*(2), 137.

Mori, S. C. (2000). Addressing the mental health concerns of international students. *Journal of Counseling & Development, 78*(2), 137–144.

Nadelson, L. S., Semmelroth, C., Martinez, G., Featherstone, M., Fuhrlman, C. A., & Sell, A. (2013). Why did they come here? The influences and expectations of first-year students' college experience. *Higher Education Studies, 3*, 50–62.

Orchowski, M. S. (2008). *Immigration and the American dream: Battling the political hype and hysteria.* Lanham, MD: Rowman & Littlefield.

O'Reilly, A., Ryan, D., & Hickey, T. (2010). The psychological well-being and sociocultural adaptation of short-term international students in Ireland. *Journal of College Student Development, 51*(5), 584–598.

Pittman, L. D., & Richmond, A. (2008). University belonging, friendship quality, and psychological adjustment during the transition to college. *The Journal of Experimental Education, 76*(4), 343–362.

Poyrazli, S., Kavanaugh, P. R., Baker, A., & Al-Timimi, N. (2004). Social support and demographic correlates of acculturative stress in international students. *Journal of College Counseling, 7*(1), 73–83.

Rajapaksa, S., & Dundes, L. (2002). It's a long way home: International student adjustment to living in the United States. *College Student Retention, 4*(1), 15–28.

Ramsay, S., Jones, E., & Barker, M. (2007). Relationship between adjustment and support types young and mature-aged local and international first year university students. *Higher Education, 54*(2), 247–265.

Rice, K. G., Choi, C. C., Zhang, Y., Morero, Y. I., & Anderson, D. (2012). Self-critical perfectionism, acculturative stress, and depression among international students. *The Counseling Psychologist, 40*(4), 575–600.

Rienties, B., & Nolan, E. M. (2014). Understanding friendship and learning networks of international and host students using longitudinal social network analysis. *International Journal of Intercultural Relations, 41*, 165–180.

Rose-Redwood, C. R., & Rose-Redwood, R. S. (2013). Self-segregation or global mixing? Social interactions and the international student experience. *Journal of College Student Development, 54*(4), 413–429.

Sandhu, D. S., & Asrabadi, B. R. (1994). Development of an acculturative stress scale for international students: Preliminary findings. *Psychological Reports, 75*(1), 435–448.

Sawir, E., Marginson, S., Deumert, A., Nyland, C., & Ramia, G. (2008). Loneliness and international students: An Australian study. *Journal of Studies in International Education, 12*(2), 148–180.

Searle, W., & Ward, C. (1990). The prediction of psychological and sociocultural adjustment during cross-cultural transitions. *International Journal of Intercultural Relations, 14*(4), 449–464.

Slaten, C. D., Elison, Z. M., Lee, J. Y., Yough, M., & Scalise, D. (2016). Belonging on campus a qualitative inquiry of Asian international students. *The Counseling Psychologist, 44*(3), 383–410.

Slaten, C. D., Ferguson, J. K., Allen, K. A., Brodrick, D. V., & Waters, L. (2016). School belonging: A review of the history, current trends, and future directions. *The Educational and Developmental Psychologist, 33*(1), 1–15.

Slaten, C. D., Yough, M. S., Shemwell, D. A., Scalise, D. A., Elison, Z. M., & Hughes, H. A. (2014). Eat, sleep, breathe, study: Understanding what it means to belong at a university from the student perspective. *Excellence in Higher Education, 5*(1), 1–5.

Smart, J. F., & Smart, D. W. (1995). Acculturative stress of hispanics: Loss and challenge. *Journal of Counseling and Development: JCD, 73*(4), 390.

Smith, R. A., & Khawaja, N. G. (2011). A review of the acculturation experiences of international students. *International Journal of Intercultural Relations, 35*(6), 699–713.

Soria, K. M., Troisi, J. N., & Stebleton, M. J. (2012). Reaching out, connecting within: Community service and sense of belonging among college students. *Higher Education in Review, 9*, 65–85.

Strayhorn, T. L. (2012). *College students' sense of belonging: A key to educational success for all students.* New York, NY: Routledge.

Suarez-Morales, L., Dillon, F. R., & Szapocznik, J. (2007). Validation of the acculturative stress inventory for children. *Cultural Diversity and Ethnic Minority Psychology, 13*(3), 216.

Sullivan, C., & Kashubeck-West, S. (2015). The interplay of international students' acculturative stress, social support, and acculturation modes. *Journal of International Students, 5*(1), 1–11.

Swagler, M. A., & Ellis, M. V. (2003). Crossing the distance: Adjustment of Taiwanese graduate students in the United States. *Journal of Counseling Psychology, 50*(4), 420.

Tan, S. A., & Liu, S. (2014). Ethnic visibility and preferred acculturation orientations of international students. *International Journal of Intercultural Relations, 39*, 183–187.

Telbis, N. M., Helgeson, L., & Kingsbury, C. (2014). International students' confidence and academic success. *Journal of International Students, 4*(4), 330–341.

Torres, K. (2009). 'Culture shock': Black students account for their distinctiveness at an elite college. *Ethnic and Racial Studies, 32*(5), 883–905.

Wang, C. C. D., & Mallinckrodt, B. (2006). Acculturation, attachment, and psychosocial adjustment of Chinese/Taiwanese international students. *Journal of Counseling Psychology, 53*(4), 422.

Wang, K. T., Heppner, P. P., Fu, C. C., Zhao, R., Li, F., & Chuang, C. C. (2012). Profiles of acculturative adjustment patterns among Chinese international students. *Journal of Counseling Psychology, 59*(3), 424.

Wong, J. K. K. (2004). Are the learning styles of Asian international students culturally or contextually based? *International Education Journal, 4*(4), 154–166.

Yoon, E., Lee, R. M., & Goh, M. (2008). Acculturation, social connectedness, and subjective well-being. *Cultural Diversity and Ethnic Minority Psychology, 14*(3), 246.

Young, T. J., Sercombe, P. G., Sachdev, I., Naeb, R., & Schartner, A. (2013). Success factors for international postgraduate students' adjustment: Exploring the roles of intercultural competence, language proficiency, social contact and social support. *European Journal of Higher Education, 3*(2), 151–171.

Bini Sebastian
Department of Educational, School, and Counseling Psychology
University of Missouri-Columbia
USA

Christopher D. Slaten
Department of Educational, School, and Counseling Psychology
University of Missouri-Columbia
USA

SUE ROFFEY AND CHRISTOPHER BOYLE

9. BELIEF, BELONGING AND THE ROLE OF SCHOOLS IN REDUCING THE RISK OF HOME-GROWN EXTREMISM

INTRODUCTION

Recent world events have led to an increased sense of collective fear directed to those perceived as outside the mainstream. This chapter posits that much of that fear is generated by beliefs about others, often stirred by a negative media and political interests. This is also true of those who engage in terrorism – their acts are driven by beliefs that comprise not so much religious faith but as a way of making sense of the world. There is much evidence to suggest that military responses to terrorism are counter-productive as are programs aimed at identifying at risk individuals (Byrne, 2017). It has been suggested that more effective anti-terrorism strategies need to focus on the 'normality' of people who commit atrocities and intervene early. This includes both community engagement and building an educational climate that breaks down stereotypes and addresses both values and compassion (Singer & Bolz, 2013).

There has been much debate across the world about the radicalisation of young men and women, some of them committing horrific acts of violence in the name of religion. Because this is their stated purpose, millions of peace-loving people become erroneously associated with these acts, compounding a negative cycle of mistrust and blame.

This chapter explores alternative constructions of motivation and how important a sense of belonging and purpose may be. It may not make sense to most of us, but when young people come to believe that they can achieve 'significance' and belonging by acts of terror we need to consider what is happening that makes them more open to adopting this stance and what might be done to reduce their vulnerability to persuasion. We make links with those who have committed acts of mass murder in schools in the US and what the research has to say about this. As many acts of terrorism are perpetrated by 'home-grown' terrorists most of whom have been educated in the country in which these acts take place, we suggest what schools might do to reduce the risk – especially in promoting a culture of inclusive belonging.

THE DICHOTOMY BETWEEN BELIEF AND EVIDENCE AND HOW THIS IMPACTS ON BEHAVIOUR

Although policy makers talk about the need for evidence based practice, the reality is that it is belief that often determines behaviour. This is not necessarily religious

© KONINKLIJKE BRILL NV, LEIDEN, 2018 | DOI:10.1163/9789004386969_009

faith but a conceptual construction about how the world works, how people are or should be, and what values predominate. It is also about what you believe about yourself – and your place in the world. Kelly's personal construct theory (1955) posits that such constructs provide a filter through which experiences are both anticipated and perceived. The same experience may be interpreted differently by individuals, depending on the lens each has developed over time – predominantly in their interactions with others and the cultures in which these are embedded. One example of this is 'Belief in a Just World' (Lerner, 1980) that says people get what they deserve. This underpins the American Dream; if you work hard you will be successful, if you fail you have only yourself to blame. It follows, therefore, that no matter the background, everyone has the chance to be successful if they put in the effort. Although there are elements of reality here, this fails to account for chance, including to whom and where you were born and consequent opportunity. It risks demonising those who fall on hard times despite their efforts and does not acknowledge that some people begin life with a significant advantage. You can see the impact of this belief on individual, community and federal decisions, reinforced in the media and in certain political rhetoric (Benabou & Tirole, 2006).

In the absence of scientific evidence, past communities have chosen to believe what makes sense to them – such as the earth is flat. With greater knowledge and evidence this particular belief has changed. However, we appear to be coming full circle, with the establishment of a 'post-truth' era where evidence is not only slanted but replaced by statements of what others would have us believe. One example is climate change. Those with a vested interest in the coal industry are more likely to be cynical about the raft of scientific evidence warning us of the dangers of anthropomorphic global warming – and will choose to believe those public voices who support their position.

But maybe it has always been the case that we believe what suits our purpose and/or fits with the dominant culture – or at least the one we feel an attachment to. If the rhetoric engages emotions that promote a sense of belonging and purpose, this can build motivation to engage with a shared endeavour. When young people are told that they will achieve 'glory' if they kill those who represent 'western' values and practices, and there are few other avenues open to their feeling important, then fighting for such a cause may be appealing. Millions of young men died in the First World War doing their patriotic duty. So strong was the sense of shared belief in doing 'their part' that conscientious objectors were despised and vilified. These comparisons may be uncomfortable but perhaps bring greater understanding on which we can begin to build a useful response to the threats facing us.

We all live in something called 'society'. It is a term often used to convey a collective whole, but difficult to define as a place where we, as a group of people, exist. The collective notion of society eludes definition because the strands that intertwine form such a 'complexity of detail' (Steele, 2009). Therefore, when we read such terms as 'the effect on society' we know that at face value this holds little meaning. Nevertheless, we do have commonalities which bind certain aspects of our functioning such as schools, neighbourhoods and families.

Many nations today are built on historical immigration and therefore a powerful mix of culture, religion, language and DNA. There is a collective notion that others 'unlike us' are to be feared and that we have to protect what has become our own 'collective' interests. We create borders, security, tariffs, controls especially applied to people or organisations who are seen as attempting to gain access to whatever it is 'we' have. By doing this we advance the potential to feel unsafe, untrusting and in fear of others. This political zeitgeist exists in various forms and operates at different levels within structural units. The obvious and visible creations are that of the army and the need to have a large military to protect ourselves, and 'of course' they also must have nuclear weapons to be effective. This is done in the name of peace, as protection is supposedly the key to this. There are cameras in every location said to be for public protection. In schools, children are warned from an early age, of the dangers of strangers and in some schools there are security personnel on campus. Doors are locked and it is hard for anyone to gain entry without permission. All of this creates a level of fear, despite the overarching message about protection and safety. The issue of terrorism in the UK (and elsewhere) has increased the perception of a lack of safety.

Alongside the raised security/fear levels, a 'them and us' construct has been perpetrated that seeks to put whole sections of the community 'outside' the collective norm. Beliefs perpetrated in the media for instance often include the motivations, intentions and characters of others – such as refugees, asylum seekers and those from minority groups. The aberrant behaviour of one, or a few, can perpetrate beliefs about all others within the same category.

BELIEFS ABOUT HUMAN NATURE – ARE WE SELFISH OR ALTRUISTIC?

What we believe – not just about certain groups but about human nature itself – colours our world and how we position others, determining our actions towards them. There has long been a wide spectrum of views about one of the most fundamental tenets of human nature. Has selfishness or sharing determined the path of evolution? One belief, long held in Western individualist culture, is that human beings are basically self-interested. This is at the basis of assertions that competition is more 'natural' than collaboration and life is about the 'survival of the fittest'. From Hobbes in *Leviathan* (1651) to Dawkins (1976) this position has often been taken as a 'given'. In *The Selfish Gene* (1976) Dawkins states "*If you wish, as I do, to build a society in which individuals cooperate generously and unselfishly towards a common good, you can expect little help from biological nature ... we are born selfish*". At the other end of the spectrum are those who believe that human beings are basically altruistic and that the human race would have long died out if collaborative effort was not a fundamental for survival. Selfishness and actions taken solely for personal gain put the group at risk.

The argument put forward in Dawkins' seminal work suggests that we are all only 'replicating machines' and that the really important aspect of our existence is that of carrying, protecting, and passing on our genes. If this argument is agreed upon then it would suggest that we are inherently selfish beings. Dobbs (2013) suggests that this theory has no scientific or mathematical basis and that the original work of W. D. Hamilton (1964) was based on flawed assumptions. That aside, the notion put forward of *inclusive fitness* and thus the basis of kin altruism suggests that we calculate our work with others based on what we can gain or more accurately, what our genes can gain. The overarching theme is that we may work collectively but only if it is in the interests of the individual. The notion of human selfishness is clearly not a new concept and Plato (1955) in *The Republic* wrote about the nature of human nature being 'good' unless it was believed that 'nobody is watching' "… and then they can act without fear of retribution or besmirching of their own character, thus with impunity" (Boyle, 2014a, p. 170). Plato explained this in the story of *The Ring of Gyges* (Plato, 1955) and whilst he was mostly discussing ethical and moral issues it clearly applies to the notion of inclusive fitness and the selfish gene argument. However, and quite importantly, none of these explain general acts of altruism where someone with no familial (and thus genetic) connection saves another and puts their own life in extreme danger.

Despite Dawkins' original theory that in evolutionary terms our genes are 'born selfish', and Plato's assertion that we can act unethically if we have the opportunity, the evidence indicates that human beings are fundamentally social animals and this is evident from birth. Social connection is essential for optimal development, not only for survival into adulthood but also our ability to flourish and learn. Unless a human carer responds to their baby's attempts to engage them in social interaction the synapses between brain cells make fewer connections and both social and emotional development and learning are inhibited (Gerhardt, 2006). A baby's smile at six weeks is a survival mechanism as this fosters and rewards response in adults. Empathetic, supportive attachments and relationships are essential to optimize brain development and maturity (Seigel, 2012).

Magnetic resonance imaging shows we are hard-wired to connect with each other in many ways, confirming what psychologists have long known from observational studies – that we are interdependent beings and this is not restricted to childhood. We now know from epigenetic studies that what happens in the environment not only changes behaviour but may also alter the structure of our brains. It appears that the way others behave towards us may serve to enable or inhibit genetic pre-dispositions (Huttenlocher, 2002). The quality of our relationships with others matters even more than we imagined (Johnson, 2008; Roffey, 2017).

The human brain is not only primed for connection but also favours pro-social interactions. Although the hormone oxytocin has a primary function in the reproductive system, researchers are increasingly interested in its influence on social behaviour. Although still under investigation there is evidence not only for its essential role in maternal bonding (Feldman et al., 2007) but also increasing trust (Kosfield et al., 2005), increasing positive communication (Ditzen et al., 2009), and reducing stress and anxiety, making it more possible to take risks in interactions (Heinrichs et al., 2003). There appears to be increasing evidence for a positive feedback loop at play in social interactions (Crockford et al., 2013). Positive interactions raise oxytocin levels that then foster greater warmth and cooperation between people. The mirror neurons in our brain make emotions contagious and these may transfer beyond individual relationships to those that determine cultural norms. This is evident in political rallies where the power of leaders is often determined by how much they can stir an audience and then shape mass thought and behaviour.

FEELING YOU BELONG

If our biology so clearly primes us for social connection it is unsurprising that feeling accepted within your social group is a factor for healthy functioning. Baumeister and Leary (1995) argue that it counts as one of our basic human needs, along with sustenance and shelter. Identities are formed in our relationship with others – the groups to whom we are affiliated, shapes who we are and who we become.

A sense of belonging has multiple domains. It can exist within families, both close and extended, within friendship groups or within workplace or professional networks. Where cultures put a higher value on interdependence rather than autonomy belonging to the group can override individual considerations (Markus & Kitayama, 1991)

Positive membership of groups, whether they be friendship networks, strong families or healthy communities can provide social and psychological support, protect and aid in times of need and facilitate access to resources (Duncan et al., 2007). There is evidence that feeling you belong, promotes resilience and mental health (Oliver et al., 2006; Werner & Smith, 2001) and where connections to *positive* groups are actively fostered this may inhibit violence and anti-social behaviour (Wilson, 2004; Wolfe et al., 1997).

Also, relevant in a discussion on belonging is what happens when people experience rejection. People have a powerful, negative, deep-rooted reaction to being socially rejected. The brain treats social pain and physical pain in similar ways and this is particularly evident in the emotional response to social exclusion (Macdonald & Leary, 2005). Unlike physical sensations however, this pain can return whenever the incident is remembered (Williams & Nida, 2011).

Social exclusion has been shown to quickly induce negative moods within most people (Baumeister & Leary, 1995) and inhibit feelings of belonging, self-esteem, perceptions of control over the environment, and perceptions of leading a meaningful existence (Williams & Zadro, 2005). Bernstein et al. (2010) review research that supports the view that negative feelings are elicited just as strongly by being actively excluded from groups to which the individual does not have or seek a particular affiliation as by a group in which he or she seems themselves as an "in-member".

Inclusive and Exclusive Belonging

Exclusive belonging occurs when only those who 'fit' the group are seen as worthy of membership. Putnam (2000) refers to this as 'bonding' social capital. "[This] is a term used to describe the particular features of social relationships within a group or community" (Catholic Education Office, 2007). Feeling that you are one of a select group can be a powerful agent for the wellbeing and self-esteem of those inside (Hewstone et al., 2002) but may be devastating for those outside. In order to maintain inner group cohesion, those outside can be positioned as inferior and possibly as 'objects', making them 'legitimate' targets for abuse. Students who are most vulnerable to being bullied in Australia are those against whom there is social prejudice related to race, disability, obesity, homophobia, and material deprivation (Rigby & Johnson, 2016).

Inclusive belonging, on the other hand, places a high value on welcoming others, celebrating diversity and facilitating the active participation of all. It acknowledges and values individual strengths whilst seeking commonalities. Putnam (2000) refers to this as 'bridging social capital' – bringing people together in the interest of achieving mutually agreed goals. In Buber's (1923/1996) therapeutic dialogue such relationships are referred to as having an 'I-you' orientation. Goleman (2007) says that this is demonstrated in everyday actions of respect and courtesy moving to affection and admiration in closer relationships. In order to have an 'I-you' orientation you need to believe that others have value simply by virtue of being a fellow human being.

HOW THIS PLAYS OUT IN THE RADICALISATION OF YOUNG PEOPLE

Many of the atrocities perpetrated in the name of a religious group are by young men – or sometimes women – who have mostly been living in the country of the crime they commit (Stuart, 2017). Evidence is strong that religion is not the primary motivator for joining violent extremists like ISIS (Butler, 2015) but more likely to be used to 'legitimize personal and collective frustrations and justify violent ideologies' (Lyons-Padilla et al., 2015, p. 2). When there is a call for jihad, for example, very few individuals respond – for most people this is antithetical to their faith. Extremists are therefore not acting on the basis of religious belief but the belief that they need to matter. They are seeking a sense of meaning, of connection and of giving their lives some significance (Kruglanski et al., 2014).

The Australian Policy Unit found three shared characteristics of those young people who become violent extremists (Jennings, 2015). They had a sense of injustice or humiliation, they had a need for identity and purpose and a need to belong. Most had completed school with qualifications but that evidently wasn't enough. "Overall, our assessment shows a group of people clearly failing to gain satisfaction or friendship in mainstream Australian life" (p. 13). Williams et al. (2015) also highlight the importance of friendships for countering the risk of radicalisation.

An individual example of this is Mohammed Emwazi, who later became known as Jihadi John. He achieved notoriety being filmed carrying out a beheading. Following this atrocity, he was reported in the UK media to have been a 'good student' who went to university and then worked successfully as an IT salesman in Kuwait (Chulov, 2015). In current educational terms, he was a success. It was also reported, however, that he was smaller and weaker than most students, was regularly bullied outside the school gates, had low self-esteem and at some point was given help with anger management (Topping, Halliday, & Ismail, 2015).

There is some synergy between the genesis of radicalization and other incidents of mass violence. Wike and Fraser (2009) explored similarities in the incidents of 109 killings in US schools since 1999, and found there had been high levels of social stratification where some students were seen as stars and others rejected as losers. The primary recommendation from this research is strengthening school attachment.

A review of 'zero tolerance policies' by the American Psychological Association (Skiba et al., 2006), found that schools who quickly exclude students, not only perpetrate a 'school to prison pipeline' for disadvantaged youth, but that both behavioural standards and academic attainment deteriorate throughout the school. This is attributed to reduced trust and relational quality between students and staff. This study recommends promoting stronger community connections.

Other studies show that schools with less violence tend to have students who are aware of school rules and believe they are fair, have positive relationships with their teachers, feel that they have ownership in their school, feel that they are in a classroom and school environment that is positive and focused on learning, and in an environment that is orderly (Johnson, 2007).

Relational quality in a school therefore matters not only for academic outcomes (Hattie, 2009) but also for how people feel about themselves and their developing identity. It is the micro-moments of interactions that can make the difference and although often seen as the soft side of education it is becoming clearer that this has far more impact than hitherto acknowledged. Programmes in school that focus on wellbeing through utilising positive psychology (Seligman et al., 2009; Roffey, 2014; Chodkiewicz & Boyle, 2017) and attributions retraining (Bosnjak et al., 2017; Chodkiewicz & Boyle, 2014, 2016) alongside many others, demonstrate there is much more awareness of the importance of social interaction and wellbeing in schools nowadays. The school experience at the individual level is paramount. No matter how visible government initiatives may be, it is about the level of marginality that students experience from their own perspective; whether they are included or not within their peer group (Boyle, 2014b). In schools there can be different social groups that are created through social interaction and this can lead to some students being classified as popular and others who would be rejected (Boyle, 2015). This is especially relevant for students who have sought asylum in a new country and must join the schooling system and who will face difficulties achieving satisfactory belonging in school (Gunasekera et al., 2014). This potential for marginalisation is high within some school situations. The culture within the school can be crucial to ensuring that students are able to feel a sense of belonging.

THE CULTURE OF SCHOOLS

Schools often promote a sense of group identity that may be demonstrated in uniform policies, support for sporting teams and pride in academic successes. Honour boards list the names of star students. Whether everyone in a school experiences a sense of belonging however, depends on the beliefs and practices that predominate in school culture. Where that culture is positioned as the only one which is 'correct', and that 'others' need to conform to specific values, expectations and behaviours in order to be fully accepted as a member of that community, some students may experience marginalisation, or even rejection.

The cultural norms of schools are usually those of the dominant society. Through the hidden curriculum, students often receive messages that re-inforce the values, beliefs and ideologies of mainstream society (Sari & Dogenay, 2009). Teachers who select classroom resources that reflect the majority culture may send a message to students that minority cultures are perhaps less valued. Students who are considered 'non-traditional' may not have that sense of belonging and feel disengaged or alienated (Dei et al., 1997). Whereas Aldridge and colleagues (2016) found that school connectedness positively and directly influenced students' life satisfaction and sense of wellbeing, affirming diversity was negatively correlated. The authors cite Deardoff (2006), who asserts that although schools may welcome students from diverse backgrounds, the school community may lack the knowledge, skills and attitudes to meaningfully harmonise this diversity. Processes need to be put into place to develop the intercultural competencies within a school population in order to affect a fully inclusive culture (Kickett-Tucker & Coffin, 2011).

Chiu and colleagues (2015) explored a sense of belonging in school with 193,841 fifteen-year-old students in 41 countries, and found that the quality of relationships with teachers and peers accounted for most of the variance. Specifically, students' perceptions of their teacher – encouraging participation, enthusiasm, friendliness, helpfulness, organisation, and preparation – accounted for nearly half of the variance in students' sense of belonging in class (Freeman et al., 2007).

More hierarchical cultures, however, had weaker relationships with teachers and this led to a lower sense of belonging at school. A lower sense of belonging was particularly noted for students who were first-generation immigrants, spoke a foreign language at home, were poorer or had less books at home. More similarity between students also increased a sense of connectedness at school (Thompson et al., 2006).

Beliefs about students and the purpose of education, the vision of school leaders and the level of focus on relational values and skills determine whether or not social capital in schools is actively fostered – and the extent to which this is used for the common good or to privilege those who can succeed and boost the school's reputation (Roffey, 2013). There have been multiple nuanced definitions over time but social capital is not a new concept. In 1916, Dewey suggested social capital was a valuable resource that would develop when individuals connected to others in meaningful ways. He went on to say that social capital is lost to any society that does not provide the environment and education necessary to bring out the best in any individual.

> Men (*sic*) live in a community in virtue of the things which they have in common; and communication is the way in which they come to possess things in common. What they must have in common in order to form a community or society are aims, beliefs, aspirations, knowledge – a common understanding – likemindedness as the sociologists say. (Dewey, 1916, p. 4)

The link between the individual and the system that people operate within is fundamental to psychological wellbeing and psychology in general. If we consider it at the human level, then Maslow's theory about human needs (Maslow, 1943) comes to the fore in the context of this discussion. According to Maslow an individual has different levels of need from basic needs such as food and water through other levels to those of self-fulfillment. As we have discussed in this chapter (and the theme throughout the book), the importance of belonging cannot be underestimated. In a school context in order to fulfil overall psychological needs there has to be some sort of relationship within the school, whether that be with peers, staff, or a combination. But in essence the person needs to have friendships and feel that their presence matters. This is so that a connection becomes possible and thus, the all-important sense of belonging. Without this then it becomes difficult to realise other, more complex, needs such as Maslow's well known higher need of self-actualisation. This requires opportunities to achieve one's potential and could apply to various aspects of development including social and/or academic. If these needs are not met then there is the potential for a disconnect with school and possibly the wider community. It could be argued that the longer this goes on, the higher the possibility that disaffection will become an issue first within school and then potentially in the wider community.

SO HOW CAN SCHOOLS MAKE A DIFFERENCE?

The well-being of students in the school community is promoted through developing connectedness and social capital. Social capital is a term used to describe the particular features of social relationships within a group or community. This includes such things as the extent of trust between people; whether they have a shared understanding of how they should behave toward, and care for one another (Catholic Education Office, 2007).

Human beings are primed to prefer associations with 'those like us' (Mitchell et al., 2006) which poses challenges for the healthy functioning of our multi-cultural world and an inclusive sense of belonging in schools. We do however know that there are differences between institutions and those that actively promote inclusion have higher levels of wellbeing and fewer incidents of violence (Johnson, 2009).

Catalano and colleagues (2004) define school connectedness as two interrelated components. The first is affective, supportive relationships, and the second is commitment – where students perceive themselves as doing well and have an investment in being there. Schools need to provide a learning environment that is not only safe, caring and supportive, but also one where student strengths are identified so each individual sees themselves as progressing and achieving.

To feel a sense of belonging at school students need to believe that they matter, that their contributions are valued and others care about them (Boyle, 2007; Osterman, 2000; Solomon et al., 1996). In 2003, a National Strategy for School Connectedness in the US entitled the Wingspread Declaration asserted that:

> Students are more likely to succeed when they feel connected to school. School connection is the belief by students that adults in the school care about their learning as well as about them as individuals.

Students who feel more accepted and connected in school are more likely to experience positive academic emotions, including pride, happiness, hope, satisfaction, calmness and relaxation (Lam et al., 2015) and less likely to feel bored, fatigued, anxious, ashamed or hopeless (Pekrun et al., 2002). A greater sense of school belonging and positive academic emotions may work together to create a positive appraisal of students' beliefs about their own learning abilities that consequently contribute to student academic success.

Students who feel rejected in school often feel depressed and helpless while learning because of social isolation (Buhs et al., 2006). This may undermine students' cognitive appraisal of their control over learning-related tasks because of their perception of a lack of support from their peers and teachers in school. This perceived lack of support may subsequently disturb the positive and stable emotional states (e.g. calm or satisfied) that are helpful for academic achievement.

Feeling connected at a school, however goes way beyond academic achievement. Students with higher sense of school belonging have also been found to have better psychological health, including less depression, lower rates of delinquency, stronger peer acceptance, fewer incidences of dropping out of school and less use of illicit drugs (Anderman, 2002; Finn, 1989).

Congruent with Bronfenbrenner's ecological theory (2005) relationships in schools are bi-directional and nested. A sense of belonging contributes to positive psychological and social factors while psychological and social factors influence a sense of belonging (e.g. Willms, 2003; Anderson, Boyle, & Deppeler, 2014). Family and community contexts also impact on how connected students feel at school.

INTERVENTIONS

Inclusive belonging within the learning environment does not develop by chance. It requires the following:

- Leadership that honours and values the whole child and every child (Roffey, 2007; Hattie, 2009).
- School and student wellbeing as core school business (Wyn et al., 2000).
- Intercultural understanding that includes the skills to critically reflect on one's own culture as well as positive, cooperative, and respectful interactions between people of diverse cultural backgrounds at both an institutional and interpersonal level (DEEWR, 2009).
- A focus on how intra and interpersonal understanding and skills determine the quality of relationships and the level of social capital across the organisation (Bird & Sultman, 2010).
- Social and emotional learning within an appropriate pedagogy (Roffey & McCarthy, 2013; Roffey, 2014).

When both students and staff develop a sense of shared humanity, focusing on and actively exploring commonalities, then it is possible that beliefs about the 'other' will change.

In Australia, many Indigenous students find school difficult, discouraging and alienating, and many respond to their disaffection from school by withdrawing or resisting education (Partingon & Gray, 2003). Resistance to formal education by Aboriginal students is often seen as a cultural response to schooling occurring when there are perceptions of inequality in the classroom (Rahman, 2013).

One way to foster resilience in young people is through meaningful youth participation. Over four years, more than 50 young women have been part of the Aboriginal Girls Circle initiative and there is evidence (Dobia et al., 2014) that there have been significant improvements in confidence, a sense of connection, relational skills and leadership qualities in some, if not all, of the participants. Several girls have changed their aspirations about their own future. Staff have seen positive changes in behaviour, attendance and engagement. Most of the adults involved have not only identified changes in the girls but also in themselves. This initiative has thrown up issues about the need for intercultural awareness and greater community engagement at the whole school level. Fiske (quoted in Byrne, 2017) also comments of the value of similar projects where people are working together to achieve a common goal. In order to break down stereotypes she says that it has to be something people care about and are prepared to invest in. "Success depends on understanding the minds of your collaborators – "rehumanising them" (p. 34).

WHERE TO FROM HERE?

Although direct and indirect political responses to terrorism have been documented, the psychological mechanisms underlying these responses remain isolated and less well understood (Stevens, 2013). We need to use the evidence that is available to develop a multi-faceted and long-term approach to make our communities safer for everyone.

Institutional cultures are key to student engagement and wellbeing. Culture is created in the way people talk to and about each other. It is demonstrated in the micro-moments of interaction and what can be heard in classrooms and seen on the walls of corridors. It is about what is both overtly and covertly valued. It is the opportunities people have to contribute, and whether or not they have an authentic voice.

The pathways to wellbeing identified in the Australian scoping study on student wellbeing (Noble et al., 2008) include: physical and emotional safety, pro-social values, a supportive and caring school community, a strengths-based approach and social and emotional learning. These pathways address various interrelated aspects of connectedness within an ecological framework, including both the content and the context for learning positive relationships (Roffey, 2010, 2012).

Although not offered as an answer to the complex issue of radicalisation, it is valid to question what schools might do to enhance a sense of wellbeing and inclusion within the educational environment that will reduce the need for individuals to find a sense of significance by committing atrocities. They may not do this whilst still at school but what they have learnt about themselves, their fellow learners and their teachers in those institutions will have far reaching outcomes for their future.

It is also relevant to ask whether education needs to re-prioritise social and emotional learning and the promotion of shared humanity – exploring what we have in common as well as valuing unique differences. One answer is to provide an environment in which students are not only treated equally and with respect but that there is a focus on connecting with each other by focusing on what they share. The overriding focus on academic outcomes has undermined the significance of learning about each other – and the development of empathy.

CONCLUSION

This chapter has shown that human beings are social creatures with a need to belong and to feel that they matter. Schools are one of the many sites that young at-risk people find themselves. Sometimes we know which students are vulnerable but more often it is those who keep their head down and are given little attention who end up as home-grown terrorists. Research suggests that schools that find ways for these individuals to gain a sense of significance, honour their culture and promote a sense of 'shared humanity' with others that encourages understanding and empathy might just help make us all just that bit safer.

REFERENCES

Aldridge, J. M., Fraser, B. J., Fozdar, F., Ala'i, K., Earnest, J., & Afari, E. (2016). Students' perceptions of school climate as determinants of wellbeing, resilience and identity. *Improving Schools, 19*(1), 5–26. doi:10.1177/1365480215612616

Anderman, E. M. (2002). School effects on psychological outcomes during adolescence. *Journal of Educational Psychology, 94*(4), 795–809. doi:10.1037/0022-0663.94.4.795

Anderson, J., Boyle, C., & Deppeler, J. (2014). The ecology of inclusive education: Reconceptualising Bronfenbrenner. In Z. Zhang, P. W. K. Chan, & C. Boyle (Eds.), *Equality in education: Fairness and inclusion* (pp. 23–34). Rotterdam, The Netherlands: Sense Publishers.

Baumeister, R. F., & Leary, M. R. (1995). The need to belong: Desire for interpersonal attachments as a fundamental human motivation. *Psychological Bulletin, 117*(3), 497–529. doi:10.1037/0033-2909.117.3.497

Benabou, R., & Tirole, J. (2006). Belief in a just world and redistributive politics. *The Quarterly Journal of Economics, 121*(2), 699–745.

Bernstein, M. J., Sacco, D. F., Young, S. G., Hugenberg, K., & Cook, E. (2010). Being "in" with the in-crowd: The effects of social exclusion and inclusion are enhanced by the perceived essentialism of ingroups and outgroups. *Personality and Social Psychology Bulletin, 36*(8), 999–1009. doi:10.1177/0146167210376059

Bird, K. A., & Sultmann, W. F. (2010). Social and emotional learning: Reporting a system approach to developing relationships, nurturing wellbeing and invigorating learning. *Educational and Child Psychology, 27*(1), 143–155.

Bosnjak, A., Boyle, C., & Chodkiewicz, A. R. (2017). An intervention to retrain attributions using CBT: A pilot study. *The Educational and Developmental Psychologist, 34*(1), 21–32. doi:10.1017/edp.2017.1

Boyle, C. (2014a). Professional and interprofessional ethical considerations for practising psychologists in Australia. In D. Jindal-Snape & B. Hannah (Eds.), *Exploring the dynamics of ethics in practice: Personal, professional and interprofessional dilemmas* (pp. 167–179) Bristol: Policy Press.

Boyle, C. (2014b). Labelling in special education: Where do the benefits lie? In A. Holliman (Ed.), *The Routledge international companion to educational psychology* (pp. 213–221). London: Routledge.

Boyle, C. (2015). Social and interpersonal development in schools. In A. Ashman (Ed.), *Education for inclusion and diversity* (5th ed., pp. 367–400). Frenchs Forest: Pearson Australia.

Boyle, C. M. (2007). An analysis of the efficacy of a motor skills training programme for young people with moderate learning difficulties. *International Journal of Special Education, 22*(1), 11–24.

Bronfenbrenner, U. (2005). The developing ecology of human development: Paradigm lost or paradigm regained. In U. Bronfenbrenner (Ed.), *Making human beings human: Bioecological perspectives on human development* (pp. 94–105). Thousand Oaks, CA: Sage Publications.

Buber, M. (1996). *I and thou* (W. Kauffman, Trans.). New York, NY: Simon and Schuster. (Original work published, 1923)

Buhs, E. S., Ladd, G. W., & Herald, S. H. (2006). Peer exclusion and victimisation: Processes that mediate the relation between peer group rejection and children's classroom engagement and achievement. *Journal of Educational Psychology, 98*(1), 1–13. doi:0.1037/0022-0663.98.1.1

Butler, D. (2015). Terrorism science: 5 insights into jihad in Europe. *Nature, 528,* 20–21. doi:10.1038/528020a

Byrne, P. (2017, August). Anatomy of terror: What makes normal people become extremists? *New Scientist.* Retrieved from https://goo.gl/aZ2AmE

Catalano, R. F., Haggerty, K. P., Oesterle, S., Fleming, C. B., & Hawkins, J. D. (2004). The importance of bonding to school for healthy development: Findings from the social development research group. *Journal of School Health, 74*(7), 252–261. doi:10.1111/j.1746-1561.2004.tb08281.x

Catholic Education Office. (2007). *Enhancing Relationships in School Communities (ERIS). Phase 1 report (2004–2006).* Melbourne: University of Melbourne.

Chiu, M. M., Chow, B. W.-Y., McBride, C., & Mol, S. T. (2016). Students sense of belonging at school in 41 countries: Cross-cultural variability. *Journal of Cross-Cultural Psychology, 47*(2), 175–196. doi:10.1177/0022022115617031

Chodkiewicz, A. R., & Boyle, C. (2014). Exploring the contribution of attribution retraining to student perceptions and the learning process. *Educational Psychology in Practice, 30*(1), 78–87. doi:10.1080/02667363.2014.880048

Chodkiewicz, A. R., & Boyle, C. (2016). Promoting positive learning in students aged 10–12 years using attribution retraining and cognitive behavioural therapy: A pilot study. *School Psychology International, 37*(5), 519–535. doi:10.1177/0143034316667114

Chodkiewicz, A. R., & Boyle, C. (2017). Positive psychology school-based interventions: A reflection on current success and future directions. *Review of Education, 5*(1), 60–86. doi:10.1002/rev3.3080

Chulov, M. (2015, March 2). The best employee we ever had: Mohammed Emwazi's former boss in Kuwait. *The Guardian.* Retrieved from https://goo.gl/9b1Ud4

Crockford, C., Deschner, T., Zeigler, T. E., & Wittig, R. M. (2013). Endogenous peripheral oxytocin measures can give insight into the dynamics of social relationships: A review. *Frontiers in Behavioural Neuroscience, 8*, 68. doi:10.3389/fnbeh.2014.00068

Dawkins, R. (1976). *The selfish gene.* New York, NY: Oxford University Press.

Deardorff, D. (2006). Identification and assessment of intercultural competence as a student outcome of inter-nationalization. *Journal of Studies in International Education, 10*(4), 241–266. doi:10.1177/1028315306001000409

DEEWR. (2009). *Teaching for intercultural understanding: Professional learning program.* Canberra: Commonwealth Government of Australia.

Dei, G. J. S., Mazzuca, J., McIsaac, E., & Zine, J. (1997). *Reconstructing 'drop-out': A critical ethnography of Black students disengagement from school.* Toronto: University of Toronto Press.

Dewey, J. (1916). *Democracy and education.* New York, NY: Macmillan.

Ditzen, B., Schaer, M., Gabriel, B., Bodenmann, G., Ehlert, U., & Heinrichs, M. (2009). Intranasal oxytocin increases positive communication and reduces cortisol levels during couple conflict. *Biological Psychiatry, 65*(9), 728–731. doi:10.1016/j.biopsych.2008.10.011

Dobbs, D. (2013, December). Die, selfish gene, die. *Aeon.* Retrieved from https://aeon.co/essays/the-selfish-gene-is-a-great-meme-too-bad-it-s-so-wrong

Dobia, B., Bodkin-Andrews, G., Parada, R., O'Rourke, V., Gilbert, S., Daley, A., & Roffey, S. (2014). *Aboriginal girls' circle: Enhancing connectedness and promoting resilience for Aboriginal girls* (Final Pilot Report). Penrith: University of Western Sydney.

Duncan, P. M., Garcia, A. C., Frankowski, B. L., Carey, P. A., Kallock, E. A., Dixon, R. D., & Shaw, J. S. (2007). Inspiring healthy adolescent choices: A rationale for and guide to strength promotion in primary care. *Journal of Adolescent Health, 41*(6), 525–535. doi:10.1016/j.jadohealth.2007.05.024

Feldman, R., Weller, A., Zagoory-Sharon, O., & Levine, A. (2007). Evidence for a neuroendocrinological foundation of human affiliation: Plasma oxytocin levels across pregnancy and the postpartum period predict mother-infant bonding. *Psychological Science, 18*(11), 965–970. doi:10.1111/j.1467-9280.2007.02010.x

Finn, J. (1989). Withdrawing from school. *Review of Educational Research, 59*(2), 117–142. doi:10.3102/00346543059002117

Freeman, T. M., Anderman, L. H., & Jensen, J. M. (2007). Sense of belonging in college freshmen at the classroom and campus levels. *Journal of Experimental Education, 75*(3), 203–220. doi:10.3200/JEXE.75.3.203-220

Gerhardt, S. (2006). *Why love matters: How affection shapes a baby's brain.* London: Taylor & Francis.

Goleman, D. (2007). *Social intelligence.* London: Arrow Books.

Gunasekera, S., Houghton, S., Glasgow, K., & Boyle, C. (2014). From stability to mobility: African secondary school aged adolescents' transition to mainstream schooling. *The Australian Educational and Developmental Psychologist, 31*(1), 1–17. doi:10.1017/edp.2014.4

Hamilton, W. D. (1964). The genetical evolution of social behaviour. I. *Journal of Theoretical Biology, 7*(1), 1–16. doi:10.1016/0022-5193(64)90039-6

Hattie, J. (2009). *Visible learning: A synthesis of over 800 meta-analyses relating to achievement.* London: Routledge.

Heinrichs, M., Baumgartner, T., Kirschbaum, C., & Ehlert, U. (2003). Social support and oxytocin interact to suppress cortisol and subjective responses to psychosocial stresss. *Biological Psychiatry, 54*(12), 1389–1398. doi:10.1016/S0006-3223(03)00465-7

Hewstone, M., Rubin, M., & Willis, H. (2002). Intergroup bias. *Annual Review of Psychology, 53*(1), 575–604. doi:10.1146/annurev.psych.53.100901.135109

Hobbes, T. (1651/2010). *Leviathan* (Rev. ed.). Peterborough, ON: Broadview Press.

Huttenlocher, P. R. (2002). *Neural plasticity: The effect of the environment on the development of the cerebral cortex.* Cambridge, MA: Harvard University Press.

Jennings, P. (Ed.). (2015). *Gen Y Jihadists: Preventing radicalisation in Australia.* Canberra: Australian Strategic Policy Institute.

Johnson, B. (2008). Teacher-student relationships that enhance resilience at school: A micro-level analysis of students' views. *British Journal of Guidance and Counselling, 36*(4), 385–398. doi:10.1080/03069880802364528

Johnson, L. (2007). Re-thinking successful school leadership in challenging US schools: Culturally responsive practices in school-community relationships. *International Studies in Educational Administration, 35*(3) 49–59.

Johnson, S. L. (2009). Improving the school environment to reduce school violence: A review of the literature. *Journal of School Health, 79*(10), 451–465. doi:10.1111/j.1746-1561.2009.00435.x

Kelly, G. (1955–1991). *The psychology of personal constructs* (Vol. I, II). New York, NY: Norton.

Kickett-Tucker, C. S., & Coffin, J. (2011). Aboriginal self-concept and racial identity: Practical solutions for teachers. In N. Purdie, G. Milgate, & H. R. Bell (Eds.), *Two-way teaching and learning: Toward culturally reflective and relevant education* (pp. 154–170). Melbourne: ACER Press.

Kosfeld, M., Heinrichs, M., Zak, P. J., Fischbacher, U., & Fehr, E. (2005). Oxytocin increases trust in humans. *Nature, 435,* 673–676. doi:10.1038/nature03701

Kruglanski, A. W., Gelfand, M. J., Bélanger, J. J., Sheveland, A., Hettiarachchi, M., & Gunaratna, R. (2014). The psychology of radicalization and deradicalization: How significance quest impacts violent extremism. *Political Psychology, 35,* 9–93. doi:10.1111/pops.12163

Lam, U. F., Chen, W. W., Zhang, J., & Liang, T. (2015). It feels good to learn where I belong: School belonging, academic emotions, and academic achievement in adolescents. *School Psychology International, 36*(4), 393–409. doi:10.1177/0143034315589649

Lerner, M. J. (1980). *The belief in a just world: A fundamental delusion.* New York, NY: Plenum.

Lyons-Padilla, S., Gelfand, M. J., Mirahmadi, H., Farooq, M., & van Egmond, M. (2015). Belonging nowhere: Marginalization & radicalization risk among Muslim Immigrants. *Behavioral Science & Policy, 1*(2), 1–12. doi:10.1353/bsp.2015.0019

MacDonald, G., & Leary, M. R. (2005). Why does social exclusion hurt? The relationship between social and physical pain. *Psychological Bulletin, 131*(2), 202–223. doi:10.1037/0033-2909.131.2.202

Markus, H. R., & Kitayama, S. (1991). Culture and the self: Implications for cognition, emotion and motivation. *Psychological Review, 98,* 224–253.

Maslow, A. H. (1943). A theory of human motivation. *Psychological Review, 50*(4), 370–396. Retrieved from http://dx.doi.org/10.1037/h0054346

Mitchell, J. P., Macrae, C. N., & Banaji, M. R. (2006). Dissociable medial pre-frontal contributions to judgements of similar and dissimilar others. *Neuron, 50*(4), 655–663.

Noble, T., McGrath, H., Roffey, S., & Rowling, L. (2008). *A scoping study on student wellbeing.* Canberra: Department of Education, Employment & Workplace Relations (DEEWR).

Oliver, K. G., Collin, P., Burns, J., & Nicholas, J. (2006). Building resilience in young people through meaningful participation. *Australian e-Journal for the Advancement of Mental Health, 5*(1), 34–40. doi:10.5172/jamh.5.1.34

Osterman, K. F. (2000). Students' need for belonging in the school community. *Review of Educational Research, 70*(3), 323–367. doi:10.3102/00346543070003323

Partington, G., & Gray, J. (2003). Classroom management and Aboriginal students. In Q. Beresford & G. Partington (Eds.), *Reform and resistance in Aboriginal education: The Australian experience* (pp. 164–184). Perth: University of Western Australia Press.

Pekrun, R., Goetz, T., Titz, W., & Perry, R. (2002). Academic emotions in students' self-regulated learning and achievement: A program of qualitative and quantitative research. *Educational Psychologist, 37*(2), 91–105. doi:10.1207/S15326985EP3702_4

Plato. (1955). *The republic* (D. Lee, Trans.). Middlesex: Penguin.

Putnam, R. D. (2000). *Bowling alone: The collapse and revival of American community.* New York, NY: Simon and Schuster.

Rahman, K. (2013). Belonging and learning to belong in school: The implications of the hidden curriculum for indigenous students. *Discourse: Studies in the Cultural Politics of Education, 34*(5), 660–672. doi:10.1080/01596306.2013.728362

Rigby, K., & Johnson, K. (2016). *The prevalence and effectiveness of anti-bullying strategies employed in Australian schools*. Adelaide: University of South Australia.

Roffey, S. (2007). Transformation and emotional literacy: The role of school leaders in developing a caring community. *Leading and Managing, 13*(1), 16–30.

Roffey, S. (2010). Content and context for learning relationships: A cohesive framework for individual and whole school development. *Educational and Child Psychology, 27*(1), 158–167.

Roffey, S. (2012). Developing positive relationships in schools. In S. Roffey (Ed.), *Positive relationships: Evidence-based practice across the world* (pp. 181–196). Rotterdam: Springer.

Roffey, S. (2013). Inclusive and exclusive belonging: The impact on individual and community wellbeing. *Educational and Child Psychology, 30*(1), 38–48.

Roffey, S. (2014). *Circle solutions for student wellbeing*. London: Sage Publications.

Roffey, S. (2017). Ordinary magic needs ordinary magicians: The power and practice of positive relationships for building youth resilience and wellbeing. *Kognition und Paedagogik, 103*, 38–57.

Roffey, S., & McCarthy, F. (2013). Circle solutions: A philosophy and pedagogy for learning positive relationships. What promotes and inhibits sustainable outcomes? *International Journal of Emotional Education, 5*(1), 36–55.

Sari, M., & Dogenay, A. (2009). Hidden curriculum on gaining the value of respect for human dignity: A qualitative study in two elementary schools in Adana. *Educational Sciences: Theory and Practice, 9*(2), 925–940.

Seligman, M. E. P., Ernst, R. M., Gillham, J., Reivich, K., & Linkins, M. (2009). Positive education: Positive psychology and classroom interventions. *Oxford Review of Education, 35*(3), 293–311. doi:10.1080/03054980902934563

Siegel, D. (2012). *The developing mind: How relationships and the brain interact to shape who we are*. New York, NY: Guildford Press.

Singer, T., & Bolz, M. (Eds.). (2013). *Compassion: Bridging practice and science*. Leipzig: Max Planck Institute for Human Cognitive and Brain Sciences.

Skiba, R., Reynolds, C. R., Graham, S., Sheras, P., Close Conely, J., & Garcia-Vasquez, E. (2006). *Are zero tolerance policies effective in the schools? An evidentiary review and recommendations*. Zero Tolerance Task Force Report for the American Psychological Association.

Solomon, D., Watson, M., Battistich, V., Schaps, E., & Delucchi, K. (1996). Creating classrooms that students experience as communities. *American Journal of Community Psychology, 24*(6), 719–748.

Steele, G. R. (2009). There is no such thing as society [blog post]. Retrieved from https://iea.org.uk/blog/there-is-no-such-thing-as-society

Stevens, M. J. (2013). Negative emotions and political engagement. In S. Sinclair & D. Antonius (Eds.), *The political psychology of terrorism fears* (pp. 51–66). New York, NY: Oxford University Press.

Stuart, H. (2017). *Islamist terrorism: Analysis of attacks and offences in the UK, 1998–2015*. London: Henry Jackson Society.

Thompson, D. R., Iachan, R., Overpeck, M., Ross, J. G., & Gross, L. A. (2006). School connectedness in the health behaviour of school-aged children study: The role of school, student and school neighbourhood characteristics. *Journal of School Health, 76*(7), 379–386. doi:10.1111/j.1746-1561.2006.00129.x

Topping, A., Halliday, J., & Ismail, N. (2015, November 13). Who is Mohammed Emwazi? *The Guardian*. Retrieved from http://bit.ly/1WWBqOz

Werner, E., & Smith, R. (2001). *Journeys from childhood to the midlife: Risk, resilience, and recovery*. New York, NY: Cornell University Press.

Wike, T. L., & Fraser, M. W. (2009). School shootings: Making sense of the senseless. *Aggression and Violent Behavior, 14*(3), 162–169. doi:10.1016/j.avb.2009.01.005

Williams, K. D., & Nida, S. A. (2011). Ostracism: Consequences and copings. *Current Directions in Psychological Science, 20*(2), 71–75. doi: 10.1177/0963721411402480

Williams, K. D., & Zadro, L. (2005). Ostracism: The indiscriminate early detection systems. In K. D. Williams, J. P. Forgas, & W. von Hippel (Eds.), *The social outcast: Ostracism, social exclusion, rejection, and bullying* (pp. 19–34). New York, NY: Psychology Press.

Williams, M. J., Horgan, J. G., & Evans, W. P. (2015). The critical role of friends in networks for countering violent extremism: Toward a theory of vicarious help-seeking. *Behavioral Sciences of Terrorism and Political Aggression, 8*(1), 45–65. doi:10.1080/19434472.2015.1101147

Willms, J. D. (2003). *Student engagement at school: A sense of belonging and participation.* Paris: Organization for Economic Cooperation and Development.

Wilson, D. (2004). The interface of school climate and school connectedness and relationships with aggression and victimization. *Journal of School Health, 74*(7), 293–299. doi:10.1111/j.1746-1561.2004.tb08286.x

Wingspread Declaration on School Connections. (2004). Wingspread declaration on school connections. *Journal of School Health, 74*(7), 233–234. doi:10.1111/j.1746-1561.2004.tb08279.x

Wolfe, D. A., Wekerle, C., & Scott, K. (1997). *Alternatives to violence: Empowering youth to develop healthy relationships.* Thousand Oaks, CA: Sage Publications.

Wyn, J., Cahill, H., Holdsworth, R., Rowling, L., & Carson, S. (2000). Mindmatters, a whole school approach promoting mental health and wellbeing. *Australian and New Zealand Journal of Psychiatry, 34*(4), 594–601. doi:10.1080/j.1440-1614.2000.00748.x

Sue Roffey
Graduate School of Education
University of Exeter
England

Christopher Boyle
Graduate School of Education
University of Exeter
England

165

DANIEL MAYS, SEBASTIAN FRANKE, FRANKA METZNER,
CHRISTOPHER BOYLE, DIVYA JINDAL-SNAPE,
LISA SCHNEIDER, HOLGER ZIELEMANNS,
SILKE PAWILS AND MICHELLE WICHMANN

10. SCHOOL BELONGING AND SUCCESSFUL TRANSITION PRACTICE

*Academic Self-Concept, Belonging, and Achievement Motivation
in Primary School Students*

INTRODUCTION

Academic transitions, such as those between nursery to primary school, primary to secondary school or the return from special education to general education, can be key factors that affect a young person's feeling of school belonging. The professional organisation of these transitions is the key factor shaping whether these transitions have a positive effect on student self-concept and academic motivation in children and adolescents. If transitional phases in childhood and adolescence are poorly implemented, adjustment difficulties can be a consequence, which may result in socio-emotional or behavioural issues, such as maladaptive coping, truancy, and school attrition (Rosenkoetter, Schroeder, Rous, Hains, Shaw, & McCormick, 2009; Mays, Jindal-Snape, & Boyle, 2019). This chapter considers the question of whether students identified by their primary school teachers as having issues with socio-emotional development will show changes in their self-concept and achievement motivation during the transition from Grade 4 to Grade 5. It was anticipated that academic self-concept and achievement motivation would decrease during the transition for students identified as having social-emotional development issues. Using a pre-post study design, students aged between 9 to 11 years in 4th grade were monitored across one year in regular primary schools in Germany. The social-emotional development of 33 students identified by teachers as having difficulties in this area were assessed across the year and compared with a similar aged control sample in 4th grade (n=531) and 5th grade (n=611) over the course of a year.

TRANSITIONS AND SCHOOL

Since a transition-specific theoretical structure is missing in research on special education, the term academic transition will be explained using definitions from

© KONINKLIJKE BRILL NV, LEIDEN, 2018 | DOI:10.1163/9789004386969_010

education and psychology. According to Welzer (1993, p. 37), transitions are "complex, merging and cross-fading transformation processes" in which one's life experiences a massive reorganisation. Such processes of change can happen when a child in pre-school moves to the first grade of primary school, or when a student transfers from a special educational setting to a mainstream education environment. Academic transitions can be understood as processes describing the transfer from one educational context – including existing interpersonal relationships – into another (Jindal-Snape, 2010). These transfers can happen within one educational system as well as between educational institutions. Transitional phases are characteristically periods of rapid change and times of intense learning. Transitions are therefore social processes, which condense and accelerate phases of change in one's life (Griebel & Niesel, 2004; Griebel, 2005; Mays, 2014) and through which a variety of stress factors accumulate.

Transitions are typically accompanied by a range of clear changes. For example, "abandoning" the old peer group, building new relationships with people in the new environment, and changes regarding one's own identity (Bronfenbrenner, 2009). More subtle or hidden changes may also occur during transitional phases, such as changes in behavioural expectations and compliance with rules in the new context. While some studies report school transitions result in positive developmental outcomes for students (Jindal-Snape & Foggie, 2008; Akos, 2010; Jindal-Snape, 2010), other studies note negative factors related to these transitions, describing student fears regarding the size, location and structure of the new school, the loss of friendships and the new teachers' expectations (Galton, 2010). There is currently a lack of empirical research focusing on this topic in the context of inclusion (Hughes, Banks, & Terras, 2013; Mays, 2016).

The changes that occur during transitions force one to confront conflicts in his or her environment on a number of levels, which can have both a positive and negative impact on an individual's general development (Bronfenbrenner, 1993). Nickel (1990) distinguishes three processes of transition depending on the requirements of the new environment as well as the individual's coping resources: a) a delay of development when demands are too low, b) failure or, in extreme cases, developmental regression when demands are too high, and c) a satisfying developmental course when demands meet the individual's capacity. Positively experienced transitions can promote a child's development, while negative transitional experiences can impair social and emotional well-being and lead to a decline in academic performance and achievement motivation (Galton & Hargreaves, 2002; Jindal-Snape, 2016).

Research findings suggest that many children and adolescents successfully navigate transitions (Lucey & Reay, 2000; Jindal-Snape & Foggie, 2008). For most children, the adjustment process is completed after about one year at a new school. Some students, however, lack the resources needed to cope with transitional phases. Students with identified difficulties in the areas of social behaviour and emotional regulation are likely to be among the students who struggle with transitions.

Transitions and Self-Concept

In educational psychology research, self-concept is a factor found to influence psychological well-being in childhood and adolescence. Saarni (2002) defines self-concept as the "heartpiece of emotional self-efficacy" and describes the ability with which children and adolescents tolerate intense negative emotions (like despair, melancholy, rage or fear), accepting these emotions without allowing them to become overpowering (Saarni, 2002). Cole and colleagues (2001) point out that the self-concept of children and adolescents is unstable and easily malleable, especially during transition from nursery to primary school (between ages 5 and 8), and during the onset of puberty. According to Trautwein (2003) complex expressions of self-concept – where gender-specific tasks, parental expectations and peer influence are in conflict – can lead to considerable insecurity and confusion in adolescents. By overcoming obstacles, children and adolescents can develop confidence in their ability to meet challenges. This can lead to further development in some, but not all, areas. Transitions can therefore result in an increased self-efficacy across a range of specific areas in addition to an overall boost in self-concept (Mruk, 2006). Mruk (2006, p. 184) uses the term "self-esteem-moments" for the sensitive transitional phases. Mruk believes that self-concept is both influencing and influenced by an individual's ability to successfully transition into a new context.

According to Shavelson, Hubner and Stanton (1976), the individual competency self-concepts are based on concrete performance feedbacks as well as on the resulting social comparisons and causal attributions (Marsh & Shavelson, 1985). For children and adolescents, the primary framework for social comparisons is the class to which they belong. The big-fish-little-pond effect and peer group effect illustrate the impact of social comparison on the self-concept of children and adolescents (Schwarzer, 1979; Schwarzer, Lange, & Jerusalem, 1982; Schwarzer & Jerusalem, 1983; Marsh, 1990). According to the socialisation theory by Fend (1989), various "subcultural" normative systems of social peer groups may also influence the development of self-concept. These systems are not necessarily oriented towards school performance. Problem behaviour, such as classroom disruptions, may in fact enhance self-esteem if such behaviour leads to a student receiving attention or gaining approval from his or her peer group (Trautwein, 2003). The involvement in problem behaviour can therefore contribute to an increase of self-esteem in students with low self-concept. As such, students with learning and behavioural difficulties may actually profit from problem behaviour during the transition to secondary school (ibid.). Similarly, Trautwein, Köller, and Baumert (2004) also found a connection between the involvement in problem behaviour and increased student self-concept.

An academic transition can affect self-concept not only positively, but also negatively. Mruk (2006) names three essential experiences connected with the developmental dynamics during a transition that can negatively shape a student's self-concept: (1) the experience of being exposed to a new environment, (2) the challenge of having to find one's own answers to a set of new questions and (3) finding ways to either maintain friendships during the transitional phase or manage the loss of close relationships as a result of the transition.

With the transition from primary to secondary school, students are required to become more independent and are usually required to spend longer periods of time sitting still. They are forced to find new ways to interact with adults and meet changing expectations. They also need to manage new restrictions to their movements and new forms of assessment. At the same time the structure of a student's class group, the group with which one compares him or herself, is also changing. These changes include implicit messages that affect the students' self-concept. The "Fresh-Start-Approach" explicitly does not prepare for the transition but instead assumes a positive start in the new school. It can have lasting effects on low – as well as high-performing children. Moreover, Newman and Blackburn (2002) refer to a transfer dilemma, proposing that transitions are accompanied with both negative feelings of loss and at the same time positivity about the prospect of change.

Hattie (2013) investigated the results of 181 studies and three meta-analyses concerning relevant factors for a successful school transition. Finding new friends within the first month was identified as the deciding predictor for a successful transition. At the same time, it became apparent that school transitions had a negative effect on academic achievement (ibid.) and consequently on students' feeling of being part of the new school. The acknowledgement and rejection experienced in the new environment defines the perception of one's own worth and competence (Jindal-Snape & Miller, 2010). The change of schools can temporarily challenge one's self-image and lead to internal insecurity. In transition, new friends need to be found, fears and worries need to be confronted and suitable coping strategies need to be developed. As such, it is likely more difficult for children and adolescents with additional social-emotional support needs (ASN) to transition than their peers. In response to these feelings of insecurities, students may demonstrate noticeable temporary behavioural changes. Such changes are especially likely to occur in students with identified emotional regulation difficulties.

School Belonging and Transitions

Schools can be complex and difficult places for many students. The levels of social complexity can be overpowering before the issues of academic achievement and expectation are even taken into consideration. Allen and Boyle (2016, p. i) define school belonging as being "… generally regarded as a student's sense of affiliation or connection to his or her school". With the increasing prominence of wellbeing in schools and the understanding that academic success is not the only measure of achievement in education, school belonging is a crucial component in the makeup of schools. Slaten, Ferguson, Allen, Brodrick, and Waters (2016) discuss Maslow's original assertion of belonging being an important, if not crucial, psychological need. The notion of school belonging and feeling part of a wider community can be detrimental to the psychological needs of students. If this need is not met, the individual and collective wellbeing of students can be affected, which in turn may contribute to poorer academic achievement within the school system. Children need support in social and emotional learning, particularly at crucial stages in schooling e.g. at the transition from primary to secondary school. It is paramount that students are able to enjoy their education and do not feel isolated at school. A sense of belonging and positive wellbeing should contribute a great deal in developing symbiotic, appropriate and necessary friendships and connections (Jindal-Snape, 2016). Uwah, McMahon, and Furlow (2008) found that feeling encouraged to participate in school was a significant, positive predictor of pupils' academic self-efficacy. Anderman and Anderman (1999) examined school belonging and achievement goal orientation of students at the transition from 5th to 6th grade and showed that the sense of being respected and able to "be yourself" in school is associated with achievement motivation. The longitudinal study carried out by Gillen-O'Neel and Fuligni (2013) revealed that when students felt that school was more enjoyable and more useful they also had a higher level of school belonging.

Transitions and Achievement Motivation

Besides the changes seen in students' self-concept during academic transitions, changes in students' achievement motivation can also occur. It can be assumed that a negative change to a student's self-concept is accompanied by a decrease in achievement motivation. Achievement motivation can be defined as striving to reach, or exceed, individual or societal expectations (Schiefele & Schaffner, 2015, p. 160). Achievement motivation is comprised of both the desire to succeed (approximation achievement goal) and the fear of failure (avoidance achievement goal). There does not always exist a simple correlation between the goals one sets and the goals one believes he or she can achieve, rather the amount of effort required to successfully reach a goal must also be considered. Spinath, Stiensmeier-Pelster, Schöne, and Dickhäuser (2012) defined learning goals (mastery goals) as goals that prioritise the mastery of a new skill instead of simply completing a single task. Contrastingly avoidance goals are more general in nature, for example being purely hedonistic (Stiensmeier-Pelster et al., p. 14). It is assumed that an orientation towards master goals (self-orientation) is linked to improved academic achievement. Students who set mastery goals typically: attribute their achievement to their own effort; show more positive affect; demonstrate a greater interest in the topic and task; and use superior problem solving skills to overcome barriers to success. Spinath and colleagues (2012) report a correlation between achievement goals and self-concept. The link between goal setting and self-concept could play an important role during times of academic transition. It may therefore be that focused intervention targeting a student's goal orientations can positively impact both their self-concept and their academic achievement (Spinath et al., 2012).

Research Questions

The following research questions were examined in this study:

a. What kind of changes to self-concept and achievement motivation (goal-orientation) are observed among students with identified socio-emotional difficulties when transitioning from primary school (4th grade) to secondary school (5th grade)?
b. Does the self-concept and achievement motivation of children with identified socio-emotional difficulties differ from their typically developing peers during the transition from primary school (4th grade) to secondary school (5th grade)?

METHODS

Sample

Teachers were asked to predict students competencies in the area of socio-emotional development. Those students identified as having low socio-emotional skills were selected for examination in this study. Students were drawn from the 4th grade and were between the ages of 9 and 11 years. They attended regular primary schools in Germany between 2014 and 2016. Just over half of the students came from rural areas. A control condition of students with typical levels of socio-emotional skills was also included, with a selection of control condition students being drawn from each class. In line with German research ethics requirements, parents were asked for written informed consent for the students' participation.

Instruments

The *Child Behaviour Checklist – Teacher's Report Form* (CBCL-TRF; Döpfner, Plück, & Kinnen, 2014), the *Scales for Assessment of Academic Self-Concept* (SESSKO; Schöne, Dickhäuser, Spinath, & Stiensmeier-Pelster, 2012) and the *Scales for Assessment of Learning and Achievement Motivation* (SELLMO; Spinath et al., 2012) were used as instruments. All instruments have been proven reliable and valid.

The *CBCL-TRF* (Döpfner et al., 2014) is comprised of 113 items which can be assigned to six symptom scales (affective, anxiety, physical, attention-deficit, hyperactivity, oppositional behavior and dissocial symptoms) according to the classification system for psychological diseases the Diagnostic and Statistical Manual of Mental Disorders (DSM-5; APA, 2013) as well as three superordinate scales (internal problems, external problems, overall conspicuity). Each item is answered on a 3-point-scale from 0=*not accurate* to 2=*exactly or often accurate*. The questionnaire takes 15 to 20 minutes to complete.

The *SESSKO* (Schöne et al., 2012) assesses academic self-concept of students in Years 3 to 10 using 22 items which are answered on a 5-point-scale (from *strong rejection* to *strong agreement*). The items are assigned to four scales, one of which is not specific to a reference norm (*academic self-concept – absolute*) and a further three assess self-concept with regard to a specific reference norm (*social, criterial* and *individual*). The four scales do not form an overall value. The focus of assessment is the cross-disciplinary self-concept of cognitive competency. The items of the "criterial" scale assess e.g. the estimation of one's own competence measured against educational requirements. A prototypical item of this scale is "If I look at what we need to know at school, I feel not competent/very competent". The scales take 7 to 15 minutes to complete.

The *SELLMO* (Spinath et al., 2012) is a standardised instrument for individual diagnostics regarding various aspects of achievement motivation. They are comprised of 31 items for the assessment of learning goals (LG; learning as a challenge), approximation achievement goals (ApAG; proactively demonstrating knowledge and skills), avoidance achievement goals (AvAG; concealing lack of knowledge and skills) and a tendency towards work avoidance (WA; minimal effort). The items are answered using a 5-point-scale (from 1=*not true at all* to 5=*completely true*). The scales take 8 to 15 minutes to complete.

Procedures

In October of 2014 teachers were asked to make predictions about the socio-emotional skills of their students and their transition to secondary school. A total of 33 members of the project team were each assigned to monitor a single ASN student from the middle of the fourth grade. All members of the project team attended a training course before beginning the role. Student self-report measures were administered at two time points. Time 1 measurements were taken during the middle of the 4th grade. Time 2 measurements were taken approximately 4–6 months later, following the transition to 5th Grade – with the exception of one case in which the second interview was possible only after 9 months. Throughout the study, the project team members offered parents and children short-term support, e.g. tutoring or supervision for homework.

Data Analysis

The collected data were entered, coded and analysed using the statistical data analysis software SPSS (Version 18.0; SPSS Inc., 2009). Absolute and relative frequencies were described using median, range and percentages. Potential changes of academic self-concept and achievement motivation of the mentored students with need for support from T1 to T2, as well as potential differences between this group of students and their classmates regarding academic self-concept and achievement motivation in T1 and T2 were analysed. For the statistical significance test regarding changes in ASN students from T1 to T2, the non-parametrical method of the Sign Test for paired samples was used. For the statistical significance test regarding potential differences between this group of students and their classmates in T1 and T2, the

Mann-Whitney-U-Test for independent samples was utilised. These methods were chosen as an alternative for a t-test for paired or independent samples due to a small sample size and lack of normal distribution of the data. Effect sizes were estimated using Cohen's d and following thresholds according to Cohen (1988) applied for the interpretation: small (d $\geq$ .10), medium (d $\geq$ .30), and large (d $\geq$ .50). In order to take type I errors into account, the results were Bonferroni-corrected and interpreted based on adjusted significance levels of $p^*<.006$ for the Sign Test and $p^{**}<.003$ for the Mann-Whitney-U-Test.

RESULTS

Sample Description

The sample was comprised of n=33 students (82% male) with ASN during transition from overall 31 primary schools to the same number of secondary schools. Special educational needs identified through an official assessment were present in 19 children (58%). Need for additional support was present in n=11 children regarding socio-emotional development, n=7 children regarding learning and in one child regarding language. A non-standardised assessment of ASN in the area of socio-emotional development was made by teachers for n=10 students (30%). Four of the accompanied and assessed children (12%) displayed "slight" deviance and learning difficulties (e.g. dyslexia) according to teacher report.

The assessed children were between 9 and 11 years old at T1 and between 10 and 12 years old at T2. After primary school, the majority of mentored students with ASN transferred to a secondary modern school, comprehensive school or a high school (see Table 10.1). Compared to the values of a norm sample (Döpfner et al., 2014, p. 157 ff.), 3% of mentored students with ASN displayed prominent internalising problems (9% in critical range), 21% displayed prominent externalising problems (9% in critical range) and 15% displayed a prominent total score (12% in critical range) in the CBCL-TRF. Thus, 69% of the mentored students were in an at least critical range towards behavioural problems. Classmates from 4th (T1) and 5th grade (T2) were used as comparison groups. 4th grade consisted of a total of n=531 children between ages 7 and and in 5th grade were n=611 children between ages 9 and 13 (see Table 10.1).

Development of Academic Self-Concept of Students with Additional Support Needs from T1 to T2

The t-values students with ASN reached on the SESSKO scales at T1 and T2 are displayed in Table 10.2. The t-values changed only marginally from T1 to T2 in a relative comparison. The statistical significance test resulted in no significant change of t-values from T1 to T2 (see Table 10.2).

Table 10.1. Sociodemographic characteristics of the assessed sample and comparison groups (T1 and T2)

	Pre-measurement (T1)				Post-measurement after 4–6 months (T2)			
	Stdnt with ASN (n = 33)		4th grade (n = 531)		Stdnt with ASN (n = 33)		5th grade (n = 611)	
	n	%	n	%	n	%	n	%
Gender								
male	27	82%	242	46%	27	82%	252	41%
female	6	18%	237	45%	6	18%	215	35%
n.a.	–	–	52	10%	–	–	144	24%
Age (Md [Range])	10.0 [9–11]		10.0 [7–12]		11.0 [10–12]		10.0 [9–13]	
n.a.	3	9%	83	16%	13	39%	197	32%
Secondary schools								
Realschule (Secondary modern school)	–	–	–	–	8	24%	134	22%
Gesamtschule (Comprehensive school)	–	–	–	–	5	16%	122	20%
Gymnasium (High school)	–	–	–	–	4	13%	93	15%
Sekundarschule (secondary school)	–	–	–	–	3	10%	75	12%
Realschule Plus (secondary modern school)	–	–	–	–	2	6%	37	6%
Hauptschule (lower secondary school/main school)	–	–	–	–	1	3%	19	3%
Gemeinschaftsschule (secondary school)	–	–	–	–	1	3%	16	3%
n.a.	–	–	–	–	9	27%	115	19%

Notes: Stdnt with ASN = students with additional support needs; Md = median; n.a. = not available; percentages may not add up to 100 due to rounding

Comparison of Academic Self-Concept between Students with Additional Support Needs and Their Classmates at T1 and T2

In relative comparison with the academic self-concept of their classmates at T1, the majority of students with ASN displayed a tendentially lower t-value on the absolute, criterial and social scales. None of these comparisons reached statistical significance in accordance with the adjusted significance level of $p** < .003$ (see Table 10.3).

Table 10.2. Pre-post-comparison of academic self-concept of students with additional support needs from T1 to T2 (n=33)

Scales of SESSKO	T-values at pre-measurement (T1)			T-values at post-measurement after 4–6 months (T2)			Change of academic self-concept from T1 to T2							
							decrease		increase		no change		Sign Test	
	Md	Range	n.a. as n (%)	Md	Range	n.a. as n (%)	n	%	n	%	n	%	p^a	d^b
criterial	44.0	25–59	3 (9%)	42.0	15–71	10 (30%)	10	30%	11	33%	–	–	1.000	-
individual	48.5	27–70	3 (9%)	45.0	29–65	14 (42%)	8	24%	9	27%	–	–	1.000	-
social	44.0	24–63	3 (9%)	45.0	25–71	10 (30%)	10	30%	10	30%	1	3%	1.000	-
absolute	46.0	26–71	3 (9%)	44.0	26–70	10 (30%)	10	30%	9	27%	2	6%	1.000	-

Notes: Md = median; [a] adjusted significance level of p*<.006; [b] effect size (Cohen's d): small (d ≥ .10), medium (d ≥ .30), large (d ≥ .50); n.a. = not available; percentages may not add up to 100 due to rounding

Table 10.3. Comparison between students with additional support needs and their classmates regarding academic self-concept at T1 and T2

Scales of SESSKO	t-values of students with ASN			t-values of classmates			Comparison between students with ASN and classmates								
							above Md of classmates		under Md of classmates		same Md as classmates		Mann-Whitney-U-Test		
	Md	Range	n.a. as n (%)	Md	Range	n.a. as n (%)	n	%	n	%	n	%	z^a	p^b	d^c
Measurement point T1	n = 33			n = 531											
criterial	44.0	25–59	3 (9%)	46.0	26–72	91 (17%)	13	39%	17	52%	3	9%	−2.488	.013	–
individual	48.5	27–70	3 (9%)	48.0	23–70	92 (17%)	18	55%	14	42%	1	3%	−0.902	.367	–
social	44.0	24–63	3 (9%)	47.0	16–70	91 (17%)	15	46%	16	49%	2	6%	−1.613	.107	–
absolute	46.0	26–71	3 (9%)	48.0	21–71	92 (17%)	14	42%	18	55%	1	3%	−1.687	.092	–
Measurement point T2	n = 33			n = 611											
criterial	42.0	15–71	10 (30%)	53.0	12–71	156 (26%)	12	36%	20	61%	1	3%	−3.366	.001	.59
individual	45.0	29–65	14 (42%)	53.0	19–67	236 (39%)	19	58%	13	39%	1	3%	−2.632	.008	–
social	45.0	25–71	10 (30%)	52.0	15–76	159 (26%)	13	39%	17	52%	3	9%	−2.693	.007	–
absolute	44.0	26–70	10 (30%)	53.0	15–70	160 (26%)	14	42%	18	55%	1	3%	−2.730	.006	–

Notes: ASN = additional support needs; Md = median; ^{a} z-value; ^{b} adjusted significance level of p **<.003; ^{c} effect size (Cohen's d): small (d ≥ .10), medium (d ≥ .30), large (d ≥ .50); n.a. = not available; percentages may not add up to 100 due to rounding

177

At T2, 61% of students with ASN displayed a significantly lower t-value on the criterial scale than their classmates ($z=-3.366$, $p^{**}=.001$) with large effect size (Cohen's $d=.59$). Furthermore, the majority of students with ASN displayed a relatively lower t-value on the absolute and social scales as well as a relatively higher t-value on the individual scale than their classmates. These three comparisons approached statistical significance in accordance with the adjusted significance level of $p^{**}<.006$ (see Table 10.3). The t-values of students with ASN and of their classmates regarding academic self-concept at T1 and T2 are displayed in Figures 10.1 and 10.2.

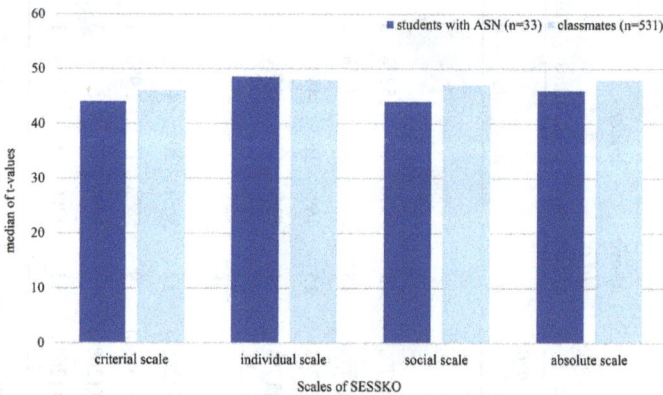

Figure 10.1. T-values of students with Additional Support Needs (ASN) and of their classmates regarding academic self-concept at T1

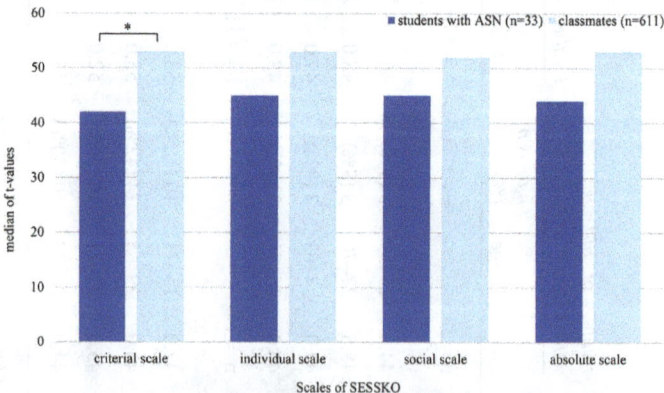

Figure 10.2. T-values of students with Additional Support Needs (ASN) and of their classmates regarding academic self-concept at T2. A significantly lower t-value in 61% of students with ASN is represented by the asterisk (*)

Development of Achievement Motivation of Students with Additional Support Needs from T1 to T2

The t-values students with ASN reached on the SELLMO scales at T1 and T2 are displayed in Table 10.4. In a relative pre-post comparison of the t-values, a tendential increase of t-values on the scales LG, ApAG and AvAG, as well as a tendential decrease of t-values on the WA-scale at T2 became apparent in some students. However, these comparisons did not reach statistical significance in accordance with the adjusted significance level of p*<.006 (see Table 10.4).

Comparison of Achievement Motivation between Students with Additional Support Needs and Their Classmates at T1 and T2

Compared with their classmates at T1, 70% of the students with ASN displayed a significantly lower t-value on the LG-scale (z=-3.253, p**=.001) with large effect size (Cohen's d=.57) (see Table 10.5). Furthermore, in a relative comparison, about half of the students with ASN displayed a lower t-value than their classmates on the ApAG-scale as well as the majority a higher t-value on the WA- and AvAG-scales than their classmates. These comparisons did not reach statistical significance in accordance with the adjusted significance level of p**<.003 (see Table 10.5).

At T2, almost half of the students with ASN reached a lower t-value than their classmates on the WA- and ApAG-scales, as well as the majority a higher t-value on the LG- and ApPG-scales in a relative comparison. However, there were no significant differences between students with ASN and their classmates with regard to their achievement motivation (all p**>.003; see Table 10.5). The t-values of students with ASN and of their classmates regarding achievement motivation at T1 and T2 are displayed in Figures 10.3 and 10.4.

Limitations.   The present study is a complex project with methodological limitations due to its design in a research field that is difficult to measure. The eligibility criterion for the children was predicted ASN in socio-emotional development based on teacher reports. A more objective measure would have strengthened this research. Collecting information about individual students was also challenging. Some secondary schools did not permit or only partially permitted data acquisition, so there was a high proportion of missing values. Because the students were mentored over the course of a year, the participating schools had to be located in an area accessible for the project team members and thus were selected based on this criterion. As a result, there was a broad geographical dispersion of participating schools. The mentoring of students with ASN by research members furthermore is a substantial confounding variable on the observed outcomes. Due to the research team's direct involvement with students it is not possible to make statements about the causality of the changes and differences. It is possible that without this intervention, students

Table 10.4. Pre-post-comparison of achievement motivation of students with additional support needs between T1 and T2 (n=33)

Scales of SELLMO	t-values at pre-measurement (T1)			t-values at post-measurement after 4-6 months (T2)			Change of achievement motivation from T1 to T2							
							decrease		increase		no change		Sign Test	
	Md	Range	n.a. as n (%)	Md	Range	n.a. as n (%)	n	%	n	%	n	%	p^a	d^b
LG	43.0	19–71	1 (3%)	49.0	23–71	9 (27%)	8	24%	14	42%	1	3%	.286	—
ApAG	49.5	23–68	1 (3%)	52.0	30–66	8 (24%)	8	24%	16	48%	–	–	.152	—
AvAG	53.0	33–74	1 (3%)	53.0	34–71	8 (24%)	9	27%	13	39%	2	6%	.523	—
WA	54.0	35–71	2 (6%)	53.0	36–61	8 (24%)	13	39%	8	24%	2	6%	.383	—

Notes: Md = median; [a] adjusted significance level of p* < .006; [b] effect size (Cohen's d): small (d ≥ .10), medium (d ≥ .30), large (d ≥ .50); n.a. = not available; LG = Learning Goals, ApAG = Approximation Achievement Goals, AvAG = Avoidance Achievement Goals, WA = Work Avoidance; percentages may not add up to 100 due to rounding

Table 10.5. *Comparison between students with additional support needs and their classmates regarding their achievement motivation at T1 and T2*

Scales of SELLMO	t-values of students with ASN			t-values of classmates			Comparison between students with ASN and classmates								
							above Md of classmates		under Md of classmates		same Md as classmates		Mann-Whitney-U-Test		
	Md	Range	n.a. as n (%)	Md	Range	n.a. as n (%)	n	%	n	%	n	%	z^a	p^b	d^c
Measurement point T1	n = 33			n = 508											
LG	43.0	19–71	1 (3%)	49.0	19–71	16 (3%)	8	24%	23	70%	2	6%	−3.253	.001	,57
ApAG	49.5	23–68	1 (3%)	50.0	20–68	17 (3%)	14	42%	16	49%	3	9%	−1.031	.302	—
AvAG	53.0	33–74	1 (3%)	51.0	29–74	16 (3%)	18	55%	14	42%	1	3%	−0.334	.738	—
WA	54.0	35–71	2 (6%)	50.0	31–74	36 (7%)	20	61%	10	30%	3	9%	−1.678	.093	—
Measurement point T2	n = 33			n = 606											
LG	49.0	23–71	8 (26%)	49.0	27–71	141 (23%)	21	64%	12	36%	—	—	−0.788	.431	—
ApAG	52.0	30–66	7 (23%)	54.0	20–68	140 (23%)	16	49%	15	46%	2	6%	−0.619	.536	—
AvAG	53.0	34–71	7 (23%)	53.0	29–74	140 (23%)	20	61%	12	36%	1	3%	−0.672	.502	—
WA	53.0	36–61	7 (23%)	54.0	31–74	141 (23%)	16	49%	15	46%	2	6%	−2.197	.028	—

Notes: ASN = additional support needs; Md = median; [a] z-value; [b] adjusted significance level of p**<.003; [c] effect size (Cohen's d): small (d ≥ .10), medium (d ≥ .30), large (d ≥ .50); n.a. = not available; LG = Learning Goals, ApAG = Approximation Achievement Goals, AvAG = Avoidance Achievement Goals, WA = Work Avoidance; percentages may not add up to 100 due to rounding

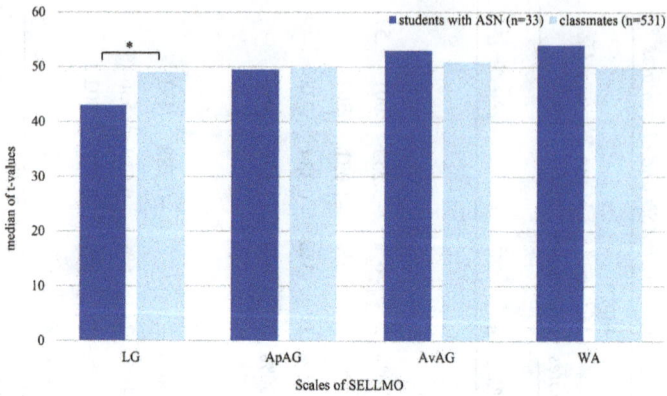

Figure 10.3. T-values of students with Additional Support Needs (ASN) and of their classmates regarding achievement motivation at T1. LG = Learning Goals, ApAG = Approximation Achievement Goals, AvAG = Avoidance Achievement Goals, WA = Work Avoidance. A significantly lower t-value in 70% of students with ASN is represented by the asterisk (*)

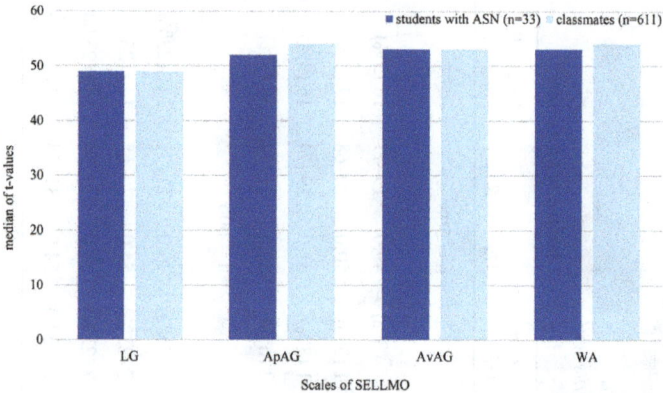

Figure 10.4. T-values of students with Additional Support Needs (ASN) and of their classmates regarding achievement motivation at T2. LG = Learning Goals, ApAG = Approximation Achievement Goals, AvAG = Avoidance Achievement Goals, WA = Work Avoidance

with ASN may have shown greater difficulty during the transition period. The utilised questionnaires SESSKO and SELLMO are self-assessment questionnaires that might have exceeded the self-reflection capabilities of some students. Inclusion of corroborating data, from teacher or parent reports, would have strengthened the results of this study.

DISCUSSION AND CONCLUSIONS

This study assessed the impact that a transition from primary to secondary education has on students' academic self-concept and motivation, with a specific focus on students with ASN. The study aimed to identify whether the academic self-concept and motivation of students with ASN changes during the first semester following this transition. The study was also interested in identifying whether students with ASN showed different changes in academic self-concept and motivation during transitions to their non-ASN classmates.

A marginal change of academic self-concept from T1 to T2 was observed for students with ASN. Regarding achievement motivation, a tendential increase in the areas of LG, ApAG and AvAG as well as a tendential decrease in the area of WA became apparent. No significant changes were seen over the period of research. This study suggests, therefore, that academic self-concept and motivation may remain stable across academic transition for students with ASN. Further research is needed in order to better understand the trajectory of academic self-concept and motivation during transitions for students with ASN.

When students with ASN were compared to their classmates, students with ASN were identifying as significantly lower levels of academic self-concept at T2. This suggests that already at the beginning of secondary school students with ASN may be feeling less capable of meeting the new educational requirements than their peers.

Regarding their achievement motivation, students with ASN displayed a significantly lower LG-orientation as well as a tendentially lower ApAG-orientation, a tendentially higher AvAG-orientation and a tendentially stronger inclination to work avoidance compared with their classmates at T1. According to Spinath et al. (2012), a high learning-goal orientation has a positive effect on educational engagement and achievement. In order to explain the significant differences in the examined sample, information about the students (e.g., cognitive capacity), the teaching structure, the class leadership style of the primary school teacher, the schools' catchment area and staff resources needs to be included in future research. The group of students with ASN examined in this study already has a lower base motivation for independent learning than the simultaneously examined group of classmates at the end of 4th grade. The higher avoidance tendencies in the group with ASN possibly indicate that some students have already developed strategies in order not to stand out too much in the group while their aversion to work has increased at the same time. This observation needs to be verified in further studies. The emerging tendencies and supposed contradictions, e.g. students with ASN showing higher LG-values (learning as challenge) but also higher AvAG-values (concealing lack of knowledge and skills) in relative comparison at T2, do not withstand a statistical significance test and need to be examined more in-depth in further studies.

Pathways to a successful transition. The present results may provide indications that it is important to support the academic transition of students from primary to

183

secondary education, especially for students with ASN. It is possible that the first units taught at the beginning of secondary schools may have an impact on a students' transition, and should be used to strengthen students' academic self-concept and achievement motivation. However, secondary teachers will require information about the relative competencies of their new students before the beginning of the school year in order to develop appropriate lesson plans. In the Anglo-American language area, this issue is addressed in some schools using a 'Transition-Plan', in which relevant information about the student is communicated across systems. It is important to remove administrative barriers, e.g. restrictions due to privacy policies, and develop secondary school transition sensitively, in cooperation with the primary schools. A system-linking preparation of lessons might be an important component for a developmentally productive transition design and may preventively counteract the feeling of being left behind. Moreover, service facilities for the transition management between schools is advised. The functions of these facilities should include system-linking networking, consulting and diagnostic tasks as well as supporting subject-specific didactical differentiation. This way, teachers in the entry grades of secondary schools could receive consultation and assistance in the preparation of lessons, especially for children and adolescents with ASN. At the same time, a reliable contact person should be available for primary schools. This contact person would actively influence the transition process on an educational, organisational and socio-emotional level to support the sense of belonging as early as the second semester of 4th grade. Furthermore, a reliable reference teacher acting as important support for transition management in the first weeks and months of re-orientation would help students as they transition into secondary school. These measures should also contribute to good emotional well-being and to strengthening the sense of school belonging especially for students with ASN.

REFERENCES

Akos, P. (2010). Moving through elementary, middle, and high schools: The primary to secondary shifts in the United States. In D. Jindal-Snape (Ed.), *Academic transitions: Moving stories from around the world* (pp. 125–142). New York, NY: Routledge.

Allen, K., & Boyle, C. (2016). Pathways to school belonging. *The Australian Educational and Developmental Psychologist, 33*(1), ii–iv. doi:10.1017/edp.2016.13

American Psychological Association. (2013). *Diagnostic and statistical manual of mental disorders: DSM-5* (5th ed.). Washington, DC: Author.

Anderman, L. H., & Anderman, E. M. (1999). Social predictors of changes in students' achievement goal orientations. *Contemporary Educational Psychology, 25*, 21–37.

Bronfenbrenner, U. (1993). *Die Ökologie der menschlichen Entwicklung: Natürliche und geplante Experimente* [The ecology of human development: Experiments by nature and design]. Frankfurt am Main: Fischer.

Bronfenbrenner, U. (2009). *The ecology of human development: Experiments by nature and design.* Cambridge, MA: Harvard University Press.

Cohen, J. (1988). *Statistical power analysis for the behavioral sciences* (2nd ed.). Abingdon-on-Thames: Routledge.

Cole, D. A., Maxwell, S. E., Martin, J. M., Peeke, L. G., Seroczynski, A. D., Tram, J. M., Hoffman, K. B., Ruiz, M. D., Jacquez, F., & Maschmann, T. (2001). The development of multiple domains of child and adolescent self-concept: A cohort sequential longitudinal design. *Child Development, 72*, 1723–1746.

Döpfner, M., Pflück, J., & Kinnen, C. (2014). *CBCL/6-18R, TRF/6-18R, YSR/11-18R. Deutsche Schulalter-Formen der Child Behavior Checklist von Thomas M. Achenbach* [CBCL/6-18R, TRF/6-18R, YSR/11-18R. German school-age forms of the Child Behavior Checklist by Thomas M. Achenbach]. Göttingen: Hogrefe.

Fend, H. (1989). Pädagogische Programme und ihre Wirksamkeit. Das Beispiel der Umdeutung schulischer Normen und Erwartungen in der Altersgruppe [Paedagogic programs and their effectiveness. The example of reinterpretating of academic norms and expectations within the age-group]. In W. Breyvogel (Ed.), *Pädagogische Jugendforschung* (pp. 187–200). Opladen: Leske + Budrich.

Galton, M. (2010). Moving to secondary school: What do pupils in England say about the experience? In D. Jindal-Snape (Ed.), *Academic transitions: Moving stories from around the world* (pp. 107–123). New York, NY: Routledge.

Galton, M., & Hargreaves, L. (2002). Transfer: A future agenda. In M. Galton & L. Hargreaves (Eds.), *Transfer from primary classroom: 20 years on* (pp. 185–208). London: Routledge Falmer.

Gillen-O'Neel, C., & Fuligni, A. (2013). A longitudinal study of school belonging and academic motivation across high school. *Child Development, 84*(2), 678–692.

Griebel, W. (2005). Übergang von Kindertagesstätte in die Schule: Nicht nur Kompetenzen des Kindes sind gefordert, sondern die seines sozialen Systems. Impulsreferat im Rahmen der Tagung „Unterschiedliche Begabungen und differenzierte Förderung in der Schule" in der katholischen Akademie in Berllin am 14.11.2005 und 15.11.2005 [Transition from nursery into school: not only competencies from the child are required, but those of its social system. A talk at the conferenct „Different talents and differentiated support at school" at the catholic academy in Berlin on 14 and 15 November 2005]. Retrieved July 27, 2011, from http://berliner-runde.net/Fleyer/Kirche%20und%20 Bildung%20II%20Beitrag_Griebel.pdf

Griebel, W., & Niesel, R. (2004). *Transitionen. Fähigkeit von Kindern in Tageseinrichtungen fördern, Veränderungen erfolgreich zu bewältigen* [Transitions. Promoting abilities of children in day-care facilities to successfully manage changes]. Weinheim: Beltz.

Hattie, J. (2013). *Lernen sichtbar machen. Überarbeitete deutschsprachige Ausgabe von Visible Learning. Übersetzt und überarbeitet von W. Beywel, & K. Zierer.* Baltmannsweiler: Schneider.

Hughes, L. A., Banks, P., & Terras, M. (2013). Secondary school transition for children with special educational needs. A literature review. *Supporting for Learning, 28*(1), 24–34.

Jindal-Snape, D. (2010). *Academic transition: Moving stories from around the world.* New York, NY: Routledge.

Jindal-Snape, D. (2016). *A-Z of transitions.* Basingstoke: Palgrave.

Jindal-Snape, D., & Foggie, J. (2008). A holistic approach to primary-secondary transitions. *Improving Schools, 11*, 5–18.

Jindal-Snape, D., & Miller, D. J. (2010). Understanding transitions through self-esteem and resilience. In D. Jindal Snape (Ed.), *Education transition: Moving stories from around the world* (pp. 11–32). New York, NY: Routledge.

Lucey, H., & Reay, R. (2000). Identities in transition: Anxiety and excitement in the move to secondary school. *Oxford Review of Education, 26*, 191–205.

Marsh, H. W. (1990). A multidimensional, hierarchical model of self-concept: Theoretical and empirical justification. *Education Psychology Review, 2*, 77–172.

Marsh, H. W., & Shavelson, R. J. (1985). Self-concept: Its multifaceted hierarchical structure. *Educational Psychologist, 20*, 107–125.

Mays, D. (2014). *In Steps! – wirksame Faktoren schulischer Transition. Gestaltung erfolgreicher Übergänge bei Gefühls- und Verhaltensstörungen* [In steps! – Effective factors of academic transition. Designing successful transitions with emotional and behavioural disorders]. Bad Heilbrunn: Klinkhardt.

Mays, D. (2016). Transparenz als wirksamer Faktor schulischer Transition [Transparency as effective factor of academic transition]. In K. Moegling & S. Schude (Eds.), *Transparenz im Unterricht und*

185

in der Schule. Theorie und Praxis transparenten Unterrichts und transparenter Schulorganisation [Transparency in education and at school theory and practice of transparent education and transparent school organisation]. Immenhausen: Prolog-Verlag.

Mays, D., Jindal-Snape, D., & Boyle, C. (2019). Academic transitions and inclusion. In C. Boyle, S. Mayropoulou, & J. Anderson (Eds.), *Inclusive education: Global issues & controversies. Studies in inclusive education.* Boston, MA: Brill.

Mruk, C. J. (2006). *Self-esteem: Research, theory and practice: Toward a positive psychology of self-esteem* (3rd ed.). New York, NY: Springer.

Newman, T., & Blackburn, B. (2002). *Interchange 78: Transitions in the lives of children and young people: Resilience factors.* Edinburg: The Scottish Executive Education Department.

Nickel, H. (1990). Das Problem der Einschulung aus ökologisch-systemischer Perspektive [The problem of school enrolment from an ecological-systemic perspective]. *Psychologie in Erziehung und Unterricht, 37,* 217–227.

Rosenkoetter, S., Schroeder, C., Rous, B., Hains, A., Shaw, J., & McCormick, K. (2009). *A review of research in early childhood transition: Child and family studies* (Technical Report #5). Lexington: University of Kentucky, Human Development Institute, National Early Childhood Transition Center. Retrieved April 27, 2017, from http://www.ihdi.uky.edu/nectc/

Saarni, C. (2002). Die Entwicklung von emotionaler Kompetenz in Beziehungen [The development of emotional competency in relationships]. In M. Salisch (Ed.), *Emotionale Kompetenz entwickeln* [Developing emotional competency]. Berlin: Kohlhammer.

Schiefele, R., & Schaffner, E. (2015). Motivation. In E. Wild & J. Möller (Eds.), *Pädagogische Psychologie* [Paedagogical psychology] (2nd ed., pp. 153–176). Berlin: Springer.

Schöne, C., Dickhäuser, O., Spinath, B., & Stiensmeier-Pelster, J. (2012). *SESSKO. Skalen zur Erfassung des schulischen Selbstkonzepts* [SESSKO. Scales for assessment of academic self-concept] (2nd ed.). Göttingen: Hogrefe.

Schwarzer, R. (1979). Bezugsgruppeneffekte in schulischen Umwelten [Big-fish-little-pond effects in educational environments]. *Zeitschrift für empirische Pädagogik, 3,* 153–166.

Schwarzer, R., & Jerusalem, M. (1983). Selbstkonzeptentwicklung in schulischen Bezugsgruppen – eine dynamische Mehrebenanalyse [Development of self-concept in educational peer-groups – A dynamic multilayer analysis]. *Zeitschrift für personenzentrierte Psychologie und Psychotherapie, 2,* 79–87.

Schwarzer, R., Lange, B., & Jerusalem, M. (1982). Selbstkonzeptentwicklung nach einem Bezugsgruppenwechsel [Development of self-concept after a change of peer-groups]. *Zeitschrift für Entwicklungspsychologie und Pädagogische Psychologie, 14,* 125–140.

Shavelson, R. J., Hubner, J. J., & Stanton, G. C. (1976). Self-concept: Validation of construct interpretations. *Review of Educational Research, 46*(3), 407–441.

Slaten, C. D., Ferguson, J. K., Allen, K.-A., Bodrick, D.-V., & Waters, L. (2016). School belonging: A review of the history, current trends, and future directions. *The Educational and Developmental Psychologist, 33*(1), 1–15. doi:10.1017/edp.2016.6

Spinath, B., Stiensmeier-Pelster, J., Schöne, C., & Dickhäuser, O. (2012). *SELLMO. Skalen zur Erfassung der Lern- und Leistungsmotivation* [SELLMO. Scales for assessment of learning and achievement motivation] (2nd ed.). Göttingen: Hogrefe.

SPSS Inc. (2009). *PASW statistics for windows* (Version 18.0) [Statistical Software]. Chicago, IL: SPSS Inc.

Trautwein, U. (2003). *Schule und Selbstwert* [School and self-esteem]. Münster: Waxmann.

Trautwein, U., Köller, O., & Baumert, J. (2004). Des einen Freud', des anderen Leid? Der Beitrag schulischen Problemverhaltens zur Selbstkonzeptentwicklung [One's joy and the other's sorrow? The contribution of academic problem behaviour in the development of self-concept]. *Zeitschrift für Pädagogische Psychologie, 18*(1), 15–29.

Uwah, C. J., McMahon, H. G., & Furlow, C. F. (2008). School belonging, educational aspirations, and academic self-efficacy among African American male high school students: Implications for school counselors. *Professional School Counseling, 11*(5), 296–305.

Welzer, H. (1993). *Transitionen. Zur Sozialpsychologie biographischer Wandlungsprozesse* [Transitions. About the social psychology of biographic transformation processes]. Tübingen: Edition discord.

Daniel Mays
University of Siegen
Germany

Sebastian Franke
Developmental Science and special education (Inclusion)
University of Siegen
Germany

Franka Metzner
Department of Medical Psychology
University Medical Centre Hamburg-Eppendorf
Germany

Christopher Boyle
Graduate School of Education
University of Exeter
England

Divya Jindal-Snape
University of Dundee
Scotland

Lisa Schneider
University of Siegen
Germany

Holger Zielemanns
University of Siegen
Germany

Silke Pawils
Department of Medical Psychology
University Medical Centre Hamburg-Eppendorf
Germany

Michelle Wichmann
Department of Medical Psychology
University Medical Centre Hamburg-Eppendorf
Germany

PART 4

INTERVENTIONS FOR SCHOOL BELONGING

KELLY-ANN ALLEN, DIANNE VELLA-BRODRICK
AND LEA WATERS

11. RETHINKING SCHOOL BELONGING

A Socio-Ecological Framework

INTRODUCTION

Belonging has been described as the need for positive regard from others (Rogers, 1951), affiliation motivation (McClelland, 1987), and the desire for relatedness (Vallerand, 1997). Friedman (2007) described a sense of belonging as the development of the self and identity building. It is well accepted that sense of belonging is not dependent on participation with, or proximity to, others. Rather, it relies on perceptions about the quality of social interactions (Baumeister & Leary, 1995). Therefore, belonging could be considered as one's perception of his or her involvement in a social system or environment (Hagerty, Lynch-Sauer, Patusky, Bouwsema, & Collier, 1992).

An extensive review of the literature demonstrates that belonging is an important construct, not only at a theoretical level, but also at an empirical level (Hagerty, Williams, & Oe, 2002; Hale, Hannum, & Espelage, 2005). A marked proportion of the psychological literature suggests that general belonging is a vital component of psychological and physical health and these effects are typically sustained (Daley & Buchanan, 1999; Poulton, Caspi, & Milne, 2002; Wadsworth, Thomsen, Saltzman, Connor-Smith, & Compas, 2001).

A sense of belonging is considered to play a fundamental role in adolescent development, particularly in respect to identity formation (Brechwald & Prinstein, 2011; Davis, 2012), psychosocial adjustment, and transition to adulthood (O'Connor et al., 2010). The literature has also demonstrated that *school belonging*, more specifically, is an important factor in the successful psychosocial adjustment of young people and presents a purpose for schools to engage in interventions and strategies that might promote belonging to school (Lonczak, Abbott, Hawkins, Kosterman, & Catalano, 2002; Nutbrown & Clough, 2009; O'Connor, 2010; O'Connor, Sanson, & Frydenberg, 2012; Sari, 2012).

It has been argued that schools play an important role in fostering a sense of belonging for students (Allen & Bowles, 2013) because they are important institutions that can build social networks for young people. Yet, in a review of the literature concerned with school belonging, Allen and Bowles (2013) have argued that the importance of a student's sense of belongingness to school has not been

© KONINKLIJKE BRILL NV, LEIDEN, 2018 | DOI:10.1163/9789004386969_011

given the same degree of attention as a student's academic success. This finding is consistent with the lower level of attention devoted to other areas of preventive interventions in schools such as health promotion and social and emotional learning (Collaborative for Academic Social and Emotional Learning [CASEL], 2003; Hagerty et al., 1992; West, Sweeting, & Leyland, 2004). Very few examples of interventions aimed at specifically increasing a student's sense of belonging can be found at the secondary school level in Australian schools (e.g., SenseAbility; Beyond Blue, 2014), however the absence of school belonging in whole-school intervention programs appears to be a universal issue with very few examples in the literature (e.g., Centres for Disease Control and Prevention [CDC], 2009). One reason why school belonging is seldom examined in schools could be due to the absence of a model or framework that schools can employ to foster belonging in students. The field of school belonging research in this respect, is largely theoretical and this may be one factor that restricts the development of belongingness interventions (e.g., in addition to definitional and measurement issues).

Clearly, there is a need for frameworks that assist schools to foster school belonging. Yet, only a small number of conceptual frameworks have focused on school belonging at the student level (e.g., motivation, individual characteristics, emotional instability) (Brendtro, Brokenleg, & VanBockern, 2002; Connell & Wellborn, 1991; Malti & Noam, 2009; Ryan & Deci, 2000). Furthermore, these frameworks are limited because they have focused on school belonging as an internal, intra-individual phenomenon and, thus, have not accounted for relational factors and broader aspects in the school environment that influence a student's sense of belonging. While a few frameworks have recognised the importance of school resources and support (e.g., CDC, 2009; McMahon et al., 2008; Wallace, Ye, & Chhuon, 2012), very few of these frameworks have presented school belonging as a multidimensional construct within a multilayered social ecology based on empirical evidence (e.g., Rowe, Stewart, & Patterson, 2007; Waters, Cross, & Reunion, 2009).

THE SOCIO-ECOLOGICAL FRAMEWORK OF SCHOOL BELONGING

We propose that school belonging is a student's sense of affiliation to his or her school, influenced by individual, relational, and organisational factors inside a broader school community and within a political, cultural, and geographical landscape unique to each school setting (Allen, Kern, Vella-Brodrick, Hattie, & Waters, 2016). Put more simply, school belonging is one's feeling of being connected to a school within a school social system.

In this conceptual chapter, we propose that school belonging is a multi-layered socio-ecological phenomena and we apply Bronfenbrenner's (1979) ecological framework for human development to school belonging in order to explore the various layers that affect a student's sense of school belonging. Bronfenbrenner's (1979) ecological framework for human development is concerned with systems in society and suggests that for young people, the family is the first unit to which children belong. This is followed by school and community, with each student belonging to a broader network of groups and systems.

All children are at the centre of multiple levels of influence (i.e., the microsystem, mesosystem, exosystem, and macrosystem) and schools can have a significant effect on their development and psychosocial adjustment (Bronfenbrenner, 1979). Bronfenbrenner's (1979) ecological framework for human development serves as a reminder that within any school setting, each student is a part of a greater whole influenced by formal and informal groupings and overarching systems that are common and typically represented within all schools.

Socio-ecological frameworks such as Bronfenbrenner's (1979), emphasise the importance of social relationships, but also include tangible environmental, physical, and ecological variables, such as classrooms and resources (Bronfenbrenner, 1979). The socio-ecological layers represented in such frameworks may provide a structure for schools to improve school belonging by working at the level of the individual, working with interpersonal relationships (e.g., peer, teacher, and parent), and addressing whole school approaches (Saab, 2009; Waters et al., 2009; Waters, Cross, & Shaw, 2010).

Bronfenbrenner's (1979) ecological framework for human development provides the most widely applied theoretical construct to date with which to investigate belonging in an organisational setting such as a school, while acknowledging the innate desire humans have to belong (Anderson, Boyle, & Deppeler, 2014; Baumeister & Leary, 1995; Saab, 2009; Waters et al., 2009; Waters et al., 2010). This may be because Bronfenbrenner's socio-ecological framework represents the varied layers and systems within a school whereas other models and frameworks may only examine constructs directly related to the individual student (Brendtro et al., 2002; Malti & Noam, 2009).

The current conceptual chapter proposes a socio-ecological framework of school belonging (Figure 11.1) to explore school belonging at the individual (through individual characteristics), microsystem (through relationships with parents, peers, and teachers), mesosystem (through school rules and practices), exosystem (through the extended school community), and macrosystem levels (through legislation, social norms, and government initiatives such as the nationally collected data on academic achievement).

The framework can be used by educators, school leaders, and school psychologists to intervene at various levels across the school to enhance school belonging. It also provides an organising framework for researchers in the field to categorise the many different research findings on school belonging at the individual, classroom, and organisational levels. Such a classification system will benefit schools and shed light on which layers within the schools should be prioritised.

While there is plenty of research supporting the importance of school belonging, very few attempts have been made to understand *how it can be fostered*. Previous studies (Goodenow, 1992; Hurtado & Carter, 1997; Juvonen, 2006) have only focused on the definition, measurement, and importance of school belonging without

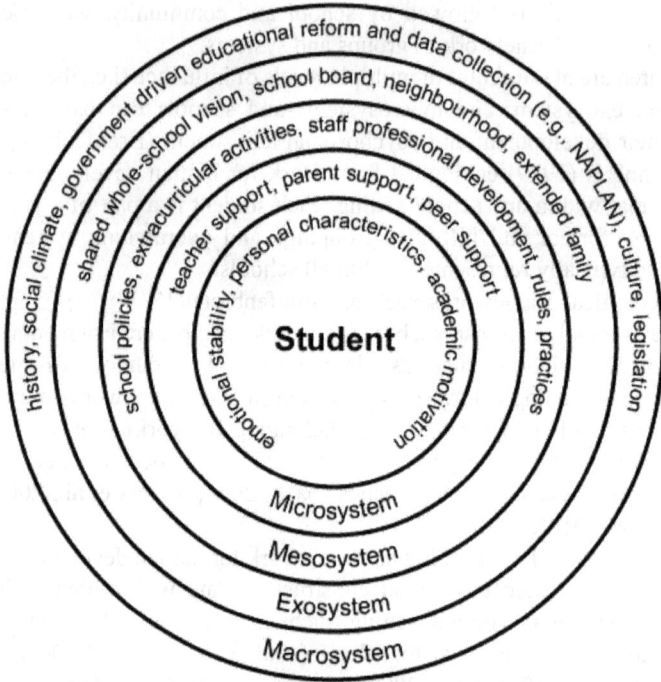

Figure 11.1. The socio-ecological framework of school belonging

identifying the precursors and methods for fostering a sense of belonging in school settings. Therefore, this chapter attempts to address this research-practice gap in schools by specifically looking at the themes that foster school belonging through Bronfenbrenner's (1979) socio-ecological framework for human development. This chapter also endeavours to draw upon existing empirical research to support the development of a framework. The translation of findings into an evidence-based framework can assist schools to address the research-practice gap and provide the necessary antecedent conditions for fostering school belonging (Hirschkorn & Geelan, 2008; Rowe & Stewart, 2011). Conceptual frameworks can be viewed as theories in their early stages, according to Sharma and Romas (2008), and as such, they should use empirical evidence and be subject to on-going testing to further develop an evidence base.

The framework used to support the socio-ecological framework of school belonging is based on the work of Wingspread Declaration on School Connections (2004), the Centers for Disease Control and Prevention (2009), as well as other research and various measurement instruments of school belonging (Appleton, Christenson, Kim, & Reschly, 2006; Goodenow, 1993; Libbey, 2004; McNeely, Nonnemaker, & Blum, 2002). This thematic framework represents a sample of important tiers in the literature on school belonging to broadly explore the question: *What themes influence school belonging?* The studies that informed the development of the socio-ecological framework of school belonging were sourced from electronic databases such as EBSCO's Discovery search layer, including Ovid Medline, Mental Health Abstracts, PsycINFO, Social Sciences Abstracts, Sociological Abstracts via SocioFile, Academic Search Premier, Social Sciences Citation Index, and ERIC. Studies were sourced from English speaking countries and published within the last 20 years. Therefore, broad ranges of studies have been used to support the development of the socio-ecological framework of school belonging.

The Layers and Their Interactions

The socio-ecological framework of school belonging outlines five levels of interconnected layers within an *ecology* that supports school belonging. The levels start with the individual and move in concentric rings outwards through the microsystem, mesosystem, exosystem, and macrosystem. The five layers of the socio-ecological framework of school belonging and associated evidence based practices will be discussed below.

Individual. The inner portion of the socio-ecological framework of school belonging represents the individual student and associated individual-level themes that relate to his or her sense of school belonging. Past literature indicates three distinct aspects within an individual student that have been found to correlate with school belonging: academic motivation, emotional stability, and personal characteristics (social and emotional competencies).

Academic motivation includes variables related to performance, objective measures (e.g., test scores and grades), classroom engagement, and perceived value of and usefulness of the curriculum and school (Wingspread Declaration on School Connections,[1] 2004). Gillen-O'Neel and Fuligni (2013) performed longitudinal within-person analyses with 572 young people aged between 13 and 19 years over a four-year period. The results suggested that school belonging was positively associated with a higher level of perceived academic value. The authors suggest that when young people feel connected to their school, they are more likely to find school useful and be academically motivated.

Emotional stability is defined as the absence of maladaptive behaviour, psychopathology, or persistent distress, thus including the absence of mental illness (Allen & McKenzie, 2015; Cole, Llera, & Pemberton, 2009). One example of an emotional instability variable that has been studied in the literature on school belonging is anxiety where a consistent inverse relationship has been found within its association with school belonging (Williams & Galliher, 2006; Lee & Robbins, 2000). It is unlikely that schools will use the term *emotional instability* in policy and practice. Instead, schools are more likely to build *emotional stability* and use terminology based on psychological health and wellbeing (Donovan, 2011). This is

195

why the term emotional stability has been used in the framework of school belonging rather than emotional instability. Emotional stability has not been examined in previous frameworks of school belonging, therefore, the socio-ecological framework of school belonging is unique in that it represents this important theme.

The third theme at the student level that has been shown to relate to school belonging involves personal characteristics (i.e., social and emotional competencies), like coping skills, positive affect, self-efficacy, self-esteem, and self-concept (Hawkins & Weis, 1985; Faircloth, 2009; Huebner, Appleton, & Antaramian, 2008; Samdal et al., 1998; Sirin & Rogers-Sirin, 2004). Frydenberg, Care, Freeman, and Chan (2009) found that students who engaged in productive coping (i.e., the ability to successfully regulate behaviours, cognitions, and emotions in response to daily stressors) were more likely to exhibit a greater sense of belonging to their school. Other research (e.g., Reschly, Huebner, Appleton, & Antaramian, 2008; Ryzin, Gravely, & Roseth, 2009) has demonstrated that positive emotions like optimism, hope, and hopefulness are positively associated with school belonging as well. Reschly et al. (2008) identified that social and emotional competencies such as having a positive affect and productive coping skills play an important role in fostering school belonging and vice versa. Therefore, when schools engage in practices that encourage academic motivation, build emotional stability, and foster certain personal characteristics (e.g., coping skills, self-efficacy, self-esteem, and self-regulation), this will likely increase the students' sense of school belonging.

The direction of the relationships between academic motivation, emotional stability, and personal characteristics with school belonging has not been accurately determined from past research, but it is likely the relationship is bidirectional (e.g., Goodenow & Grady, 1993; Ryan, 1995; Klem & Connell, 2004; Zimmer-Gembeck, Chipuer, Hanisch, Creed, & McGregor, 2006). As such, it is suggested that while academic motivation, emotional stability, and personal characteristics may increase a sense of school belonging, school belonging may also lead to an increase in academic motivation, emotional stability, and personal characteristics (such as self-esteem and self-efficacy). Schools seeking to build school belonging can do so by creating high academic motivation, building strong emotional stability, and fostering personal characteristics of students.

Table 11.1 outlines a set of evidence-based practices designed to increase school belonging at the individual (student) level, based on the three themes of academic motivation, emotional instability, and personal characteristics (Caraway et al., 2003; Zimmer-Gembeck et al., 2006; Sirin & Rogers-Sirin, 2004). That is, these practices are directed at the student and designed to boost his or her academic motivation, cultivate emotional stability, and foster personal characteristics such as coping skills, self-esteem, positive affect, and prosocial goal behaviour. Future intervention studies are needed to confirm the potential for academic motivation, emotional stability, and personal characteristics to increase school belonging, but this table represents key independent variables found in studies that have examined school belonging that have reported a significant and positive relationship and have reported medium to

Table 11.1. Individual level practices associated with socio-ecological framework of school belonging

Target area	Evidence-based practices that can increase school belonging	Independent variables	Related studies
Academic Motivation	Encourage students to have high (developmentally appropriate) expectations of their own academic ability. Engage in practices that motivate students to aim to do well. Communicate expectations concerned with learning and behaviour. Apply flexible teaching methodologies and personalise learning. Use consistent positive messages that encourage students to achieve their personal best.	Self-academic rating and education goals	Heaven et al. (2002) Klem and Connell (2004) Guthrie and Davis (2003)
	Assist students to understand the benefit and purpose of what they are learning in relation to long- and short-term outcomes (i.e., perceived instrumentality) and lesson goals. Express a belief that what is being taught is important and valuable. Ensure that teachers are allocated to subject areas that they are interested and passionate about. Relate information to the students' real world and experiences.	Perceived Instrumentality Valuing academics	Walker (2012) Battistich, Schaps, Watson, and Solomon (1996) Whitlock (2006)
	Apply mastery goal orientation in the classroom so that students have opportunities to set goals, acquire skills to master those goals, and set further goals. Use teacher feedback to motivate students towards their goals. Emphasise student progress and help students have a good understanding of where they are in their progress and where they are headed next.	Mastery Goal Orientation	Wentzel (1998) Dweck, 1986)

(Continued)

197

Table 11.1. (Continued)

Target area	Evidence-based practices that can increase school belonging	Independent variables	Related studies
	Foster motivation through specific classroom interventions designed to motivate students (e.g., student-directed and strength-based learning). In addition, present novel and interesting learning opportunities to students that are based on student interests and abilities. Engage students through interactive approaches such as role play, group work, and problem solving. Teach skills and strategies related to academic motivation, competence and effective study (i.e., positive self-talk, goal setting, time management, organisation, help seeking). Encourage intrinsic rewards from learning by seeking feedback of student work from other students, teachers, parents, and the local school community.	Motivation	Battistich, Schaps, Watson, and Solomon (1996) Goodenow and Grady (1993) Patton, Bond, and Carlin (1996)
	Teach students skills related to self-regulation to assist in self-monitoring of their academic behaviour and motivating themselves. These skills can be taught by using reward systems and checklists to ensure they are on task and/or working towards acquiring the skills to achieve their goals. Enable students to develop skills that will assist them to prepare for class with the right material and resources.	Academic Self-Regulation	Ryzin et al. (2009)
	Provide career guidance and counselling services to students in respect to setting long-term goals and career ambitions.	Future Aspirations	Reschly et al. (2008)

| Emotional Stability | Implement mental health promotion activities and interventions using a whole-school approach (e.g., Act Belong Commit, www.actbelongcommit.org.au). Adopt specific evidence-based programs that target skills related to self-care, resiliency, social connectedness, managing stressors, and resolving conflict. Some specific examples include Mindmatters (www.mindmatters.edu.au), Coping for Success (Frydenberg, 2011), and Thinking Skills for Peak Performance (Brandon, 2012). Educate staff to identify early warning signs of mental illness, implement mental health first aid, and understand appropriate referral and response pathways for students at risk. Train key staff members in postvention (i.e., interventions conducted after a critical incident, to restore wellbeing when managing a critical incident). Encourage staff to proactively reach out to students who may be exhibiting signs of stress or distress. Encourage student help seeking behaviours across the school. Enable students to know where to access key staff members to seek personal support when needed (i.e., school counsellor, psychologist). Ensure that these individuals are known within the school community (e.g., they may participate actively in other school-based activities that are not directly related to counselling) to reduce stigma for students seeking these services. | Depressive Symptoms

Emotional Distress/problem
Stress
Fear of Failure
Psychoticism | Kaminski et al. (2010)
Kelly et al. (2012)
Kuperminc et al. (2001)
Shochet et al. (2006)
Shochet et al. (2011)

Education Development Center (2008)
Waters et al. (2010)
Wentzel (1998)
Wilkinson-Lee et al. (2011)
Roche and Kuperminc (2012)
Caraway et al. (2003)
Heaven et al. (2002) |

(Continued)

199

Table 11.1. (Continued)

Target area	Evidence-based practices that can increase school belonging	Independent variables	Related studies
Personal Characteristics	Ensure that students understand that they have a role to play in fostering their own sense of school belonging. This can be done through psychoeducational opportunities provided by the school, social and emotional learning, small group interventions, or individual counselling that specifically address the key themes found to foster school belonging (e.g., academic motivation, emotional stability, personal characteristics, and support from others) as well as boosting individual social and emotional competencies.	Self-esteem	Ryan et al. (1994) Sirin and Rogers-Sirin (2004)
			Proctor et al. (2011)
	Encourage students to identify their individual character strengths and provide opportunities for them to apply them within curricula and co-curricula activities. Character education has been shown to increase self-efficacy and self-esteem. Teach students about the benefits associated with a positive mindset (i.e., their beliefs and attitudes). For example, encourage students to view errors and mistakes as learning opportunities.		Dweck (1986)
	Engage students in setting personal goals related to their wellbeing in addition to goals set around their academic outcomes. Interventions can occur within the school that foster positive relationships, coping skills, adaptability, resilience, and positive prosocial behaviour.	Prosocial goal pursuit and behaviour	Wentzel (1998) Zimmer-Gembeck et al. (2006)
	Consider the use of positive psychology interventions to foster optimism, hopefulness, and happiness (see Seligman, 2011). These interventions can include gratitude curricula, giving to others, and savouring what went well well routines (Nielsen, 2011).	Positive affect	Heaven et al. (2002) Reschly et al. (2008) Ryzin et al. (2009) Stoddard et al. (2011)

Note: Practices are derived from the literature as indicated.

large effect sizes (medium $\geq$ .30, large $\geq$ .50, Cohen, 1988) ranging from r = .32 to r = .72. These variables are presented alongside effective evidence-based practices identified in previous research derived from the literature.

Microsystem. The importance of a student's relationship with parents, peers, and teachers has been illustrated through various frameworks incorporating school belonging (e.g., CDC, 2009; Connell & Wellborn, 1991). One example is the Self-System Process Model applied to educational settings by Connell and Wellborn (1991). Elements of this model include relationship skills with peers and adults, self-awareness of feelings, emotional regulation, and conflict resolution skills. Thus, it is clear that both the individual and microsystem levels work together to foster school belonging.

Brophy (2004) encourages educators to enhance students' positive dispositional traits such as initiative and self-perceived competence, which contribute to social interactions and relatedness to adults and peers within a school setting. Through Brophy's work, based on a systematic review of motivational literature, the findings suggest that the individual and microsystem levels of the socio-ecological framework interact, because when a school builds the personal characteristics of self-perceived competence (e.g., self-efficacy, self-esteem, and self-concept), this increases the students' relational skills. This in turn strengthens relationships within the students' microsystem (e.g., with parents, peers, and teachers).

Peer support has been found to be an important variable in influencing a sense of school belonging (Goodenow & Grady, 1993; Hamm & Faircloth, 2005; Reschly, Busch, Betts, Deno, & Long, 2009; Osterman, 2000). Libbey (2004) found this variable to be especially valid on measures that looked at school connectedness. The literature suggests that peers may facilitate adolescent students' feelings of being connected to school through social and academic support (Wentzel, 1998), acceptance (Wang & Eccles, 2012), trust (Garcia-Reid, Reid, & Peterson, 2005), or merely being present (e.g., having friends at school; Whitlock, 2006).

In the literature, parents are also found to play an important role in fostering school belonging (Brewster & Bowen, 2004; Wang & Eccles, 2012). Studies have shown that when parents provide support and show care, compassion, and encouragement towards academic endeavours, young people are more likely to exhibit greater connectedness to school (Benner et al., 2008; Brewster & Bowen, 2004; Carter, McGee, Taylor, & Williams, 2007; Wang & Eccles, 2012).

The importance of teachers, towards student outcomes has been widely studied (e.g., Anderman, 2002; Hattie, 2009; Wang & Eccles, 2012). In a large-scale synthesis of research, Hattie (2009) ranked a teacher-student relationship (large effect size, d = .72) as an important contributor to enhancing academic outcomes in students. In respect to school belonging, a study by Brewster and Bowen (2004) involving 699 high school students in the United States, likewise established that while support from others (e.g., parents) was indeed beneficial for students, teacher support was the more important factor. This finding has been widely supported by other studies (e.g., Anderman, 2003; Garcia-Reid, 2007; Johnson, 2009; Sakiz, 2012).

Table 11.2 outlines examples of evidence-based strategies that specifically target the microsystem layer of the socio-ecological framework. Similar to Table 11.1, the approaches outlined are derived from the literature as indicated in the table and developed from key independent variables found in the literature that reported a significant and positive relationship with school belonging with effect sizes ranging from medium to large strength $r = .30$ to $r = .86$ (Cohen, 1988). Future research is needed to evaluate what specific interventions are needed for the themes of peer, parent, and teacher support to increase school belonging, but this table represents some examples of approaches found in the previous literature worth exploring.

Mesosystem. The mesosystem can be seen as a by-product of the interactions among the layers in the socio-ecological framework, and thus not only represents school processes, practices, policy, and pedagogy (Libbey, 2004; Saab, 2009), but also highlights the unique bi-directional interactions of the features within the microsystem layer. Tillery, Varjas, Roach, Kuperminc, and Meyers (2013) suggested that support for others within a school system (parents, peers, and teachers), may be made stronger or weaker by aspects of the mesosystem, such as the organisational structure and practices within the school. For example, schools promote safety at the mesosystem level through school rules and policies (Saab, 2009). *Feeling safe at school* has been identified in the literature as an important factor in a student's sense of belonging to school (CDC, 2009; Samdal et al., 1998; Wingspread Declaration on School Connections, 2004; Whitlock, 2006) and has also been found to be a central theme in measures of school connectedness and school belonging (Libbey, 2004).

School vision and mission statements are another example of one element of the mesosystem in the socio-ecological framework of school belonging (Allen, Kern, Vella-Brodrick, & Waters, 2017). School vision and mission statements outline a school's purpose and they may provide a school with an opportunity to create a shared vision in respect to how school belonging is prioritised. School vision and mission statements are, therefore, appropriate to include in a socio-ecological framework specific to a school setting due to their ability to offer a vehicle to promote a school's commitment to fostering school belonging (Allen et al., 2017). The development of school vision and mission statements that prioritise school belongingness can be created by schools to promote the school's approach to fostering school belonging and assist the development of goals and objectives around creating a stronger school community (CDC, 2009).

A number of studies have explored the importance of students' belief in school rules, discipline, and fairness upon school belonging (Brown & Evans, 2002; Libbey, 2004). A review of the literature on the subject shows strong evidence for school engagement and retention in schools where discipline is enforced consistently and fairly (Finn & Voelkl, 1993; Rumberger, 1995), therefore policies concerned with these variables should be an important consideration for all schools.

Multiple group memberships, such as those provided by extracurricular activities are another example of a prevalent theme in the literature on school belonging.

Table 11.2. Microsystem level practices associated with socio-ecological framework of school belonging

Target area	Evidence-based practices that can increase school belonging	Independent variables	Related studies
Parent Support	Provide opportunities for parents to be involved in the school in meaningful ways, such as through family events and parent led committees. Enable strong communication between school staff and parents through the use of newsletters, information nights, and email correspondence. Encourage parents to feel comfortable in approaching staff members about their child's schooling. Consider disseminating information to parents that specifically provides information and strategies for supporting their child's learning and sense of belonging to the school.	Family Support for learning	Reschly et al. (2008)
	Offer parenting courses and information nights that promote ways to foster positive parent-child relationships and positive communication skills. Ensure parents are aware of school support staff and teaching staff that may be able to provide appropriate referral pathways and support to parents when there has been a breakdown in the relationship between the adolescent and the parent.	Parent–Student relationship	Brookmeyer et al. (2006) Carter et al. (2007) Henrich et al. (2005) Kelly et al. (2012) Mo and Singh (2008) Shochet et al. (2007) Stoddard et al. (2011) Waters et al. (2010) Wentzel (1998) Whitlock (2006)

(Continued)

Table 11.2. (Continued)

Target area	Evidence-based practices that can increase school belonging	Independent variables	Related studies
Peer Support	Enable multiple opportunities for students to know each other. Offer extracurricular activities, such as clubs, that can operate during lunchtimes and after school. Provide school sanctioned activities that foster social connectedness and school bonding (i.e., sports days, House activities). Encourage students to engage in these activities and ensure staff and parents model participatory behaviours.	Having friends and feeling accepted	Jennings (2003) Shochet et al. (2011) Whitlock (2006) Zimmer-Gembeck et al. (2006)
	Encourage student peers to be academically supportive towards each other. Create opportunities for study groups and peer-to-peer study support to assist homework and peer support learning. Encourage students to be inclusive, respectful, and tolerant towards the learning needs of others.	Peers are academically supportive	Goodenow and Grady (1993) Reschly et al. (2008)
	Consider formal peer mentoring and peer support programs within the school. New students, for example, may be assigned to a peer group or buddy system.	Peers are emotionally supportive	Ryzin et al. (2009)
Teacher Support	Encourage teachers to provide pastoral support to students. Allow teachers time to be available to students for personal support as well as academic support.	Positive student-teacher relationship	Anderman (2003) Bowen et al. (1998) Garcia-Reid (2007) Garcia-Reid et al. (2005) National Research Council and the Institute of Medicine (2004) Reschly et al. (2008)

Practice		References
Provide opportunities for teachers to get to know and understand their students (and at least know them by name). This can show their students that they care about them. Encourage teachers to seek feedback from students regarding their relationship and rapport. Consider structuring classes, tutorial, or home groups within the school so that teachers stay with the same students for a number of years.		Shochet et al. (2007) Shochet et al. (2011) Waters et al. (2010) Zimmer-Gembeck et al. (2006)
Demonstrate fair practices within the classroom. Teachers should model respectful behaviour towards each other and to students, and implement reasonable and consistent disciplinary procedures that are agreed upon by students and other staff. Teachers can create student led groups that provide mechanisms and pathways for student voice (e.g., student representative committee or a quality of teaching committee).	Teachers show fairness	Sakiz (2012)
Offer support for the academic learning of students. Consider implementing a tutoring program for students to seek additional support over their academic learning or extended learning opportunities after school or during the school holidays. Teachers can provide students with autonomy support and involvement over their own learning. They can use learning interactions, visible learning practices, and formative feedback (Hattie, 2009).	Academic Support	Patton, Bond, and Carlin (1996) Wentzel (1998) Ryzin et al. (2009)

Note: Practices are derived from the literature as indicated.

Researchers have found that a sense of school belonging can be positively influenced by the number of group memberships (Drolet & Arcand, 2013) and number of extracurricular activities a student may subscribe to (Dotterer, McHale, & Crouter, 2007; Libbey, 2004). One example is a study by Soria, Clark, and Koch (2011) who found that students' perceived sense of school belonging was influenced by whether or not they participated in extracurricular groups. The researchers investigated 1,865 students who participated in a range of student groups formed during orientation week activities. Results showed that students who attended these activities reported a higher sense of school belonging than those who did not. Furthermore, these students were more likely to have a higher grade point average than the respective cohort of non-participants. A similar relationship between a sense of belonging and extracurricular activities has been found in other research (Blomfield & Barber, 2010; Dotterer et al., 2007; Knifsend & Graham, 2012; Waters et al., 2010).

As well as fostering themes that positively correlate to school belonging at the individual and microsystem levels, it is clear from the literature that school leaders may also intervene at the mesosystem of the socio-ecological system. Table 11.3 outlines a set of evidence-based practices for schools derived from the past studies as outlined below. These practices aim to foster school belonging primarily at the policy and practice level. The mesosystem level can include many variables and it can be difficult for researchers to disentangle the multiple causal relationships. These practices should therefore be interpreted with some degree of caution and may serve as a source of further research.

Exosystem. The exosystem represents the community surrounding the school and encompasses the local neighbourhood, grandparents and extended families (although depending on the family structure they may also reside in the microsystem), local businesses, and community groups (Saab, 2009). Like the mesosystem, this layer is facilitated by the opportunities provided by schools that bring these groups together. Cemalcilar (2010) suggests that changing school-level practices at the exosystem level (or macro-level through reforms and laws) is a valid recommendation for interventions designed to foster school belonging. Some concrete examples would be for schools to connect with local businesses or other schools within the neighbourhood, or to implement school activities that involve the broader school community and the extended families of its students. Schools may also consider engaging with local community partners who are willing to provide a range of services within the school (e.g., a visiting GP, nurse health checks, dental services) (CDC, 2009).

Less empirical information is available for the exosystem and macrosystem levels on school belonging (Brown Kirschman & Karazsia, 2014). This is because it can be difficult to examine the exosystem or macrosystem, especially through studies concerned with preventative interventions like school belonging. These layers do not have a direct association with the student (or individual) where most studies are focused. Studies at the exosystem and macrosystem level on preventative

Table 11.3. Mesosystem level practices associated with socio-ecological framework of school belonging

Evidence-based practices	Related studies
Develop a whole-school shared vision that prioritises school belonging The development of a shared vision that prioritises school belongingness can be created by schools to promote the school's approach to fostering school belonging and assist the development of goals and objectives around creating a stronger school community (CDC, 2009). A school's vision or mission statement may be an appropriate vehicle to do this.	Bryson (2004) Legters, Balfanz, and McPartland (2002) Owings and Kaplan (2003) Stemler, Bebell, and Sonnabend (2011) Teddlie and Reynolds (2000)
Provide Staff Professional Development Provide teachers opportunities to receive professional development in the area of student school belonging that will allow them to enhance their relationships with students, foster a positive, safe, and fair classroom environment, and implement a student-centred pedagogy. Facilitate staff development through mentoring programs that are aimed at fostering student school belonging. Mentoring programs have been found to encourage teacher retention, increase job satisfaction, enhance teaching quality, as well as have positive implications for students' outcomes. Mentoring programs allow teachers to share strategies and techniques, learn from one another, and create a positive collaborative environment.	Allen et al. (2011) Ingersoll and Strong (2011) National Research Council and the Institute of Medicine (2004) Quint et al. (2005) Sherin and Han (2004)
School Policies Apply policies and practices that are concerned with student safety, discipline, and fairness (e.g., anti-bullying policies) as these variables have been found to be important for fostering school belonging. Seek input from students, parents, school staff, and community members to develop school policies. Use policies to create foundations for school rules/classroom rules that can be promulgated to create a fair and safe school climate. Ensure they are understood, and implemented by all staff members.	Hawkins, Von Cleve, and Catalano (1991). Garcia-Reid et al. (2005) Whitlock (2006)

(*Continued*)

207

Table 11.3. (Continued)

Evidence-based practices	Related studies
Ensure policies and practices are created that are concerned with staff wellbeing and connectedness to the school, which may promote whole-school belongingness, not just student belongingness. If the wellbeing and belongingness of staff members is taken into account, teachers may be more effective educators, which may enhance the student-teacher relationship found to be an important theme for fostering school belonging. One example is the Positive Educational Practices (PEPS) Framework (Noble & McGrath, 2008) which applies an optimistic approach to educational planning for school-wide wellbeing. Concepts such as positive emotions for students and teachers, social-emotional learning, focusing on ideal characteristics and strengths, and developing a sense of meaning are emphasised.	Noble (2006) Noble and McGrath (2008)
School Curricular and Extracurricular Activities	
Create school curricular and extracurricular activities that implement practices which foster school belonging. Allow for sufficient curriculum time to be available to teach social and emotional learning (SEL) found to increase school belonging. An example of such a program is MindMatters, which is a mental health program designed for Australian schools (Wyn et al., 2000). One of the objectives of the MindMatters program is to include mental health promotion and education in the school curriculum. Another example could be for schools to introduce programs and interventions in the school curriculum targeting the personal characteristics of students (e.g., coping skills and resiliency skills) as well as mental health promotion initiatives shown to foster school belonging. For instance, research using interventions on coping techniques has demonstrated that adaptive coping styles are positively related to perceived sense of school belonging (Frydenberg et al., 2009). Another example is Mindfulness-Based Education programs (Schonert-Reichl & Lawlor, 2010), adapted from the practice of mindfulness to assist socio-emotional competence and encourage positive emotions.	Frydenberg (2009) Schonert-Reichl and Lawlor (2010) Wyn et al. (2000)
Extracurricular activities have been found to be an important theme for school belonging. Aim to provide opportunities for students to join multiple groups within the school system (e.g., lunch time and afterschool activities) and offer school sanctioned groups for students to belong to (e.g., home group/tutorial groups, school house groupings).	Blomfield and Barber (2010) Dotterer et al. (2007) Shochet et al. (2007)

Note: Practices are derived from the literature as indicated.

interventions have traditionally engaged whole neighbourhoods at a considerable cost of time and resources (Brown Kirschman & Karazsia, 2014). Furthermore, publically available data concerned with the exosystem are not available as they are for other systems (e.g., mesosystem, microsystem).

Macrosystem. The macrosystem layer represents broader legislation and public policies at the federal level and includes factors such as regulations, guidelines, and government-driven initiatives and data collection (Saab, 2009) as well as the historical (e.g., past events, climate, collective attitudes, and conditions) and cultural (e.g., language, norms, customs, beliefs) context unique to each school. The macrosystem can be influential in the processes of daily school practice, particularly on how schools orient their priorities and goals. The macrosystem layer may influence a student's sense of belonging, although further research is needed to substantiate this claim. One example for this assertion can be seen in Australia, where the use of NAPLAN testing has been controversial and intertwined with debates around teacher effectiveness and performance pay. A teacher's ability to implement a curriculum or bolster the study scores of students is not reported in the literature as a concern for students, yet it can often be a pressing burden for teachers in modern-day schools (Roffey, 2012; Thompson, 2013). This is perhaps a reflection of the pressure by governments and legislation to prioritise academic outcomes at the macrosystem level, above other important factors in the school system. Roffey's (2012) Wellbeing Australia Survey found that "The additional stress on teachers working in unrealistic performance-driven environments has a negative impact on them, which in turn must impact [on the] health and wellbeing of the students in their classrooms" (p. 4). Increased teacher stress may affect the student-teacher relationship found to be important for fostering school belonging in this chapter. The absence of a positive student-teacher relationship may result in a reduction in school belonging. Therefore, schools should be mindful of the effect of government-driven initiatives and data collection and the effect this may have on the other socio-ecological layers common to schools.

Unless government bodies become aware of the growing pressure on schools and teachers from over-prioritising academic outcomes, schools may be reluctant to implement positive, proactive interventions related to school belonging or other areas (e.g., coping, resiliency, positive psychology) due to an already overcrowded curriculum (Thompson, 2013). Government bodies concerned with schools should therefore ensure that school belonging (and wellbeing more generally) is prioritised in major sources of information disseminated about schools; for example, including a school belonging measure on the *My School* website.[1] How students perceive their sense of belonging to their school may be information parents wish to seek about a school in addition to academic scores. This is particularly relevant for addressing school drop out rates and student retention at school. Given that school life generally encompasses a diverse range of outcomes and experiences for students, it seems reasonable to argue that a school's educational practices should not be reduced to a set of standardised scores based on one element of the school's performance

(Hardy & Boyle, 2011). At the school level, schools must be mindful of these macrosystem level influences from government reform and policy. It is paramount that schools set realistic and inclusive expectations for academic outcomes for their students, while being mindful of the needs of teachers (Roffey, 2012).

STRENGTHS AND LIMITATIONS OF THE FRAMEWORK

The socio-ecological framework of school belonging is based on empirical evidence derived from past literature. The framework is designed as a comprehensive way for schools to foster school belonging. While the framework itself has been developed from peer-reviewed empirical studies, the inclusion of mainly correlational findings means that the direction of the relationship between the themes found to be strongly correlated with school belonging require further analysis. An important caveat of the framework, therefore, is that the influence of themes associated with school belonging cannot be regarded as causal.

FUTURE RESEARCH

The framework and suggested evidence-based school practices would be strengthened if they were tested or evaluated using other methods of research. For example, a case study would refine the understanding of how context affects: (a) what practices are implemented, (b) how the practices are implemented, and (c) the success of the practices. A deeper understanding of the evidence-based socio-ecological framework and accompanying school practices would be gained by investigating the experiences, values, and preferences of school leaders, educators, students, and school psychologists (Dollaghan, 2004). Further research should aim to use longitudinal designs with objective measures (e.g., observation) for a more detailed understanding of school belonging.

Questions also remain about how school belonging may differ within specific populations. How does the framework apply to young people who do not belong? How does the framework apply to minority groups? While it is clear that social support is essential to improve belonging among students, this appears to be even more salient for minority groups: for example, individuals of different racial and ethnic backgrounds, persons with disabilities (McMahon et al., 2008), and students who identify themselves as having GLBTQI orientation (Aerts, Van Houtte, Dewaele, Cox, & Vincke, 2012). For these students, the acceptance of their peers, teachers, and parents has been found to be an important variable in developing prosocial behaviour and a positive attitude towards school (Galliher, Rostosky, & Hughes, 2004). Assessing the socio-ecological framework of school belonging's usefulness for specific populations can be examined by future research. Further investigation of the relationship between the broader school community, neighbourhoods, and extended families on the perceived sense of belonging by young people may yield more information on how school belonging can be fostered through a whole school approach.

Empirical evaluation of the framework in different samples would allow identification of the direction of the relationships of the various individual, microsystem, mesosystem, exosystem, and macrosystem levels with school belonging, thus creating a clearly identified pathway for fostering this construct (e.g., what layers are interdependent, how are they weighted, and what combinations are especially important for school belonging to occur?). Therefore, further research is needed to empirically validate the framework and associated evidence-based school practices and further understand the importance of school belonging and how to increase and/or maintain it in secondary school settings.

CONCLUSION

This chapter presented a new socio-ecological framework of school belonging using an ecologically oriented school perspective. The socio-ecological framework of school belonging, in its present form, extends Bronfenbrenner's (1979) ecological framework for human development and represents school belonging as a multidimensional construct. Schools may be better equipped to prioritise school belonging more effectively if they have the appropriate and accessible resources by which they could base interventions on fostering and maintaining school belonging at *multiple levels*. Therefore, the socio-ecological framework of school belonging aims to bridge research and practice through equipping schools with evidence-based information on how school belonging can be increased or maintained.

ACKNOWLEDGEMENT

This chapter is an adapted version from Allen, K., Vella-Brodrick, D., & Waters, L. (2016). Fostering school belonging in secondary schools using socio-ecological framework. *The Educational and Developmental Psychologist, 33*(1), 97–121. doi:10.1017/edp.2016.5

NOTE

[1] In 2003 the Centers for Disease Control and Prevention's (CDC) Division of Adolescent and School Health, and the Johnson Foundation, convened an international gathering of educational leaders and researchers, at the Wingspread conference centre in the United States. The *Wingspread Declaration on School Connections* (2004) was the result of a "detailed review of research and in-depth discussions across two days" (p. 233).

REFERENCES

Aerts, S., Van Houtte, M., Dewaele, A., Cox, N., & Vincke, J. (2012). Sense of belonging in secondary schools: A survey of LGB and heterosexual students in Flanders. *Journal of Homosexuality, 59*, 90–113.

Allen, J. P., Pianta, R. C., Gregory, A., Mikami, A. Y., & Lun, J. (2011). An interaction-based approach to enhancing secondary school instruction and student achievement. *Science, 333*(6045), 1034–1037.

Allen, K., & Bowles, T. (2013). Belonging as a guiding principle in the education of adolescents. *Australian Journal of Educational & Developmental Psychology, 12*, 108–119.

Allen, K., Kern, P., Vella-Brodrick, D., Hattie, J., & Waters, L. (2016). What schools need to know about belonging: A meta-analysis. *Educational Psychology Review, 30*(1), 1–34. doi:10.1007/s10648-016-9389-8

Allen, K., Kern, P., Vella-Brodrick, D., & Waters, L. (in press). School values: A comparison of academic motivation, mental health promotion, and school belonging with student achievement. *Educational and Developmental Psychologist, 34*(1), 31–47. doi:10.1017/edp.2017.5

Allen, K., & McKenzie, V. (2015). Mental health in an Australian context and future interventions from a school belonging perspective. *Special Issue on Mental Health in Australia for the International Journal of Mental Health, 44*, 80–93. doi:10.1080/00207411.2015

Anderman, E. M. (2002). School effects on psychological outcomes during adolescence. *Journal of Educational Psychology, 94*(4), 795–809.

Anderman, L. H. (2003). Academic and social perceptions as predictors of change in middle school students' sense of school belonging. *Journal of Experimental Education, 72*(1), 5–22.

Anderson, J., Boyle, C., & Deppeler, J. (2014). The ecology of inclusive education: Reconceptualising Bronfenbrenner. In Z. Zhang, P. W. K. Chan, & C. Boyle (Eds.), *Equality in education: Fairness and inclusion* (pp. 23–34). Rotterdam, The Netherlands: Sense Publishers.

Appleton, J. J., Christenson, S. L., Kim, D., & Reschly, A. L. (2006). Measuring cognitive and psychological engagement: Validation of the student engagement instrument. *Journal of School Psychology, 44*, 427–445.

Bailey, M., & McLaren, S. (2005). Physical activity alone and with others as predictors of sense of belonging and mental health in retirees. *Aging & Mental Health, 9*(1), 82–90.

Battistich, V., Schaps, E., Watson, M., & Solomon, D. (1996). Prevention effects of the child development project early findings from an ongoing multisite demonstration trial. *Journal of Adolescent Research, 11*(1), 12–35.

Baumeister, R. F., & Leary, M. R. (1995). The need to belong: Desire for interpersonal attachments as a fundamental human motivation. *Psychological Bulletin, 11*(3), 497–529.

Benner, A. D., Graham, S., & Mistry, R. S. (2008). Discerning direct and mediated effects of ecological structures and processes on adolescents' educational outcomes. *Developmental Psychology, 44*(3), 840.

Beyond Blue. (2014). *SenseAbility communications portal.* Retrieved from http://www.beyondblue.org.au/resources/schools-and-universities/secondary-schools-and-tertiary/senseability

Blomfield, C., & Barber, B. L. (2010). Australian adolescents' extracurricular activity participation and positive development: Is the relationship mediated by peer attributes? *Australian Journal of Educational & Developmental Psychology, 10*, 114–128.

Boerema, A. J. (2006). An analysis of private school mission statements. *Peabody Journal of Education, 81*, 180–202.

Bowen, G., Richman, J. M., & Bowen, N. K. (1998). Sense of school coherence, perceptions of danger at school, and teacher support among youth at risk of school failure. *Child & Adolescent Social Work Journal, 15*, 273–286.

Brandon, C., & Ivens, C. (2009). *Thinking skills for peak performance: Student workbook and coach's manual.* South Yarra: Macmillan Education Australia.

Brechwald, W. A., & Prinstein, M. J. (2011). Beyond homophily: A decade of advances in understanding peer influence processes. *Journal of Research on Adolescence, 21*(1), 166–179.

Brendtro, L., Brokenleg, M., & Van Bockern, S. (2002). *Reclaiming youth at risk: Our hope for the future* (Rev. ed.). Bloomington, IN: National Educational Service.

Brewster, A. B., & Bowen, G. L. (2004). Teacher support and the school engagement of Latino middle and high school students at risk of school failure. *Child and Adolescent Social Work Journal, 21*(1), 47–67.

Bronfenbrenner, U. (1979). *The ecology of human development: Experiments by nature and design.* Cambridge, MA: Harvard University Press.

Brookmeyer, K. A., Fanti, K. A., & Henrich, C. C. (2006). Schools, parents, and youth violence: A multilevel, ecological analysis. *Journal of Clinical Child & Adolescent Psychology, 35*(4), 504–514.

Brophy, J. (2004). *Motivating students to learn* (2nd ed.). Mahwah, NJ: Lawrence Erlbaum Associates.

Brown Kirschman, K. J., & Karazsia, B. T. (2014). The role of pediatric psychology in health promotion and injury prevention. In M. C. Roberts, B. Aylward, & Y. Wu (Eds.), *Clinical practice of pediatric psychology* (pp. 136–138). New York, NY: Guilford Press.

Brown, R., & Evans, W. P. (2002). Extracurricular activity and ethnicity: Creating greater school connection among diverse student populations. *Urban Education, 37*(1), 41–58. doi:10.1177/0042085902371004

Bryson, J. M. (2004). What to do when stakeholders matter: Stakeholder identification and analysis techniques. *Public Management Review, 6*(1), 21–53.

Caraway, K., Tucker, C. M., Reinke, W. M., & Hall, C. (2003). Self-efficacy, goal orientation, and fear of failure as predictors of school engagement in high school students. *Psychology in the Schools, 40*(4), 417–428.

Carter, M., McGee, R., Taylor, B., & Williams, S. (2007). Health outcomes in adolescence: Associations with family, friends and school engagement. *Journal of Adolescence, 30,* 51–62.

Cemalcilar, Z. (2010). Schools as socialization contexts: Understanding the impact of school climate factors on students' sense of school belonging. *Applied Psychology: An International Review, 59*(2), 243–272.

Centers for Disease Control and Prevention. (2009). *School connectedness: Strategies for increasing protective factors among youth.* Atlanta, GA: U.S. Department of Health and Human Services.

Cohen, J. (1988). *Statistical power analysis for the behavioral sciences* (2nd ed.). Mahwah, NJ: Lawrence Erlbaum.

Cole, P., Llera, S., & Pemberton, C. (2009). Emotional instability, poor emotional awareness, and the development of borderline personality. *Development and Psychopathology, 21*(4), 1293–1310.

Collaborative for Academic, Social, and Emotional Learning (CASEL). (2003). *Safe and sound: An educational leaders' guide to evidence-based Social and Emotional Learning (SEL) programs.* Retrieved from http://www.casel.org

Connell, J. P., & Wellborn, J. G. (1991). Competence, autonomy and relatedness: A motivational analysis of self-system processes. In M. R. Gunnar & L. A. Sroufe (Eds.), *Minnesota symposium on child psychology* (Vol. 22, pp. 43–77). Hillsdale, MI: Lawrence Erlbaum Associates.

Croninger, R. G., & Lee, V. E. (2001). Social capital and dropping out of high school: Benefits to at-risk students of teachers' support and guidance. *Teachers College Record, 103*(4), 548–581.

Daley, A. J., & Buchanan, J. (1999). Aerobic dance and physical self-perceptions in female adolescents: Some implications for physical education. *Research Quarterly for Exercise and Sport, 70,* 196–200.

Davis, K. (2012). Friendship 2.0: Adolescents' experiences of belonging and self-disclosure online. *Journal of Adolescence, 35*(6), 1527–1536.

Dollaghan, C. (2004). Evidence-based practice: Myths and realities. *The ASHA Leader, 12,* 4–5. Retrieved from http://www.asha.org/publications/leader/2004/040413/f040413a1.htm

Donovan, J. (2011). The role for marketing in public health change programs. *Australian Review of Public Affairs, 10,* 23–40.

Dotterer, A. M., McHale, S. M., & Crouter, A. C. (2007). Implications of out-of-school activities for school engagement in African American adolescents. *Journal of Youth and Adolescence, 36,* 391–401.

Drolet, M., & Arcand, I. (2013). Positive development, sense of belonging, and support of peers among early adolescents: Perspectives of different actors. *International Education Studies, 6*(4), 29–38.

Dweck, C. S. (1986). Motivational processes affecting learning. *American Psychologist, 41*(10), 1040–1048.

Education Development Center. (2008). *School connectedness and meaningful student participation.* Washington, DC: U.S. Department of Education. Retrieved from http://www.ed.gov/admins/lead/safety/training/connect/index.html

Faircloth, B. S. (2009). Making the most of adolescence: Harnessing the search for identity to understand classroom belonging. *Journal of Adolescent Research, 24,* 321–348.

Finn, J. D., & Voelkl, K. E. (1993). School characteristics related to student engagement. *Journal of Negro Education, 62*(3), 249–268.

Friedman, M. (2007). The role of government in education. In R. Current (Ed.), *Philosophy of education* (pp. 194–199). Oxford: Blackwell.

Frydenberg, E. (2011). *Coping for success program: Skills for everyday living.* Retrieved from http://www.coop.com.au/coping-for-success-program-skills-for-everyday-living/9780734027412

Frydenberg, E., Care, E., Freeman, E., & Chan, E. (2009). Interrelationships between coping, school connectedness and wellbeing. *Australian Journal of Education, 53*(3), 261–276.

Galliher, R. V., Rostosky, S. S., & Hughes, H. K. (2004). School belonging, self-esteem, and depressive symptoms in adolescents: An examination of sex, sexual attraction status, and urbanicity. *Journal of Youth and Adolescence, 33*(3), 235–245.

Garcia-Reid, P. (2007). Examining social capital as a mechanism for improving school engagement among low income Hispanic girls. *Youth & Society, 39*, 164–181.

Garcia-Reid, P. G., Reid, R. J., & Peterson, N. A. (2005). School engagement among Latino youth in an urban middle school context: Valuing the role of social support. *Education and Urban Society, 37*(3), 257–275.

Gillen-O'Neel, C., & Fuligni, A. (2013). A longitudinal study of school belonging and academic motivation across high school. *Child Development, 84*(2), 678–692. doi:10.1111/j.1467-8624.2012.01862.x

Goodenow, C. (1992). Strengthening the links between educational psychology and the study of social contexts. *Educational Psychologist, 27*(2), 177–196.

Goodenow, C., & Grady, K. E. (1993). The relationship of school belonging and friends' values to academic motivation among urban adolescent students. *Journal of Experimental Education, 62*(1), 60–71.

Guthrie, J. T., & Davis, M. H. (2003). Motivating struggling readers in middle school through an engagement model of classroom practice. *Reading &Writing Quarterly, 19*(1), 59–85.

Hagerty, B. M., Lynch-Sauer, J., Patusky, K., Bouwsema, M., & Collier, P. (1992). Sense of belonging: A vital mental health concept. *Archives of Psychiatric Nursing, 6*(3), 172–177.

Hagerty, B. M., Williams, R. A., & Oe, H. (2002). Childhood antecedents of adult sense of belonging. *Journal of Clinical Psychology, 58*, 793–801.

Hale, C. J., Hannum, J. W., & Espelage, D. L. (2005). Social support and physical health: The importance of belonging. *Journal of American College Health, 53*, 276–284.

Hamm, J. V., & Faircloth, B. S. (2005). The role of friendship in adolescents' sense of school belonging. *New Directions for Child and Adolescent Development, 2005*(107), 61–78. doi:10.1002/cd.121

Hardy, I., & Boyle, C. (2011). My school? Critiquing the abstraction and quantification of education. *Asia-Pacific Journal of Teacher Education, 39*(3), 211–222. doi:10.1080/1359866X.2011.588312

Hattie, J. A. (2009). *Visible learning: A synthesis of meta-analyses relating to achievement.* London: Routledge.

Hattie, J. A., & Hansford, B. C. (1984). Meta-analysis: A reflection on problems. *Australian Journal of Psychology, 36*(2), 239–254.

Hawkins, J. D., Von Cleve, E., & Catalano, R. F. (1991). Reducing early childhood aggression: Results of a primary prevention program. *Journal of the American Academy of Child and Adolescent Psychiatry, 30*(2), 208–17.

Hawkins, J. D., & Weis, J. G. (1985). The social development model: An integrated approach to delinquency prevention. *Journal of Primary Prevention, 6*(2), 73–97.

Heaven, P. C., Mak, A., Barry, J., & Ciarrochi, J. (2002). Personality and family influences on adolescent attitudes to school and self-rated academic performance. *Personality and Individual Differences, 32*(3), 453–462.

Henrich, C. C., Brookmeyer, K. A., & Shahar, G. (2005). Weapon violence in adolescence: Parent and school connectedness as protective factors. *Journal of Adolescent Health, 37*, 306–312.

Hirschkorn, M., & Geelan, D. (2008). Bridging the research-practice gap: Research translation and/or research transformation. *Alberta Journal of Educational Research, 54*(1), 1–13.

Hurtado, S., & Carter, D. F. (1997). Effects of college transition and perceptions of the campus racial climate on Latino college students' sense of belonging. *Sociology of Education, 70*(4), 324–345.

Ingersoll, R., & Strong, M. (2011). The impact of induction and mentoring programs for beginning teachers: A critical review of the research. *Review of Education Research, 81*(2), 201–233.

Jennings, G. (2003). An exploration of meaningful participation and caring relationships as contexts for school engagement. *The California School Psychologist, 8*, 43–52.

Johnson, L. S. (2009). School contexts and student belonging: A mixed methods study of an innovative high school. *The School Community Journal, 19*(1), 99–119.

Juvonen, J. (2006). Sense of belonging, social bonds, and school functioning. In P. A. Alexander & P. H. Winne (Eds.), *Handbook of educational psychology* (2nd ed., pp. 655–674). Mahwah, MH: Lawrence Erlbaum.

Kaminski, J. W., Puddy, R. W., Hall, D. M., Cashman, S. Y., Crosby, A. E., & Ortega, L. A. (2010). The relative influence of different domains of social connectedness on self-directed violence in adolescence. *Journal of Youth and Adolescence, 39*(5), 460–473.

Kelly, A. B., O'Flaherty, M., Toumbourou, J. W., Homel, R., Patton, G. C., White, A., & Williams, J. (2012). The influence of families on early adolescent school connectedness: Evidence that this association varies with adolescent involvement in peer drinking networks. *Journal of Abnormal Child Psychology, 40*(3), 437–447.

Klem, A. M., & Connell, J. P. (2004). Relationships matter: Linking teacher support to student engagement and achievement. *Journal of School Health, 74*(7), 262–273.

Knifsend, C., & Graham, S. (2012). Too much of a good thing? How breadth of extracurricular participation relates to school-related affect and academic outcomes during adolescence. *Journal of Youth and Adolescence, 41*, 379–389. doi:10.1007/s10964-011-9737-4

Kuperminc, G. P., Leadbeater, B. J., & Blatt, S. J. (2001). School social climate and individual differences in vulnerability to emotional instability among middle school students. *Journal of School Psychology, 39*(2), 141–159.

Lee, R. M., & Robbins, S. B. (2000). Understanding social connectedness in college women and men. *Journal of Counseling & Development, 78*(4), 484–491. doi:10.1002/j.1556-6676.2000.tb01932.x

Legters, N., Balfanz, R., & McPartland, J. (2002). *Solutions for failing high schools: Converging visions and promising models*. Washington, DC: U.S. Department of Education.

Libbey, H. P. (2004). Measuring student relationships to school: Attachment, bonding, connectedness, and engagement. *Journal of School Health, 74*(7), 275–283.

Lonczak, H. S., Abbott, R. D., Hawkins, J. D., Kosterman, R., & Catalano, R. (2002). The effects of the Seattle social development project: Behavior, pregnancy, birth, and sexually transmitted disease outcomes by age 21. *Archives of Pediatric Adolescent Medicine, 156*, 438–447.

Malti, T., & Noam, G. G. (2009). A developmental approach to the prevention of adolescent's aggressive behavior and the promotion of resilience. *International Journal of Developmental Science, 3*(3), 235–246.

McClelland, J. L. (1987). The case for interactions in language processing. In M. Coltheart (Ed.), *Attention and performance XII: The psychology of reading* (pp. 3–36). Hillsdale, NJ: Lawrence Erlbaum Associates.

McMahon, S., Parnes, A., Keys, C., & Viola, J. (2008). School belonging among low-income urban youth with disabilities: Testing a theoretical model. *Psychology in the Schools, 45*(5), 387–401.

McNeely, C. A., Nonnemaker, J. M., & Blum, R. W. (2002). Promoting school connectedness: Evidence from the national longitudinal study of adolescent health. *Journal of School Health, 72*, 136–146.

Mensah, F. K., Bayer, J. K., Wake, M., Carlin, J. B., Allen, N. B., & Patton, G. C. (2013). Early puberty and childhood social and behavioral adjustment. *Journal of Adolescent Health, 53*(1), 118–124.

Mo, Y., & Singh, K. (2008). Parents' relationships and involvement: Effects on students' school engagement and performance. *Research in Middle Level Education Online, 31*(10), 1–11.

National Research Council and the Institute of Medicine. (2004). *Engaging schools: Fostering high school students' motivation to learn*. Washington, DC: National Academies Press.

Nielsen, T. W. (2011). A curriculum of giving for student wellbeing and achievement – 'How to wear leather sandals on a rough surface' (Ch. 15). In D. Wright, C. Camden-Pratt, & S. Hill (Eds.), *Social ecology: Applying ecological understanding to our lives and our planet* (pp. 151–164). Stroud: Hawthorn Press.

Noble, T. (2006). Core components of a school-wide safe schools curriculum. In H. McGrath & T. Noble (Eds.), *Bullying solutions: Evidence-based approaches to bullying in Australian schools* (pp. 36–62). Sydney: Pearson Education.

Noble, T., & McGrath, H. (2008). The positive educational practices framework: A tool for facilitating the work of educational psychologists in promoting pupil wellbeing. *Educational and Child Psychology, 25*(2), 119–134.

Nutbrown, C., & Clough, P. (2009). Citizenship and inclusion in the early years: Understanding and responding to children's perspectives on 'belonging'. *International Journal of Early Years Education, 17*(3), 191–206. doi:10.1080/09669760903424523

O'Connor, M. (2010). Life beyond school: The role of school bonding in preparing adolescents for adulthood. *Independence, 35*(1), 24–28.

O'Connor, M., Sanson, A., & Frydenberg, E. (2012). The relationship between positive development during the transition to adulthood and temperament, personality, and educational outcomes. In E. Frydenberg & G. Reevy (Eds.), *Personality, stress, and coping: Implications for education* (Vol. VI, pp. 111–130). Charlotte, NC: Information Age.

Osterman, K. F. (2000). Students' need for belonging in the school community. *Review of Educational Research, 70*(3), 323–367.

Owings, W. A., & Kaplan, L. S. (2003). *Best practices, best thinking, and emerging issues in school leadership.* Thousand Oaks, CA: Corwin Press.

Patton, G. C., Bond, L., Carlin, J. B., Thomas, L., Butler, H., Glover, S., Catalano, R., & Bowes, G. (2006). Promoting social inclusion in schools: A group-randomized trial of effects on student health risk behavior and well-being. *American Journal of Public Health, 96*(9), 1582–1587.

Poulton, R., Caspi, A., & Milne, B. J. (2002). Association between children's experience of socioeconomic disadvantage and adult health: A life-course study. *Lancet, 360*(9346), 1640–1645.

Quinn, S., & Oldmeadow, J. A. (2013). Is the igeneration a 'we' generation? Social networking use among 9- to 13-year-olds and belonging. *British Journal of Developmental Psychology, 31*(1), 136–142.

Quint, J., Bloom, H., Black, A., Stephens, L., & Akey, T. (2005). *The challenge of scaling up educational reform. Findings and lessons from first things first.* New York, NY: MDRC.

Reschly, A. L., Busch, T. W., Betts, J., Deno, S. L., & Long, J. D. (2009). Curriculum-based measurement oral reading as an indicator of reading achievement: A meta-analysis of the correlational evidence. *Journal of School Psychology, 47*(6), 427–469.

Reschly, A. L., Huebner, E. S., Appleton, J. J., & Antaramian, S. (2008). Engagement as flourishing: The contribution of positive emotions and coping to adolescents' engagement at school and with learning. *Psychology in the Schools, 45*(5), 419–431.

Roche, C., & Kuperminc, G. P. (2012). Acculturative stress and school belonging among Latino youth. *Hispanic Journal of Behavioral Sciences, 34*(1), 61–76.

Roffey, S. (2012). Pupil wellbeing – Teacher wellbeing: Two sides of the same coin? *Educational & Child Psychology, 29*(4), 8–17.

Rogers, C. R. (1951). *Client-centered therapy: Its current practice, implications, and theory.* Oxford: Houghton Mifflin.

Rowe, F., & Stewart, D. (2011). Promoting connectedness through whole-school approaches: Key elements and pathways of influence. *Health Education, 111*(1), 49–65.

Rowe, F., Stewart, D., & Patterson, C. (2007). Promoting school connectedness through whole-school approaches. *Health Education, 107*, 524–542.

Rumberger, R. (1995). Dropping out of middle school: A multilevel analysis of students and schools. *American Educational Research Journal, 32*, 583–625.

Ryan, R. M. (1995). Psychological needs and the facilitation of integrative processes. *Journal of Personality, 63*(3), 397–427.

Ryan, R. M., & Deci, E. L. (2000). Self-determination theory and the facilitation of intrinsic motivation, social development, and wellbeing. *American Psychologist, 55*, 68–78.

Ryan, R. M., Stiller, J. D., & Lynch, J. H. (1994). Representations of relationships to teachers, parents, and friends as predictors of academic motivation and self-esteem. *Journal of Early Adolescence, 14*(2), 226–249.

Ryzin, M. J., Gravely, A. A., & Roseth, C. J. (2009). Autonomy, belongingness, and engagement in school as contributors to adolescent psychological wellbeing. *Journal of Youth and Adolescence, 38*(1), 1–12.

Saab, H. (2009). *The school as a setting to promote student health.* Retrieved from http://qspace.library.queensu.ca

Sackett, D. L., Rosenberg, W. M. C., Gray, J. A. M., Haynes, R. B., & Richardson, W. S. (1996). Evidence-based medicine: What it is and what it isn't. *British Medical Journal, 312*, 71–72.

Sakiz, G. (2012). Perceived instructor affective support in relation to academic emotions and motivation in college. *Educational Psychology: An International Journal of Experimental Educational Psychology, 32*(1), 63–79.

Samdal, O., Nutbeam, D., Wold, B., & Kannas, L. (1998). Achieving health and educational goals through schools: A study of the importance of the climate and students' satisfaction with school. *Health Education Research, 3*, 383–397.

Sari, M. (2012). Sense of school belonging among elementary school students. *Çukurova University Faculty of Education Journal, 41*(1), 1–11.

Schonert-Reichl, K., & Lawlor, M. (2010). The effects of a mindfulness-based education program on pre and early adolescents' well-being and social and emotional competence. *Mindfulness, 1*(3), 137–151.

Seligman, M. (2011). *Flourish.* New York, NY: Free Press.

Sharma, M., & Romas, J. A. (2008). *Theoretical foundations of health: Education and health promotion.* Sudbury, MA: Jones & Bartlett.

Sherin, M., & Han, S. (2004). Teacher learning in the context of a video club (PDF). *Teaching and Teacher Education, 20*(2), 163–183.

Shochet, I. M., Dadds, M. R., Ham, D., & Montague, R. (2006). School connectedness is an underemphasized parameter in adolescent mental health: Results of a community prediction study. *Journal of Clinical Child and Adolescent Psychology, 35*(2), 170–179.

Shochet, I. M., Smith, C. L., Furlong, M. J., & Homel, R. (2011). A prospective study investigating the impact of school belonging factors on negative affect in adolescents. *Journal of Clinical Child & Adolescent Psychology, 40*(4), 586–595. doi:10.1080/15374416.2011.581616

Shochet, I. M., Smyth, T. L., & Homel, R. (2007). The impact of parental attachment on adolescent perception of the school environment and school connectedness. *Australian and New Zealand Journal of Family Therapy, 28*(2), 109–118.

Sirin, S. R., & Rogers-Sirin, L. (2004). Exploring school engagement of middle-class African American adolescents. *Youth & Society, 35*(3), 323–340.

Soria, K. M., Lingren Clark, B., & Coffin Koch, L. (2013). Investigating the academic and social benefits of extended new student orientations for first-year students. *The Journal of College Orientation and Transition, 20*, 33–45.

Stemler, S., Bebell, D., & Sonnabend, L. A. (2011). Using school mission statements for reflection and research. *Educational Administration Quarterly, 47*(2), 383–420.

Stoddard, S. A., McMorris, B. J., & Sieving, R. E. (2011). Do social connections and hope matter in predicting early adolescent violence? *American Journal of Community Psychology, 48*(3–4), 247–256.

Teddlie, C., & Reynolds, D. (2000). *The international handbook of school effectiveness research.* New York, NY: Falmer Press.

Thompson, G. (2013). NAPLAN, my school and accountability: Teacher perceptions of the effects of testing. *The International Education Journal: Comparative Perspectives, 12*, 62–84.

Tillery, A. D., Varjas, K., Roach, A. T., Kuperminc, G. P., & Meyers, J. (2013). The importance of adult connections in adolescents' sense of school belonging: Implications for schools and practitioners. *Journal of School Violence, 12*(2), 134–155. doi:10.1080/15388220.2012.762518

Vallerand, R. J. (1997). Towards a hierarchical model of intrinsic and extrinsic motivation. *Advances in Experimental Social Psychology, 29*, 271–360.

Wadsworth, M. E., Thomsen, A. H., Saltzman, H., Connor-Smith, J. K., & Compas, B. E. (2001). Coping with stress during childhood and adolescence: Problems, progress, and potential in theory and research. *Psychological Bulletin, 127*(1), 87–127.

Wallace, T. L., Ye, F., & Chhuon, V. (2012). Subdimensions of adolescent belonging in high school. *Applied Developmental Science, 16*, 122–139.

Walker, C. O. (2012). Student perceptions of classroom achievement goals as predictors of belonging and content instrumentality. *Social Psychology of Education, 15*(1), 97–107.

Wang, M., & Eccles, J. S. (2012). Social support matters: Longitudinal effects of social support on three dimensions of school engagement from middle to high school. *Child Development, 83*(3), 877–895.

Waters, S., Cross, D., & Runion, K. (2009). Social and ecological structures supporting adolescent connectedness to school: A theoretical model. *Journal of School Health, 79*(11), 516–524. doi:10.1111/j.1746-1561.2009.00443.x

Waters, S., Cross, D., & Shaw, T. (2010). Does the nature of schools matter? An exploration of selected school ecology factors on adolescent perceptions of school connectedness. *British Journal of Educational Psychology, 80*(3), 381–402. doi:10.1348/000709909X484479

Wentzel, K. R. (1998). Social relationships and motivation in middle school: The role of parents, teachers, and peers. *Journal of Educational Psychology, 90*(2), 202–209.

West, P., Sweeting, H., & Leyland, A. (2004). School effect on pupils' health behaviours: Evidence in support of the health promoting school. *Research Papers in Education, 19*, 261–291. doi:10.1080/0267152042000247972

Whitlock, J. (2006). The role of adults, public space, and power in adolescent community connectedness. *Journal of Community Psychology, 35*, 499–518.

Wilkinson-Lee, A. M., Zhang, Q., Nuno, V. L., & Wilhelm, M. S. (2011). Adolescent emotional distress: The role of family obligations and school connectedness. *Journal of Youth and Adolescence, 40*, 221–230. doi:10.1007/s10964-009-9494-9

Williams, K. L., & Galliher, R. V. (2006). Predicting depression and self-esteem from social connectedness, support, and competence. *Journal of Social and Clinical Psychology, 25*, 855–874. doi:10.1521/jscp.2006.25.8.855

Wingspread Declaration on School Connections. (2004). Wingspread declaration on school connections. *Journal of School Health, 74*(7), 233–234.

Wyn, J., Cahill, H., Holdsworth, R., Rowling, L., & Carson, S. (2000). Mindmatters, a whole-school approach promoting mental health and wellbeing. *Australian and New Zealand Journal of Psychiatry, 34*, 594–601.

Zimmer-Gembeck, M., Chipuer, H., Hanisch, M., Creed, P., & McGregor, L. (2006). Relationships at school and stage-environment fit as resources for adolescent engagement and achievement. *Journal of Adolescence, 29*, 911–933.

Kelly-Ann Allen
The Melbourne Graduate School of Education
The University of Melbourne
Australia

Dianne Vella-Brodrick
The Melbourne Graduate School of Education
The University of Melbourne
Australia

Lea Waters
The Melbourne Graduate School of Education
The University of Melbourne
Australia

CHRISTOPHER BOYLE AND KELLY-ANN ALLEN

12. THE PATH LEAST FOLLOWED

*Moving into the Future of School Belonging Research
and towards Clearer Interventions*

INTRODUCTION

As we have seen in this authoritative book, as well as that of the wider literature, school belonging is generally regarded as a student's sense of affiliation or connection to his or her school. Anyone who has personally navigated the sometimes-difficult terrain of secondary school is able to have some level of direct understanding as to the importance that belonging and identifying with a school holds for most people. Educators and practitioners often work with young people who feel that they do not belong to the school community that they attend. An absence of belonging can manifest itself in mental health concerns, school attrition and risk-taking behaviours. Opportunities for early intervention through fostering school belonging are born from a greater understanding and awareness of what school belonging is and how it is contextualised and fostered. School belonging is perennially important and marks a significant social issue of our time. The aim of this final chapter is to consider the key messages of the foregoing chapters, as well as relating them to the wider literature on school belonging.

This book, through 12 chapters, demonstrates that school belonging research is diverse. This collection of chapters presents a collection of mixed research designs, methodologies, and participants.

PATHS TO SCHOOL BELONGING

Students who may be marginalised or excluded may find it difficult to experience a strong sense of school belonging (Slaten et al., 2015). For example, students with special educational needs, low social and economic background. It is clear that students at the periphery of social acceptance may struggle to fully belong in a regular school setting. An important finding from Slaten et al.'s study (Chapter 2) is the lack of focus in school belonging literature on actual interventions in order to improve outcomes for students who require extra support in accessing school (e.g., social and emotional learning interventions). The fields of educational psychology and school belonging are complementary in nature and gaining a better understanding of the psychological aspects and consequences of students not achieving school belonging success is mutually beneficial.

© KONINKLIJKE BRILL NV, LEIDEN, 2018 | DOI:10.1163/9789004386969_012

Gowing and Jackson's main findings centre around the understanding that school connectedness is somewhat of a fluid concept that is affected by students' individual circumstances. In a similar way to the principles of inclusive education (Boyle, 2007; Boyle, Topping, & Jindal-Snape, 2013), a key aspect is about individualising the educational experience and adapting the school structure to take account of the student participants. As Gowing and Jackson (Chapter 3) state "the key challenge for schools is to become places of opportunity for every young person". It seems obvious, yet we know that with the increased focus on 'attainment or nothing' many young people can become disconnected from the school experience.

Gowing and Jackson (Chapter 3) discuss the importance of involving both teachers and students in school decision-making as this greatly improved the richness of the school environment (Simmons, Graham, & Thomas, 2015). Putting it simply, school connectedness cannot be regarded as existing properly if peer relationships are poor. It is clear that dialogue between all parties involved in a functioning school environment must be able to understand the goals and perspectives of each other.

The National School Climate Center (2015) discuss the main components of school climate through an emphasis on extracurricular activities. As has been emphasised earlier in this chapter and elsewhere in this book, the importance of *meaningfully* involving all parties in a school provides a much higher likelihood of success. Coker et al. (Chapter 4) states that this should "include systemically engaging all members of the school community, focusing on instruction that promotes prosocial development (e.g., collaboration, co-leadership), and meaningful relationships". The thesis that Coker and colleagues put forward for achieving this laudable goal is to make use of the curricular activities as a method of energising the life of students and staff in the school in order to facilitate a high degree of school belonging.

Again, the common theme in developing a positive progressive environment for school belonging is about building collaborations between all players in the school arena (Monahan, Oesterle, & Hawkins, 2010). Successful interventions in school need to be broader than just the school but should involve the wider community so that support can be readily provided by various groups (Boyle, 2007; Boyle et al., 2013). Moffa and colleagues (in Chapter 5) discuss the issue of the importance of ensuring quality interventions in order to enhance school belonging in schools. As with many areas of education various interventions are put forward to purportedly improve the social outcomes of students in schools and Moffa et al., whilst acknowledging the variance in programmes of this type, make the useful suggestions that further study into understanding whether being involved in school belonging interventions improves longer term mental health may be worth pursuing.

Attaining a positive school environment and taking cognisance of school belonging principles becomes more complex when support is required for students who are entering the system as refugees. Apart from the potential for severe psychological trauma (Gunasekera, Houghton, Glasgow, & Boyle, 2014), students who are refugees may have multi-faceted needs. In Chapter 6, Due, Riggs and Augoustinos highlight

THE PATH LEAST FOLLOWED

different considerations for this student population, which is much more pronounced than that of the general school population. The particular nature of refugee students in a new, and more than likely, culturally diverse situation indicates the importance of being able to experience a sense of belonging, in all aspects of the school. Research has shown the importance of Intensive English Language Centres (IELCs) in South Australia (de Heer, Due, & Riggs, 2016) of fostering as sense of school belonging in the schools where they were part of the setup. As Due and colleagues indicate, the students were able to build up their social skills and sense of belonging through the safe facility of the IELC. The research is not clear whether this would have been possible for refugee students in the general mainstream environment. In order to establish a strong sense of belonging, it is necessary to ensure that the individual needs of students, especially those who are described as being vulnerable and neglected, are fully taken into consideration.

In Chapter 7, McKenzie and Smead suggest that student mastery may be influenced by self-efficacy and optimism. It follows that developmental aspects outside school may be highly influential vis-à-vis school belonging. The results from this research seems to indicate that students who can be regarded as having "positively functioning parents" may have more positive attributions for success and failure in learning and other events (Bosnjak et al., 2017; Chodkiewicz & Boyle, 2014, 2017). Furthermore, it could be argued that if a person's self-efficacy is strong when dealing with negative situations, which invariably will occur, will then be better prepared to positively deal with any arising difficulties.

The findings in McKenzie and Smead's study link to other research (e.g. Renzaho, Mellor, McCabe, & Powell, 2013), which demonstrates the importance of resilience of the individual in that their ability to experience positive school belonging is far greater than could be expected otherwise. The study also suggests that experiencing strong school belonging can enhance students' ability to afford greater coping in those who may be experiencing a somewhat dysfunctional family environment. Furthermore, a key aspect is the availability of quality programmes to improve resilience, which counteract a poor familial situation. Overall, McKenzie and Smead's findings indicated that there is a benefit of making the most of programmes that enhance school connectedness. This is especially the case where family functioning for some students may have gone somewhat awry.

One of the roles of schools is to ensure belongingness for all its students and this is especially true for international students who are involved in an acculturation process. Rose-Redwood and Rose-Redwood (2013) suggest that there are still issues with host institutions not establishing and encouraging reasonable communication between international students and the host institution. Sebastian and Slaten (Chapter 8) suggest that by focussing on enabling international students to positively feel belongingness facilitates an understanding of the importance of diversity and inclusion across the school community.

The issue of disconnection from schooling and in more extreme cases that of society is an issue that requires successful interventions. Roffey and Boyle, in

Chapter 9 of this book, highlight some interventions which can be effective in respect of improving belonging in schools, especially targeting those who can become marginalised from their peers and possibly society. The question of what exactly is society must be considered, after all, it is a completely anomalous and arguably vacuous term. Sometimes it can be used to subjugate a population or make people feel more together; a sense of being closer to each other in that society. Skiba et al. (2006) found that schools who embraced a zero-tolerance policy ensured that a perceived breach of trust between students and management ensued, in effect decreasing any feeling of belonging and security which the policy attempted to facilitate.

Roffey and Boyle (Chapter 9, this book) remind us that school belonging goes beyond the school gates. Students who become negatively affected through isolation and a failure to belong in school, will have difficulties in general and not only in school. The stronger the feeling of belonging is directly related to improvements in well-being and self-esteem (Allen, Vella-Brodrick, & Waters, 2017). The family context influences school belonging just as much as school belonging affects the family context. School interventions to promote school belonging provide a strong tool in ensuring that fewer become disillusioned with 'society' and feel the need to disengage from others (Allen, Kern, Vella-Brodrick, Hattie, & Waters, 2016).

An issue, which many students experience in their schooling journey is, that of transitioning between schools. This can be natural progression from primary to secondary or it can be related to a change of school for other reasons (e.g., house or aspirational move). This can be a point in life where someone can be extremely vulnerable and the usual difficulties of finding belonging in schools may be exacerbated. The consequences associated with transitional difficulties can be high. In Chapter 10, Mays et al. highlight the importance of providing an effective plan to ensure that transition planning leads to a robust feeling of school belonging for those students. Building into the planning the recognition that there may be issues with acceptance and self-esteem as students' transition is fundamental to an effective psychologically safer school. Students who may have additional support needs are the clear and obvious beneficiaries of this type of well thought out programme.

There can be little argument that schools are a results-driven business. With countries (e.g., PISA) and schools (e.g. NAPLAN, cf. Hardy & Boyle, 2011) becoming the comparison points, individual schools are finding it more difficult to accommodate wellbeing interventions. As Allen, Vella-Brodrick and Waters (Chapter 11) discuss, the ramifications of not being able to develop strong interventions to enhance school belonging can be detrimental to student wellbeing but also to academic results. Often the schools are unable or reluctant to facilitate wellbeing programmes due to the already crowded school curriculum (Allen, Kern, Vella-Brodrick, & Waters, 2017; Thompson, 2013).

School life and experience is more important than scores, yet the government driven education system continues to espouse this somewhat discredited approach. School life is holistic; it is not only results nor is it only wellbeing. Through properly integrated school belonging programmes, both can be achieved. They are not mutually exclusive.

CONCLUSION

An issue highlighted through the chapters of this text is that school belonging research has suffered markedly by the diverse ways in which the construct is described – especially in regards to the mixed terminology used – not only by researchers – but also educators and school leaders. The field of school belonging research could be improved if researchers took more time to clearly define their constructs as has been allowed to develop in this book.

Future researchers interested in school belonging are able to extend our understanding of this construct within an ephemeral political and social landscape. Advances in technology and the change in how young people connect and seek meaningful friendships and opportunities to belong, provide opportunities to examine social media and online social behaviours (Allen, Ryan, Gray, McInerney, & Waters, 2014; Ryan, Allen, Gray, & McInerney, 2017).

The world has watched media channels report the lived experiences of young individuals recruited to extremist groups. These groups offer, to their members, an opportunity to belong, but perhaps those members were attracted to such groups after failing to belong in other areas.

School belonging in the university sector also offers another pathway in which researchers can study belonging. Distance education in particular is often troubled by high attrition rates and difficulty for students to find meaningful ways to connect with their studies, other students and staff while studying in an online context.

This book was developed to provide a collection of new research in the area of school belonging to create accessible information for school leaders, educators, school psychologists and other professionals who work with or are interested in schools. It is hoped that readers of this book can take away a greater understanding of school belonging to apply empirically founded strategies within their own settings.

REFERENCES

Allen, K., Kern, P., Vella-Brodrick, D., & Waters, L. (2017). School values: A comparison of academic motivation, mental health promotion, and school belonging with student achievement. *Educational and Developmental Psychologist, 34*(1), 31–47. doi:10.1017/edp.2017.5

Allen, K., Vella-Brodrick, D., & Waters, L. (2017). School belonging and the role of social and emotional competencies in fostering an adolescent's sense of connectedness to their school. In E. Frydenberg & A. Martin (Eds.), *Social and emotional learning in the Australasian context* (pp. 83–99). Melbourne: Springer Social Sciences.

Allen, K., Kern, P., Vella-Brodrick, D., & Hattie, J., & Waters, L. (2016). What schools need to know about belonging: A meta-analysis. *Educational Psychology Review, 30*(1), 1–34. doi:10.1007/s10648-016-9389-8

Allen, K., Ryan, T., Gray, D., & McInerney, D., & Waters, L. (2014). Social media use and social connectedness in adolescents: The positives and the potential pitfalls. *Australian Educational and Developmental Psychologist, 31*, 18–33. Retrieved from http://dx.doi.org/10.1017/edp.2014.2

Bosnjak, A., Boyle, C., & Chodkiewicz, A. R. (2017). An intervention to retrain attributions using CBT: A pilot study. *The Educational and Developmental Psychologist, 34*(1), 21–32. doi:10.1017/edp.2017.1

Boyle, C. M. (2007). An analysis of the efficacy of a motor skills training programme for young people with moderate learning difficulties. *International Journal of Special Education, 22*(1), 11–24.

Boyle C., Topping, K., & Jindal-Snape, D. (2013). Teachers' attitudes towards inclusion in high schools. *Teachers and Teaching: Theory and Practice, 19*(5), 527–542. doi:10.1080/13540602.2013.827361

Chodkiewicz, A. R., & Boyle, C. (2014). Exploring the contribution of attribution retraining to student perceptions and the learning process. *Educational Psychology in Practice, 30*(1), 78–87. doi:10.1080/02667363.2014.880048

Chodkiewicz, A. R., & Boyle, C. (2017). Positive psychology school-based interventions: A reflection on current success and future directions. *Review of Education, 5*(1), 60–86. doi:10.1002/rev3.3080

de Heer, N., Due, C., & Riggs, D. W. (2016). "It will be hard because I will have to learn lots of English": Experiences of education for children with migrant backgrounds in Australia. *The International Journal of Qualitative Studies in Education, 29*(3), 297–319. doi:10.1080/09518398.2015.1023232

Gunasekera, S., Houghton, S., Glasgow, K., & Boyle, C. (2014). From stability to mobility: African secondary school aged adolescents' transition to mainstream schooling. *The Australian Educational and Developmental Psychologist, 31*(1), 1–17. doi:10.1017/edp.2014.4

Hardy, I., & Boyle, C. (2011). My school? Critiquing the abstraction and quantification of education. *Asia-Pacific Journal of Teacher Education, 39*(3), 211–222. doi:10.1080/1359866X.2011.588312

Monahan, K. C., Oesterle, S., & Hawkins, J. D. (2010). Predictors and consequences for school connectedness: The case for prevention. *The Prevention Researcher, 17*(3), 3–7.

National School Climate Council. (2015). *School climate and prosocial educational improvement: Essential goals and processes that support student success for all.* Retrieved from https://www.schoolclimate.org/climate/documents/Essential_dimensions_Prosocial_SC_Improvement_P_3-2015.pdf

Renzaho, A., Mellor, D., McCabe, M., & Powell, M. (2013). Family functioning, parental psychological distress and child behaviours: Evidence from the Victorian child health and wellbeing study. *Australian Psychologist, 48*(3), 217–225. doi:10.1111/j.1742-9544.2011.00059.x

Rose-Redwood, C. R., & Rose-Redwood, R. S. (2013). Self-segregation or global mixing? Social interactions and the international student experience. *Journal of College Student Development, 54*(4), 413–429. doi:10.1353/csd.2013.0062

Ryan, T., Allen, K., Gray, D., & McInerney, D. (2017). How social are social networking sites? A review of online social behavior and connectedness. *Journal of Relationships Research, 8.* doi:10.1017/jrr.2017.13

Simmons, C., Graham, A., & Thomas, N. (2015). Imagining an ideal school for wellbeing: Locating student voice. *Journal of Educational Change, 16*, 129–144. doi:10.1007/s10833-014-9239-8

Skiba, R., Reynolds, C. R., Graham, S., Sheras, P., Close Conely, J., & Garcia-Vasquez, E. (2006). *Are zero tolerance policies effective in the schools? An evidentiary review and recommendations.* Zero Tolerance Task Force Report for the American Psychological Association.

Slaten, C. D., Elison, Z. M., Hughes, H., Yough, M., & Shemwell, D. (2015). Hearing the voices of youth at risk for academic failure: What professional school counselors need to know. *The Journal of Humanistic Counseling, 54*(3), 203–220. doi:10.1002/johc.12012

Thompson, G. (2013). NAPLAN, my school and accountability: Teacher perceptions of the effects of testing. *The International Education Journal: Comparative Perspectives, 12*, 62–84.

Christopher Boyle
Graduate School of Education
University of Exeter
England

Kelly-Ann Allen
The Melbourne Graduate School of Education
The University of Melbourne
Australia

INDEX

www.ingramcontent.com/pod-product-compliance
Lightning Source LLC
Chambersburg PA
CBHW071417290326
41932CB00046B/1907